MORE PRAISE FOR THE CAPITALIST SPIRIT

"*The Capitalist Spirit* is an excellent read for anyone who is looking to make a difference in their own lives and the world. Yale Hirsch is a living example that we should not allow ourselves to be shackled by the predetermined axioms of one's own limitations. AT THE MOMENT, Yale is publishing a new book, has authored and composed a musical, and is creating his own website to connect even further with his readership. Take the first step in opening your mind to what you can do by opening this book."

—John Carroll, Chief Operating Officer, Bay Crest Partner

"An intriguing assortment of wisdom regarding ways of learning, growing, investing, interacting with others, and finding inner peace. Not to mention keen observations of many significant observers regarding our planet, history, and ways that each of us can improve life on earth. Thought-provoking and highly recommended."

—Gerald Appel, President, Signalert Corporation

"*The Capitalist Spirit* should be read and studied by all those who desire to increase their perception of life, of themselves, and of the possibilities that await those who know how to seize them."

—Humphrey E. D. Lloyd, MD, MRCP, author of *Trading S&P Futures and Options* and *Taking Your IRA to the Next Level*

THE CAPITALIST SPIRIT

How Each and Every One of Us Can Make a Giant Difference in Our Fast-Changing World

YALE HIRSCH

Founder of *Stock Trader's Almanac*

Foreword by William J. O'Neil
Founder and Chairman, Investor's Business Daily

John Wiley & Sons, Inc.

Published by John Wiley & Sons, Inc., Hoboken, New Jersey.
Published simultaneously in Canada.

For general information on our other products and services or for technical support, please contact our Customer Care Department within the United States at (800) 762-2974, outside the United States at (317) 572-3993 or fax (317) 572-4002.

Wiley also publishes its books in a variety of electronic formats. Some content that appears in print may not be available in electronic formats. For more information about Wiley products, visit our Web site at www.wiley.com.

ISBN: 978-0-470-40737-0

Printed in the United States of America.

10 9 8 7 6 5 4 3 2 1

Respectfully dedicated to America, sweet land of liberty and opportunity, where an African American is now the President of the United States of America.

Give me your tired, your poor,
Your huddled masses yearning to breathe free,
The wretched refuse of your teeming shore,
Send these, the homeless, tempest-tossed to me,
I lift my lamp beside the golden door.

—Emma Lazarus (1849–1887),
American poet, from
"The New Colossus" (1883), inscribed on
a bronze plaque inside the Statue of Liberty

So at last, I was going to America!
Really, really going at last!
The boundaries burst.
The arch of heaven soared.
A million suns shone out for every star.
The winds rushed in from outer space,
Roaring in my ears,

"America! America!"

—Mary Antin (1881–1949),
immigrant writer,
from "The Promised Land" (1912)

I have a love affair with America, because there are no built-in barriers to anyone in America. I come from a country where there were barriers upon barriers.

—Michael Caine (b. 1933), British actor,
quoted in *Parade* magazine (2003)

America, brash and noble container of dreams, This muse to artists and inventors and entrepreneurs, This beacon of optimism, this dynamo of energy, This trumpet blare of liberty.

—Peter Jennings (1938–2005), anchor
ABC World News Tonight, a Canadian
gaining his U.S. citizenship in July 2003

CONTENTS

FOREWORD

Yale Hirsch's *The Capitalist Spirit* is a phenomenal book every person in America must read—especially young people. It's about the most successful nation in the world with under 5 percent of the world's population but producing 27 percent of the world's GDP. A nation of motivated immigrants who keep coming to America for our unsurpassed freedom and unlimited opportunity.

Anyone can succeed in America. All it takes is strong desire, drive, and a willingness to work and learn. In fact, your ultimate success depends almost entirely on your own attitude and determination. No one can hold you back but you yourself.

Your success depends on how you think and react to whatever happens to you. Do you react in a positive way, or by being critical, making negative complaints, blaming others? I've never met a successful pessimist, so playing victim never works.

Hirsch has gathered over 1,000 inspirational ideas, concepts, and rules for your future success, as well as motivating quotations from great people in all fields. I suggest you circle quotes that appeal to you, write them down on ten to twenty, 3 × 5 note cards to carry with you, so you can consult them when you face a problem. Problems are just opportunities in disguise.

I've been in the investment business for 50 years and started *Investor's Business Daily*® 25 years ago in 1984. We built a database on stocks from

1880 to 2009, covering 25 stock market cycles. From horse and buggy days to today's Internet, every single America cycle was led by new, innovative, entrepreneurial companies and inventions that created fast-selling, superior new products. Their big sales created big earnings increases, which created big institutional buying, which created 300 to 1,000 percent advances in these new leaders. These are the stocks you should learn to spot and buy each new cycle. Learning to read chart patterns can help you do this.

We found Apple at a split-adjusted $12 on February 27, 2004, right off a classic cup-with-handle pattern plus two quarters of earnings soaring 300 and 433 percent, respectively. So, don't let anyone convince you there is a better system for America than its freedom, democracy and capitalism.

In 1974, 86 nations in the world were free and 65 not free. Today it's 150 nations free and only 43 not. The trend is clear. So is the data in this book. History proved collectivism's poor incentives created less productivity, greater taxes, and higher unemployment, as Europe had in recent years but is now even going to the right. Our government's promotion of collective farms and communities in the late 1930s all failed. U.S. unemployment in 1939 was still around 20 percent, almost 10 years after the Stock Market Crash of 1929 that led to the Great Depression.

Socialism isn't working in Cuba or Venezuela. Soviet Communism dissolved in 1991. China, with a long border with Russia, witnessed firsthand communism's failed economic system. China, while still communist, recognized the amazing productivity of our more successful U.S. capitalistic system and is today adopting our methods with true success.

Only 19 percent of Chinese now use the Internet; by 2012, 490 million Chinese will have some form of access to the World Wide Web. Their young auto industry is where our auto market was at beginning of the Roaring Twenties.

Our 2008 financial meltdown was created by government and business. It began with the government's 1995 intervention into the mortgage market—mandating banks to make subprime loans and the government-run Freddie Mac and Fannie Mae to buy over half of these risky loans using absurd 40-to-1 leverage. Then came the rescinding of the Glass–Steagall Act in 1998. This let Wall Street join in the "anything goes" super-leveraged money-making orgy.

But cheer up . . . a new capitalist-driven stock market cycle likely started on March 12, 2009.

William J. O'Neil
Founder and Chairman
Investor's Business Daily

PREFACE

WHAT INSPIRED *THE CAPITALIST SPIRIT*

I've always looked for insights to pass along to the readers of each of the annual editions of the *Stock Trader's Almanac,* which I created years ago. Writing for each new *Almanac* required that I find words of wisdom and meaningful quotes to place on each of the 260 weekdays of the year.

The greatest and most inspirational quote I ever encountered (I have yet to find the original source) is found on page 3, though changed here for my purpose:

Inside each of us are powers so strong,
Treasures so rich, possibilities so endless,
If I command them all to action
I could make a giant difference
To millions of people in the world.

I gave it the title, "POTENTIAL," and it is **SO** true. Yet, few people realize that it applies to every human being on this planet. Finding thousands of quotations on money, power, success, motivation, ambition, and so on, to inspire and influence readers also had a magical effect on me.

Here I was providing all those "feel good about yourself" quotations, and those "there's no limit to how far you can go" sayings, and realized I was lifting myself up and benefiting from them over time. Through the years I even coined a few maxims of my own:

Life is an illusion; you are what you think you are!
Ignorance + Perseverance = $UCCE$$

I became aware that these sparks of light and inspiration were uplifting me. I thought I could also provide the impetus to millions of individuals who aspire to become a success, to make a difference, and to have a great, fulfilling life. There is a wonderful old saying, **"Some people make things happen, some watch things happen, while others sit around and wonder what happened."** I wanted to help people choose the first category. To paraphrase a great line in an ad for one of Warren Buffett's companies, **"If you are reading this page, chances are where you are heading is up."**

I am dedicating this book to "America, Sweet Land of Opportunity," because this country, while it has less than 5 percent of the world's population, has over 27 percent of the world's gross domestic product. To what can we attribute this enormous phenomenon? Capitalism of course, and several other factors:

- We were free of the religious wars that plagued many nations over the centuries.
- Thanks to our Founding Fathers, we had separation between church and state.
- There was no system of royalty and nobility and the various titles of king, prince, duke, earl, viscount, baron, and the like along with their female equivalents. It's hard to believe, but excluding the Vatican, there are still eleven monarchies in Europe: Andorra, Belgium, Denmark, Liechtenstein, Luxembourg, Monaco, the Netherlands, Norway, Spain, Sweden, and the United Kingdom.
- Progress and change under absolute monarchies with the "divine right of kings" were much slower than in a democratic society like the United States.

Why is America different? We were, and still are, a country of immigrants. Those who came and are still coming had the will to uproot themselves, to change, and to improve their lives. Children born to them were free of the customs and traditions that bound children born in most other countries.

We also benefited from the influx of multitudes of gifted people who chose to escape from countries that were persecuting certain segments of their free-minded populations.

It is my belief that Table 1.1 in the first chapter, "Capitalism Transformed the Twentieth Century," shows the dramatic changes that occurred between 1900 and today. I am sure that most people will agree that the dominant factor for our twenty-first century will be globalization. This is very likely a major factor that helped plant the seed for this book, *The Capitalist Spirit: How Each and Every One of Us Can Make a Giant Difference in Our Fast-Changing World.* This applies to you reading this, friends you will lend it to, your son, daughter, niece, nephew, and to those who may not be living up to their potential.

So . . . proceed . . . THE SKY'S THE LIMIT!

Each chapter begins with a list of the major ideas and topics covered plus a commentary and a survey of what you will read. At the start of each chapter is an inspirational poster. Leading the first chapter is the one poster that I designed, the most inspirational poster of my life.

THE CAPITALIST SPIRIT

CHAPTER 1

WHAT A DIFFERENCE A CENTURY MAKES

- POTENTIAL
- Capitalism Transformed the Twentieth Century
- Be Thankful It's Not 1910
- The "Good Old Days" of Horses and Wagons
- Engineering + Capitalism Powered the Twentieth Century
- Would You Believe Men Were Sexists in 1943?
- How "Ka-ching" (The Cash Register) Continues to Change Society (William G. Marshall)

Looking at the table in, "Capitalism Transformed the Twentieth Century" (pages 4–5), just a few items in the list demonstrate the awesome changes that we have gone through during the previous century:

- World population increased by 5 billion people, and the U.S. population quadrupled.
- Two-thirds of rural dwellers moved to cities and suburbs.
- Workers on farms shrank from 37.5 to just 2.5 percent.
- Of 4.8 people in an average household, only 2.6 remain today.
- The life expectancy of American women went from 48.3 to 80.4 years.
- Children per woman in developing countries shrank from 6.2 in 1950 to 3.2 today, and in developed countries from 2.8 to 1.5.
- And would you believe that high school enrollment went from 11 to 93 percent?

You won't believe the sexism that existed back in 1943 during World War II, when so many men were in the military and women were hired to replace them (page 11).

Can you imagine the dramatic changes that will have taken place by the end of the twenty-first century? Will you be one of those making a giant contribution to humankind—or at least make many people proud of you?

POTENTIAL

Inside each of us are powers so strong, treasures so rich, possibilities so endless, if I command them all to action I could make a GIANT DIFFERENCE to millions of people in the world.

We all have enormous potential! There is no limit to what each and every one of us can accomplish. This is my most important message to you and every other human being on planet Earth!

CAPITALISM TRANSFORMED THE TWENTIETH CENTURY

In 1900, 13 percent of people who were 65 could expect to see 85. Now, nearly half get to 85. Capitalism brought dramatic changes that raised the human spirit and quality of life higher than ever before: productivity, technology, civil rights, equality of the sexes, electrification, transportation, communication, the list is endless. The data in the following table come from *Time* magazine, *World Almanac, Parade* magazine, as well as selected U.S. government sources, and two books, *It's Getting Better All the Time* and *The First Measured Century*.

Capitalism Transformed the Twentieth Century

	1900	Today
World population	1.6 billion	6.7 billion
U.S. population (570 million est. in 2100)	76 million	306 million
Americans living in rural areas	60%	20%
Percent of workers in farming (75% in 1800)	37.5%	2.5%
People in average household	4.8	2.6
U.S. per capita Income (in current dollars)	$4,748	$36,276
Hours per average workweek	52	37.9
Percent of Americans who own stocks	1%	52%
Telephone calls per capita per year	38	2,325
Centenarians per million people	46	383
Life expectancy American women	48.3	80.4
Unmarried couples living together	>1%	7%
Children per woman (developing countries)	6.2 (1950)	3.2
Children per woman (developed countries)	2.8 (1950)	1.5
Infant deaths per 1,000 live births U.S.	140	6.3
Mothers dying out of 10,000 births (est.)	100	1

		1900	Today
Deaths from heat in Chicago (before air conditioning)		10,000	200+
High school enrollment (age 14–17)		11%	93%
Bachelor's degrees		27,410	1,500,000
B.A.'s earned by Women		19%	58%
Master's degrees		1,583	604,918
M.A.'s earned by women		19%	61%
Doctorate degrees		382	52,700
PhD's earned by women		6%	49%
Size of British Empire (sq. miles)		11 million	100,000
People living in democracies (Freedom House)		12.4%	63.2%
Lynchings in United States		94	0
Books published		6,400	65,000+
Price of 1,000 lumens of light		40 cents	1/10th cent
Cars sold worldwide		4,000	71 million
Airline passengers in the sky over the United States per day		0	1.8 million
Barrels of oil produced		150 million	31 billion
Acres of forested land worldwide		15 billion	8 billion
Where the United States gets its energy (DOE)	Wood	23%	0
	Coal	74%	22.5%
	Oil	3%	39.0%
	Gas	0	22.9%
	Nuclear	0	8.0%
	Renewables	0	7.6%

Sources: Stephen Moore and Julian L. Simon, *It's Getting Better All the Time* (Washington, D.C.: Cato Institute, 2000); Theodore Caplow, Louis Hicks and Ben J. Wattenberg, *The First Measured Century: An Illustrated Guide to Trends in America, 1900–2000* (Washington, D.C.: American Enterprise Institute, 2001); and data from *Time*, *World Almanac*, *Parade*, and U.S. government sources.

Imagine the changes that will take place in the twenty-first century!

■ BE THANKFUL IT'S NOT 1910[1]

- Average life expectancy for white males in the United States was 49 years. For black males, it was 34.
- A housewife spent 40 more hours a week doing housework. There were no washing machines, vacuum cleaners, or dishwashers.
- Few homes had a bathtub. Outhouses were normal in rural America.
- New York-to-California long-distance telephone calls began in 1915—$20.70 for the first 3 minutes, and $6.75 each additional minute.
- There were 181,000 cars manufactured in the United States. Total vehicles produced in 2007 were 10.6 million.
- The tallest structure in the world was the Eiffel Tower at 1,986 feet.
- The average Michigan male factory worker made $2.56 per day. A woman factory worker made $1.14.
- There were no refrigerators or air conditioners.
- Most births took place at home and not in maternity wards.
- Ninety percent of all U.S. doctors had no college education according to the Flexner Report.
- Sugar cost 6 cents a pound, codfish 12, and coffee was 20 cents a pound.
- To start your car you had to crank it. Self-starters became available on a limited number of cars in 1911.
- Five leading causes of death were: heart disease, pneumonia from influenza, tuberculosis, diarrhea, and stroke.
- The American flag had 46 stars. Arizona, New Mexico, Hawaii, and Alaska hadn't been admitted to the Union yet.
- The population of Las Vegas, Nevada, was only 945.
- Eleven of the 46 states were more heavily populated than California, with just 2,377,549 residents.
- There were no crossword puzzles. The first did not appear until Arthur Wynne published the first one in the *New York World* in December 1913.
- There was no Mother's Day. Congress would not make it official until 1914. (Father's Day had to wait until 1972.)
- Of those over 25 years old, only 13.5 percent had completed four years of high school.
- Many children worked fulltime. U.S. child labor laws took many years to be passed. (Today, over 250 million children, mostly in Africa, still work fulltime.)

■ THE "GOOD OLD DAYS" OF HORSES AND WAGONS

In his 1990 book, *The Automobile Age,* James Flink wrote,

> In New York City alone at the turn of the century, horses deposited on the streets every day an estimated 2.5 million pounds of manure and 60,000 gallons of urine, accounting for about two-thirds of the filth that littered the city's streets. Excreta from horses in the form of dried dust irritated nasal passages and lungs, then became a syrupy mass to wade through and track into the home whenever it rained. New York insurance actuaries had established by the turn of the century that infectious diseases, including typhoid fever, were much more frequently contracted by livery stable keepers and employees than by other occupational groups. The flies that bred on the ever present manure heaps carried more than thirty communicable diseases. Traffic was often clogged by the carcasses of overworked dray horses that dropped in their tracks during summer heat waves or had to be destroyed after stumbling on slippery payments and breaking their legs. About 15,000 dead horses were removed from the streets of New York each year. Urban sanitation departments, responsible for daily cleaning up of this mess, were not only expensive but typically graft- and corruption-ridden. These conditions were characteristic in varying degree in all large and medium-sized cities.[2]

How lucky we are we invented the automobile! Our next stop will be reducing gasoline usage and switching to hybrids and electric cars.

Daily Deposits on Streets Everywhere in 1900

1900	Population	Manure (lbs)	Urine (gals)
NYC	3,437,202	2,500,000	60,000
USA	76,212,168	55,400,000	1,320,000
World	1,600,000,000	1,163,400,000	27,720,000

What if They Hadn't Invented the Automobile?

2009 Est.	Population	Manure (lbs)	Urine (gals)
NYC	8,300,000	6,036,590	144,878
USA	305,845,034	223,226,740	5,321,703
World	6,760,000,000	4,934,800,000	117,624,000

■ ENGINEERING + CAPITALISM POWERED THE TWENTIETH CENTURY

How many of the twentieth century's greatest engineering achievements are you using today? A car? computer? Cell phone? The National Academy of Engineering's list of the top 20 achievements show how engineering shaped a century and changed the world.

Greatest Engineering Achievements of the Twentieth Century[3]

1. **Electrification.** Widespread electrification gave us power for our cities, factories, farms, and homes, and forever changed our lives. From streetlights to supercomputers, electric power makes our lives safer, healthier, and more convenient.
2. **Automobiles.** Henry Ford fine-tuned mass production and the world drove off into the age of affordable transportation—forever altering our notions of place and distance.
3. **Airplanes.** Modern air travel transports goods and people quickly around the globe, facilitating our personal, cultural, and commercial interaction.
4. **Water Supplies and Distribution.** Today a simple turn of the tap provides clean water—changing life profoundly, virtually eliminating waterborne diseases in developed nations.
5. **Electronics.** From vacuum tubes to transistors to integrated circuits, engineers have made electronics smaller, more powerful, and more efficient, paving the way for products that have improved the quality and convenience of modern life.
6. **Radio and Television.** These mediums were major agents of social change, opening windows to other lives, to remote areas of the world, and to history in the making.
7. **Agricultural Mechanization.** In 1900, four U.S. farmers could feed about 10 people. By 2000, just <u>one</u> farmer could feed more than 100 people.
8. **Computers.** Personal computers and the rise in computing power have transformed businesses and lives around the world, increased productivity, and opened access to vast amounts of knowledge.

9. **Telephones.** Nearly instant connections—between friends, families, businesses, and nations—enable communications that enhance our lives, industries, and economies.
10. **Air-Conditioning and Refrigeration.** Once luxuries, air-conditioning and refrigeration are now common necessities that greatly enhance our quality of life.
11. **Highways.** Thousands of engineers built the roads, bridges, and tunnels that connect our communities, enable goods and services to reach remote areas, facilitating commerce.
12. **Spacecraft.** Thousands of useful products and services have resulted from the space program (medical devices, improved weather forecasting, and wireless communications).
13. **Internet.** Initially a tool to link research center computers, it has become a vital force of social change, changing business practices, education, and personal communications.
14. **Imaging.** From tiny atoms to distant galaxies, imaging gives us incredible new views, both within and beyond the human body and environment.
15. **Household Appliances.** So many everyday tasks have been eliminated, enabling more people to work outside the home, and contribute significantly to our economy.
16. **Health Technologies.** Advances in medical technology have been astounding. The average longevity in the United States in 1900 was 48. Today it's about 78, a 62.5 percent increase.
17. **Petroleum and Petrochemical Technologies.** Crude oil has provided fuel for vehicles, homes, and industries, as well as the raw material for plastics, drugs, and the like—all have had an enormous effect on world economies, peoples, and politics.
18. **Laser and Fiber Optics.** Today, a single fiber-optic cable can transmit tens of millions of phone calls, data files, and video images.
19. **Nuclear Technologies.** The harnessing of the atom changed the nature of war forever, astounded the world with its awesome power, and also gave us a new source of electricity.
20. **High-Performance Materials.** From building blocks of basic materials to latest advances in polymers, ceramics, and composites, the twentieth century saw a revolution in manufacturing materials.

WOULD YOU BELIEVE MEN WERE SEXISTS IN 1943?

The following article is excerpted from *Mass Transportation Magazine* (July 1943). The article was written for male supervisors of women in the workforce during World War II.

11 Tips on Getting More Efficiency Out of Women Employees

There's no longer any question whether transit companies should hire women for jobs formerly held by men. The draft and manpower shortage has settled that point. The important things now are to select the most efficient women available and how to use them to the best advantage.

1. **Pick young married women.** They usually have more of a sense of responsibility than their unmarried sisters, they're less likely to be flirtatious, they need the work or they wouldn't be doing it, they still have the pep and interest to work hard and to deal with the public efficiently.
2. **When you have to use older women,** try to get ones who have worked outside the home at some time in their lives. Older women who have never contacted the public have a hard time adapting themselves and are inclined to be cantankerous and fussy. It's always well to impress upon older women the importance of friendliness and courtesy.
3. **General experience indicates that "husky" girls**—those who are just a little on the heavy side—are more even-tempered and efficient than their underweight sisters.
4. **Retain a physician to give each woman you hire a special physical examination—one covering female conditions**. This step not only protects the property against the possibilities of lawsuit, but reveals whether the employee-to-be has any female weaknesses which would make her mentally or physically unfit for the job.
5. **Stress at the outset the importance of time** the fact that a minute or two lost here and there makes serious inroads on schedules. Until this point is gotten across, service is likely to be slowed up.
6. **Give the female employee a definite day-long schedule of duties** so that they'll keep busy without bothering the management

for instructions every few minutes. Numerous properties say that women make excellent workers when they have their jobs cut out for them, but that they lack initiative in finding work themselves.

7. **Whenever possible, let the inside employee change from one job to another at some time during the day.** Women are inclined to be less nervous and happier with change.
8. **Give every girl an adequate number of rest periods during the day.** You have to make some allowances for feminine psychology. A girl has more confidence and is more efficient if she can keep her hair tidied, apply fresh lipstick and wash her hands several times a day.
9. **Be tactful when issuing instructions or in making criticisms.** Women are often sensitive; they can't shrug off harsh words the way men do. Never ridicule a woman—it breaks her spirit and cuts off her efficiency.
10. **Be reasonably considerate about using strong language around women.** Even though a girl's husband or father may swear vociferously, she'll grow to dislike a place of business where she hears too much of this.
11. **Get enough size variety in operator's uniforms so that each girl can have a proper fit.** This point can't be stressed too much in keeping women happy.

You've come a long way. . . . "LADY!" —*Y.H.*

■ HOW "KA-CHING" (THE CASH REGISTER) CONTINUES TO CHANGE SOCIETY[4]

by William G. Marshall

Pundits and advocate mercenaries want us to believe that great social change is the product of marches, news reports, divisive political campaigns, spin, lawsuits, and laws.

This is myth. America's greatest social change occurs via the economic ballot box.

Ka-ching at the cash register in the checkout aisle is not just the sound of votes tabulating a product's success. It is the sound of social change.

From America's first heartbeat, the economic ballot shaped our nation. Hunger for economic freedom precipitated America's most radical social change in 1775, the American Revolution.

For more than a decade prior to the Revolution, festering economic issues percolated throughout the American colonies. They included constraints on North American agricultural and mercantile trade and burdensome taxes such as the Stamp Act of 1765 and the Townshend acts of 1767. Colonial frustration led to events such as the Boston Massacre on March 5, 1770, in which British troops were attempting to enforce customs duties and the Boston Tea Party of 1773, protesting yet another tax.

These economic disputes eventually exploded into military action on April 19, 1775, first at Lexington, then at Concord. Full-scale war ensued with the rebels conducting a siege of Boston that resulted in a British defeat and evacuation on March 17, 1776.

The nine-year Revolutionary War had begun. But it was not until January 1776, nine months after the Battle of Bunker Hill and the rebels' siege of Boston, that Thomas Paine's pamphlet, *Common Sense,** provided the call and context for political freedom, and became the tipping point for broad public consensus supporting revolution and American political independence from Great Britain.

Quickly thereafter, the ka-ching of furs, free land, trade over the Santa-Fe trail with Spanish Mexico, buffalo hides, and gold led to national migration and Manifest Destiny.

---

*Common Sense sold over 100,000 copies in a country with only 3 million nonnative inhabitants, most of whom were illiterate.

During the next two centuries, the economic ballot caused the nation to evolve from a hunter-gatherer, to an agrarian to an industrial economy, and then to an information and service economy. These economic shifts produced the emergence of great cities, and the upheavals associated with new value systems, the mobility of Americans and the breakdown of traditional and extended families.

Increased discretionary income and the rise of consumer credit gave rise to the ka-ching of the consumer era and the social attitudes of the "Me" generation and the generations that followed.

As the economy transitioned to compete in the international, then global economy, different skills were demanded from employees and new methods were required for managers and employees to relate to each other—and for managers to relate to Shareowners. Methods of competition changed, industries migrated across oceans, companies failed, jobs were lost, and benefits disappeared. These changes broke down the traditional loyalty between employer and employee, employee and Shareowner. People developed new ways to relate to each other in the workplace, and learned to think about work differently. Psychologically, we became independent entrepreneurs again.

Notes

1. Data compiled and researched by the author.
2. James Flink, *The Automobile Age* (Cambridge: The MIT Press, 1990). Copyright 1988 MIT, courtesy of The MIT Press.
3. National Academy of Engineering, 2009. All rights reserved. From http://www.greatachievements.org with permission of the National Academy of Engineering.
4. Copyright 2008 by William G. Marshall (www.will-marshall.com). Mr. Marshall shows young people how to achieve financial success.

CHAPTER 2

YOUR FUTURE IN A RAPIDLY CHANGING WORLD

- PRODUCTIVITY (Roy H. Williams)
- Big Bang of Info in Constant State of Expansion (Karl Fisch)
- Free-Market Capitalism Drives Globalization (Thomas L. Friedman)
- Futurologists Technology Timeline (Ian Pearson and Ian Neild)
- The Post-American World (Fareed Zakaria)
- The World Is Flat (Thomas L. Friedman)
- The Global Achievement Gap (Tony Wagner)

Although the world population has quadrupled since 1900, it will not be growing at that rate in the current century. The United Nations Department of Economic and Social Affairs predicts that we will top out at 9.22 billion in 2075, a mere 37.6 percent higher. Population for the world in the year 2300 is expected to be only 8.97 billion.

Nowadays, while emphasis is on *globalization,* the most important information development in many centuries is *Googlization.* It's still hard to believe that you can search for so many things and get answers in a matter of seconds. What used to take hours or days at a library is now available in a flash.

Connect to a foreign site and immediately translate everything into your language. Why wait for a weather report when you can just type in your ZIP code and get your weather in an instant? Curious about a new movie in town, get recent reviews of it, one—two—three. With the Google Earth application, you can view your city from above and even zero in on your house or apartment building—even stare at your house at street level for some regions. No need to go to the library anymore when Google can let you scan over 7 million books online. Type in any address in the world and you will have a street map of the area in an instant. WOW!

PRODUCTIVITY

CEO Stephen Sanger of General Mills wanted to improve the productivity of his factories. So he sent technicians to study pit crews during a NASCAR race. When they came home, they reduced the time it took to switch a plant line by 93 percent. What used to shut down Sanger's factories for 5 LONG HOURS now takes 20 minutes.

—Roy H. Williams, *WizardofAds.com*

■ "BIG BANG" OF INFO IN CONSTANT STATE OF EXPANSION

Karl Fisch, the Director of Technology at Arapahoe High School in Littleton, Colorado, researched and came up with the following data.

- Text messages sent and received daily exceed the planet's population.
- There are about 540,000 words in the English language, about five times as many as during Shakespeare's time.
- More than 3,000 new books are published worldwide daily.
- The *New York Times* each week contains more information than a person was likely to come across in a *lifetime* in the eighteenth century.
- About 281 exabytes (that's 28.1×10^{18}) of unique new information will be generated this year worldwide. That's estimated to be more than in the previous 5,000 years.
- The amount of new technical information is doubling every two years. It's predicted to double every 72 hours by 2010.
- Third-generation fiber optics that pushes 14 trillion bits per second down one strand of fiber has recently been separately tested by communications companies NEC Electronics and Alcatel. That equals 2,660 CDs or 210 million phone calls a second. It is tripling every six months and expected to continue to do so the next 20 years.
- 38.6 million laptops were shipped worldwide in the 3Q of 2008.
- The "$100 Laptop Project" is expecting to ship between 50 and 100 million laptops a year to children in underdeveloped countries.
- By 2013, it is predicted a supercomputer will be built that exceeds the computation capability of the human brain.
- Predictions are that by 2049, a $1,000 computer will exceed the computational capabilities of the *human race*.
- One out of every eight couples married in the U.S. last year met online.
- In the next eight minutes, 60 babies will be born in the United States, 244 in China, and 351 in India.
- Name this country! It's the richest in the world, has the largest military, is the center of world business and finance, with the strongest education system and is the world center of innovation and invention.

Its currency is the world standard of value, and it has the highest standard of living. (Answer: England in 1900.)

- Over 37 billion (of 61 billion) searches are performed on Google each month. To whom were these questions addressed B.G. (i.e., *before Google*)?

FREE-MARKET CAPITALISM *DRIVES* GLOBALIZATION[1]

Thomas L. Friedman brilliantly captured the phenomenon of globalization in 1999 in *The Lexus and the Olive Tree.* The speed with which people of the world are being connected is awesome. Some pointed excerpts include:

- The driving idea behind globalization is free-market capitalism—the more you let market forces rule and the more you open your economy to free trade and competition, the more efficient and flourishing your economy will be. Globalization means the spread of free-market capitalism to virtually every country in the world. Globalization also has its own set of economic rules—rules that revolve around opening, deregulating and privatizing an economy.
- The Cold War world was like a broad plain, crisscrossed and divided by fences, walls, ditches and dead ends. It was impossible to go very far, or very fast, in that world without running into a Berlin Wall or an Iron Curtain or a Warsaw Pact or somebody's protective tariff or capital controls.
- Globalization involves the inexorable integration of markets, nation-states, and technologies to a degree never witnessed before—in a way that is enabling individuals, corporations, and nation-states to reach around the world farther, faster, deeper, and cheaper than ever before.
- While Karl Marx and John Maynard Keynes wanted to tame capitalism, economist Joseph Schumpeter and Intel's Andy Grove, preferred to unleash capitalism. According to Schumpeter, the essence of capitalism is the process of "creative destruction"—the perpetual cycle of destroying the old and less efficient product or service and replacing it with new, more efficient ones.
- The defining measurement of globalization is speed—speed of commerce, travel, communication and innovation. Globalization is about Moore's Law, which states that the computing power of silicon chips will double every eighteen to twenty-four months. Globalization also has its own demographic pattern—a rapid acceleration of the movement of people from rural areas and agricultural

lifestyles to urban areas and urban lifestyles more intimately linked with global fashion, food, markets, and entertainment trends.

- In previous eras this sort of cultural homogenization happened on a regional scale—the Hellenization of the Near East and the Mediterranean world under the Greeks, the Turkification of Central Asia, North Africa, Europe and the Middle East by the Ottomans, or the Russification of Eastern and Central Europe and parts of Eurasia under the Soviets.
- Globalization has its own defining technologies: computerization, miniaturization, digitization, satellite communications, fiber optics and the Internet. The symbol of the Cold War was a wall, which divided everyone. The symbol of globalization is a World Wide Web, which unites everyone.

FUTUROLOGISTS TECHNOLOGY TIMELINE[2]

To the Year 2030 and Beyond

What's ahead in technology, and what will it mean? A glimpse of likely developments—and of how they may change our lives—is provided by futurologists Ian Pearson and Ian Neild.

2012

- Hand-held scanner to detect tumors using tissue resonance interferometer
- Diabetes cure resulting from stem-cell research
- 60 percent of Internet accesses from mobile devices
- Bacteria used to break down explosives in mine fields
- First species brought back from extinction
- Multilayer solar cells with efficiency over 50 percent
- Solar reflector satellites bringing solar energy to major Northern Hemisphere cities
- Virtual windows enable homeowners to offset rainy-day blues

2015

- Use of individuals' own tissues to grow replacement organs
- Electronic stimulation of brain sensations as recreational substitute for drugs
- Genetic links of 90 percent of all diseases identified
- An individual's genome part of one's medical record
- Use of stem cells in brain after strokes or accidents
- Bacterial supercomputer
- Robots for guiding blind people
- Private space mission to examine asteroid with a view to space mining

2020

- Fuel cells replace internal combustion engines

2025

- Many new forms of plants and animals from genetic engineering
- Genetic, chemical and physiological bases of human behavior understood
- Fully functioning artificial eyes

- 3-D home printers
- First manned mission to Mars

2030s and Beyond

- Primate given brain implant to increase intelligence to human level
- Computer literacy reaches 95 percent in advanced nations
- Carbon dioxide–fixation technologies for environmental protection
- Space solar-power stations
- Wave energy providing up to 50 percent of British requirements
- Use of nuclear fusion as power source
- Regular manned missions to Mars
- Space elevator based on carbon nanotube cable
- Self-sustaining Mars colony
- Space solar power stations

Whether you agree or disagree with any specific prediction on the timeline, or believe its time frame to be over- or underestimated, it is important to examine the basis of the prediction and to think about and debate how it will affect you, your life, and your business. "Human technology has moved from the first flight to flying to the moon in around 60 years—which was a remarkable achievement," notes coauthor Neild. In the next 60 years, he says, "we will see nanotechnology and biotechnology making impacts on our life that might seem like magic to us but will be quite normal to our children's children."

THE POST-AMERICAN WORLD[3]

by Fareed Zakaria

In April 2008, 81 percent of the American people believed that the country is on the "wrong track." This response was by far the most negative in 25 years.

American anxiety springs from something much deeper, a sense that large and disruptive forces are coursing through the world in almost every industry, in every aspect of life.

For the first time in living memory—the United States does not seem to be leading the charge. Americans see that a new world is coming into being, but fear it is one being shaped in distant lands and by foreign people. The world has shifted from anti-Americanism to ***post***-Americanism.

1. The End of Pax Americana

We are living through the third great power shift in modern history. The first was the rise of the Western world, around the 15th century. The second shift, which took place in the closing years of the 19th century, was the rise of the United States. During this Pax Americana, the global economy has accelerated dramatically. And that expansion is the driver behind the third great power shift of the modern age—the rise of the rest.

The post-American world is naturally an unsettling prospect for Americans, but it should not be. This will not be a world defined by the decline of America but rather the rise of everyone else.

According to University of Maryland scholars, wars of all kinds have been declining since the mid-1980s and that we are now at the lowest levels of global violence since the 1950s. Harvard professor Steven Pinker speculates that we are probably living "in the most peaceful time of our species' existence."

Why do we think we live in scary times? Part of the problem is that as violence has been ebbing, information has been exploding. The last 20 years have produced an information revolution that brings us news and, most crucially, images from around the world all the time.

The threats we face are real. But it is increasingly clear that Islamic militants and suicide bombers make up a tiny portion of the world's 1.3

billion Muslims. Support for violence of any kind has dropped dramatically over the last five years in all Muslim countries. Al Qaeda in Iraq is more anti-Shiite than anti-American.

China and Russia and assorted other oil potentates are surging. But today's rising great powers are relatively benign by historical measure. In the past, when countries grew rich they've wanted to become great military powers. But, since the rise of Japan and Germany in the 1960s and 1970s, none have done this, choosing instead to get rich within the existing international order. China and India are clearly moving in this direction.

2. The Good News

Because of the Iraq War, over two million refugees have crowded into neighboring lands. Yet, little have Iraq's troubles destabilized the region. Most Middle Eastern countries are booming. Iraq's neighbors—Turkey, Jordan, and Saudi Arabia—are enjoying unprecedented prosperity. The share of people living on $1 a day has plummeted from 40 percent in 1981 to 18 percent in 2004, and is estimated to drop to 12 percent by 2015. Poverty is falling in countries that house 80 percent of the world's population. The global economy has more than doubled in size over the last 15 years and is now approaching $54 trillion! Global trade has grown by 133 percent. Wars, terrorism, and civil strife cause disruptions temporarily but eventually they are overwhelmed by the waves of globalization.

3. A New Nationalism

Of course, global growth is also responsible for some of the biggest problems in the world right now. It has produced tons of money that moves around the world. The combination of low inflation and lots of cash has meant low interest rates, which, in turn, have made people act greedily and/or stupidly. So we have witnessed over the last two decades a series of bubbles—in East Asian countries, technology stocks, housing, subprime mortgages, and emerging market equities. Growth also explains one of the signature events of our times—soaring commodity prices. $100 per barrel oil (currently in the $70s) is just the tip of the barrel. Almost all commodities are at 200-year highs. Food, only a few decades ago in danger of price collapse, is now in the midst of a scary rise. Even if people in these countries remain relatively poor, as nations their total wealth will be massive. Any number, no matter how small, when multiplied by 2.5 billion (the population of China plus India) becomes a very big number.

As economic fortunes rise, so inevitably does nationalism. Imagine that your country has been poor and marginal for centuries. Finally, things turn around and it becomes a symbol of economic progress and success. You would be proud, and anxious that your people win recognition and respect throughout the world.

Russians have long chafed over the manner in which Western countries remember World War II. Russians point out the entire Western front was a sideshow. Three quarters of all German forces were engaged on the Eastern front fighting Russian troops, and Germany suffered 70 percent of its casualties there. The Eastern front involved more land combat than all other theaters of World War II put together.

Another view from a Chinese diplomat, "When you tell us that we support a dictatorship in Sudan to have access to its oil, what I want to say is, 'And how is that different from your support of a medieval monarchy in Saudi Arabia?' We see the hypocrisy, we just don't say anything—yet."

4. The Next American Century

Many look at the vitality of this emerging world and conclude that the United States has had its day. But take a step back. Over the last 20 years, globalization has been gaining depth and breadth. America has benefited massively from these trends. It has enjoyed unusually robust growth, low unemployment and inflation, and received hundreds of billions of dollars in investment. These are not signs of economic collapse. Its companies have entered new countries and industries with great success, using global supply chains and technology to stay in the vanguard of efficiency. U.S. exports and manufacturing have actually held their ground and services have boomed.

America remains the most open, flexible society in the world, able to absorb other people, cultures, ideas, goods, and services. The country thrives on the hunger and energy of poor immigrants. Faced with the new technologies of foreign companies, or growing markets overseas, it adapts and adjusts. When you compare this dynamism with the closed and hierarchical nations that were once superpowers, you sense that the United States is different and may not fall into the trap of becoming rich, and fat, and lazy.

American society can adapt to this new world. But can the American government? Americans have not really understood the rise of "the rest." This is one of the most thrilling stories in history. Billions of people are escaping from abject poverty. The world will be enriched and ennobled as they become consumers, producers, inventors, thinkers, dreamers, and doers. This is all happening because of American ideas and actions. For 60 years, the United States has pushed countries to open their markets, free up their politics, and embrace trade and technology. American diplomats, businessmen, and intellectuals have urged people in distant lands to be unafraid of change, to join the advanced world, to learn the secrets of our success. Yet just as they are beginning to do so, we are losing faith in such ideas. We have become suspicious of trade, openness, immigration, and investment because now it's not Americans going abroad but foreigners coming to America. Just as the world is opening up, we are closing down.

Generations from now, when historians write about these times, they might note that by the turn of the 21st century, the United States had succeeded in its great, historical mission—globalizing the world. We don't want them to write that along the way, we forgot to globalize ourselves.

THE WORLD IS FLAT

New York Times columnist Thomas L. Friedman wrote an unusual—and bestselling—book *The World Is Flat*. Here are the ten major changes that are "flattening" the world from Friedman's book.

Ten Forces that Flattened the World[4]

1. **Collapse of Berlin Wall (November 9, 1989).** The collapse of the Berlin Wall revealed that the Cold War had ended and it tilted the worldwide balance of power toward democracies and free markets.
2. **Netscape goes public (August 9, 1995).** The Netscape browser made the early Internet accessible and alive for one and all.
3. **Workflow software** connected people and employees in far-flung places. Together with fiber-optic networks, workflow software created a global platform!
4. **Uploading.** This entails communities open sourcing and collaborating on online projects. Blogs are examples, as is contributing to Wikipedia and the like.
5. **Outsourcing** allowed companies to split manufacturing and service activities into separate components. Migrating business functions to India, for example, saved money and lifted a third-world economy.
6. **Offshoring.** Contract manufacturing elevated China to economic prominence. Friedman compares this to taking a factory operating in Canton, Ohio, and moving it to Canton, China.
7. **Supply-chaining.** Wal-Mart is the best example of a company using technology to streamline sales, distribution, and shipping.
8. **Insourcing.** Who would believe that UPS (United Parcel Service) employees repair Toshiba computers so they don't have to be shipped back to Japan?
9. **Informing.** In the "olden days" you could spend days trying to nail down a piece of information. With the Google search engine, you can now find it in seconds. What a phenomenal difference!

10. **"The Steroids."** Personal digital devices like mobile phones, iPods, personal digital assistants, instant messaging, and voice over Internet Protocol (VoIP). Wireless . . . wireless . . . wireless . . .

There is more than just that list in *The World Is Flat*. Friedman, for example, notes that India's 150 million Muslims live in that country peacefully participating and prospering in its secular, free-market, and democratic society. In that same country, he points out what an individual can do to transform society, a man who made a fortune in the United States and then returned to his native India to start an elementary school for "Untouchables," the lowest rung of the old caste system whose legacy persists. What a "giant difference" he is making!

Any great ideas come to your mind to help improve the world?

■ THE GLOBAL ACHIEVEMENT GAP: WHY EVEN OUR BEST SCHOOLS DON'T TEACH THE NEW SURVIVAL SKILLS OUR CHILDREN NEED—AND WHAT WE CAN DO ABOUT IT[5]

by Tony Wagner

In today's highly competitive global "knowledge economy,"*all students need new skills* for college, careers, and citizenship. The failure to give all students these new skills leaves today's youth—and our country—at an alarming competitive disadvantage.

In the 21st century . . . almost any job . . . calls for employees who know how to solve a range of intellectual and technical problems. . . . Work, learning, and citizenship in this century demand that we all know how to think—to reason, analyze, weigh evidence, problem-solve—and to communicate effectively.

While young people are learning how to read, at least at a basic level, they are not learning how to think or care about what they read; nor are they learning to clearly communicate ideas orally and in writing. They memorize names and dates in history, but they cannot explain the larger significance of historical events.

The future of our economy, the strength of our democracy, and perhaps even the health of the planet's ecosystems depend on educating future generations in ways very different from how many of us were schooled.

There are two achievement gaps in our education systems. The first is the gap between the quality of schooling that most middle-class kids get in America and the quality of schooling available for most poor and minority children-and the consequent disparity in results. The second one is the *global* achievement gap, the gap between what even our best suburban, urban, and rural public schools are teaching and testing versus what *all* students will need to succeed as learners, workers, and citizens in today's global knowledge economy.

Our system of public education—our curricula, teaching methods, and the tests we require students to take—were created in a different century for the needs of another era. They are hopelessly outdated.

The universe in which our children must compete and succeed has been rapidly transformed by groundbreaking and rapidly evolving technologies, as well as by the stunning economic growth of countries such as China, India, Thailand, the Philippines, and many more.

The Seven Survival Skills for the 21st Century

1. Critical Thinking and Problem Solving

   Asking good questions, critical thinking, and problem solving go hand in hand in the minds of most employers and business consultants, and taken together they represent the First Survival Skill for the new global "knowledge economy."
2. Collaboration Across Networks and Leading by Influence

   According to CEO Christy Pedra at Siemens, "Technology has allowed for virtual teams . . . we have teams working on major infrastructure projects that are all over the U.S. On other projects, you're working with people all around the world on solving a software problem. They don't work in the same room, they don't come to the same office, but every week they're on a variety of conference calls; they're doing web casts; they're doing net meetings.
3. Agility and Adaptability

   The shift from a hierarchal authority that tells you what to do to a team-based environment has been both rapid and profound . . . Agility and adaptability have been consistently mentioned during all of my discussions with leaders from every kind of organization.
4. Initiative and Entrepreneurialism

   Leaders today want to see individuals take more initiative and even be entrepreneurial in terms of the ways they seek out new opportunities, ideas, and strategies for improvement.

   . . . Skills needed to be a successful knowledge worker today continue to evolve and grow in importance everywhere—except in our schools.
5. Effective Oral and Written Communication

   Communication skills are a major factor highlighted in dozens of studies over the years that focus on students' lack of preparation for both college and the workplace, and these skills are only going to become more important as teams are increasingly composed of individuals from diverse cultures.

6. Accessing and Analyzing Information

   Employees in the 21st century have to manage an astronomical amount of information flowing into their work lives on a daily basis. . . . In a very short period of time, with the advent of the Internet and the increasing availability of fast connections, we have evolved from a society where only a few people had limited information to one where all of us experience information flux and glut—and can look up almost anything imaginable on our computer in a search that takes nanoseconds.

7. Curiosity and Imagination

   Creativity and innovation are key factors not only in solving problems but also in developing new or improved products and services. . . . Employees have to be new and improved knowledge workers—those who can think in disciplined ways, but also those who have a burning curiosity, a lively imagination and can engage others empathetically.

The Seven Survival Skills are for future generations what the "Three Rs" were for previous generations. They are the "new basic skills" for work, learning, and citizenship in the 21st century. —*Y.H.*

Notes

1. Excerpts from "The New System" from *The Lexus and the Olive Tree: Understanding Globalization* by Thomas L. Friedman. Copyright © 1999, 2000 by Thomas L. Friedman. Reprinted by permission of Farrar, Straus and Giroux, LLC.
2. This is only a partial listing that was originally published in *The Futurist* (www.wfs.org). Used with permission. The timeline is only a sample of the full, interactive versions of the *Technology Timeline* at http://www.btplc.com/Innovation/news/timeline/TechnologyTimeline.pdf. The sources include the preceding BT (British Telecom) timelines, the Web, magazines, interviews with world experts, and published analyses in such newsletters as the *Harrow Technology Report* (www.theharrowgroup.com), and the *Silicon.com* columns by ConceptLabs cofounder Peter Cochrane (www.cochrane.org.uk). The wild-card scenarios are based on an original idea by John Petersen, President of the Arlington Institute (www.arlingtoninstitute.org).
3. Fareed Zakaria, *The Post-American World* (New York: W.W. Norton & Company, 2008).
4. "The Ten Forces That Flattened the World" from *The World Is Flat: A Brief History of the Twenty-First Century* by Thomas L. Friedman. Copyright © 2005, 2006, 2007 by Thomas L. Friedman.
5. Excerpt from *The Global Achievement Gap: Why Even Our Best Schools Don't Teach the New Survival Skills Our Children Need—And What We Can Do About It.* Copyright 2008, by Tony Wagner. Reprinted by permission of Basic Books.

CHAPTER 3

THE ROAD TO SUCCESS

- KNOWLEDGE
- *Investor's Business Daily* 10 Secrets to Success (William J. O'Neil)
- How to Get To Where You Want To Go (Roy H. Williams)
- The Entrepreneurial Mind (Jeffry A. Timmons)
- The Entrepreneurial Spirit (George Gilder)
- Women: The Hidden Engine of World Growth (Chrystia Freeland)
- Who AM I? I am Habit

> I have a love affair with America, because there are no built-in barriers to anyone in America. I come from a country where there were barriers upon barriers.
>
> —Michael Caine

This Michael Caine quote has always impressed me. Many people feel constrained and only utilize 5 to 10 percent of their potential. However, there are no limits to how high you can climb in most of the developed countries of the world. IT'S ALL UP TO YOU!

As Thomas Edison said, "Genius is one percent inspiration and 99 percent perspiration." His patents numbered 1,093. He also added, "I never did anything worth doing by accident, nor did any of my inventions come by accident. They came by work." In other words, to be a genius you need not only to have inspiration, but also to work hard with *lots of perspiration* to make your inspiration bear fruit.

Women 65 years ago held very few positions of power. Now, in the last decade three of them held the position of U.S. Secretary of State. And who would have anticipated African American Barack Hussein Obama would be elected President of the United States of America in 2008?

> *Everything possible today was at one time impossible. Everything impossible today may at some time in the future be possible.*
>
> —Edward Lindaman (1920–1982), futurist

> *The future now belongs to societies that organize themselves for learning. What we know and can do holds the key to economic progress.*
>
> —Ray Marshall and Marc Tucker, *Thinking for a Living (1992)*

> *Change is the law of life. And those who look only to the past or present are certain to miss the future.*
>
> —John F. Kennedy (1917–1963), 35th U.S. President

KNOWLEDGE

Today we deal with 65,000 more pieces of information each day than our ancestors did 100 YEARS AGO.

INVESTOR'S BUSINESS DAILY'S 10 SECRETS TO SUCCESS[1]

by William J. O'Neil

Investor's Business Daily has spent years analyzing leaders and successful people in all walks of life. Most have 10 traits that, when combined, can turn dreams into reality.[2]

1. **HOW YOU THINK IS EVERYTHING:** Always be positive. Think success, not failure. Beware of a negative environment.
2. **DECIDE UPON YOUR TRUE DREAMS AND GOALS:** Write down your specific goals and develop a plan to reach them.
3. **TAKE ACTION:** Goals are nothing without action. Don't be afraid to get started. Just do it!
4. **NEVER STOP LEARNING:** Go back to school or read books. Get training and acquire skills.
5. **BE PERSISTENT AND WORK HARD:** Success is a marathon, not a sprint. Never give up.
6. **LEARN TO ANALYZE DETAILS:** Get all the facts, all the input. Learn from your mistakes.
7. **FOCUS YOUR TIME AND MONEY:** Don't let other people or things distract you.
8. **DON'T BE AFRAID TO INNOVATE, BE DIFFERENT:** Following the herd is a sure way to mediocrity.
9. **DEAL AND COMMUNICATE WITH PEOPLE EFFECTIVELY:** No person is an island. Learn to understand and motivate others.
10. **BE HONEST AND DEPENDABLE, TAKE RESPONSIBILITY:** Otherwise, numbers 1–9 won't matter.

■ HOW TO GET WHERE YOU WANT TO GO[3]

by Roy H. Williams

1. **See your destination in your mind.** "When you don't know where you're going, any road will get you there." —the White Rabbit in *Alice in Wonderland*
2. **Start walking.** "The journey of a thousand miles begins with a single step." —Lao Tzu (604 BCE–531 BCE)
3. **Think ahead as you walk.** "It's like driving a car at night. You can see only as far as your headlights, but you can make the whole trip that way." E. L. Doctorow (b. 1931), author of *Ragtime*
4. **Don't quit walking.** "Don't wait. Where do you expect to get by waiting? Doing is what teaches you. Doing is what leads to inspiration. Doing is what generates ideas. Nothing else, and nothing less." Daniel Quinn (b. 1935), *Ishmael*
5. **Make no deadlines.** "Patience is the best remedy for every trouble." —Titus Maccius Plautus (254 BCE–184 BCE) "I am extraordinarily patient, provided I get my own way in the end." —Margaret Thatcher (b. 1925)
6. **Look back at the progress you made each day.** "God saw all that he had made, and it was very good. And there was evening, and there was morning—the sixth day." —Genesis 1:31
7. **If evening finds you at the same place you were this morning, take a step before you lay down.** "The magic isn't in the size of your actions, but in the relentlessness of them." It is better to burn the candle at both ends, and in the middle, too, than to put it away in the closet and let the mice eat it." Henry Van Dyke (1852–1933)

Never let a day pass without making, at the very least, a tiny bit of progress. Do NOT tell yourself you'll make up for it tomorrow. (That seductive lie is the kiss of death.) Make a phone call. Lick a stamp. Correct a misspelled word. Something. Anything.

A second common mistake is to get these steps out of order. If you skip Step 1, "See your destination," and go straight to step 2, "Start walking," you'll be a wanderer, a drifter on the ocean of life, sadly on your way to lying beneath a tombstone that says, "He Had Potential."

Even more dangerous is to go from Step 1, "See your destination," directly to Step 3, "Think ahead," without ever doing Step 2, "Start walking." These are the people who never get started. Analysis paralysis. Lots of anxiety and plans and meetings and revisions and studies and evaluation and research can make you think you're getting somewhere when you're not.

Gen. George S. Patton said it best, *"A good plan today is better than a perfect plan tomorrow."* In other words, there is no perfect plan. Shut up and get started.

■ THE ENTREPRENEURIAL MIND[4]

by Jeffry A. Timmons

- It is the ability to create and build something from practically nothing.
- It is initiating, doing, achieving, and building an enterprise or organization, rather than just watching, analyzing or describing one.
- It is the knack for sensing an opportunity where others see chaos, contradiction and confusion.
- It is the ability to build a "founding team" to complement your own skills and talents.
- It is the know-how to find, marshal and control resources (often owned by others) and to make sure you don't run out of money when you need it most.
- Finally, it is a willingness to take calculated risks, both personal and financial—and then do everything possible to get the odds in your favor.
- Entrepreneurs work hard, driven by an intense commitment and determined perseverance.
- They burn with the competitive desire to excel and win.
- They use failure as a tool for learning, and would rather be effective than perfect.
- They respond to setbacks and defeats as if they were temporary interruptions, and rely on resiliency and resourcefulness to rebound and succeed.
- They have enough confidence in themselves to believe they can personally make a decisive difference in the final outcome of their ventures, and in their lives.

■ THE ENTREPRENEURIAL SPIRIT[5]

by George Gilder

Bullheaded, defiant, tenacious, creative, entrepreneurs continued to solve the problems of the world even faster than the world could create them. The achievements of enterprise remained the highest testimony to the mysterious strength of the human spirit. Confronting the perennial perils of human life, the scientific odds against human triumph, the rationalistic counsels of despair, the entrepreneur finds a higher source of hope than reason, a deeper well of faith than science, a farther reach of charity than welfare. Their success is the triumph of the spirit of enterprise—a thrust beyond the powers and principalities of the established world to the transcendent sources of creation and truth.

These men (and women) are legion, the true legislators for the silent and silenced majorities of the globe. They come by the millions and throng every mecca of freedom. Today America and the West are the prime beneficiaries of their inestimably precious gifts.

The spirit of enterprise wells up from the wisdom of the ages and the history of the West and infuses the most modern of technological adventures. It joins the old and new frontiers. It asserts a firm hierarchy of values and demands a hard discipline. It requires a life of labor and listening, aspiration and courage. But it is the source of all we are and can become, the saving grace of democratic politics and free men, the hope of the poor and the obligation of the fortunate, the redemption of an oppressed and desperate world.

WOMEN: THE HIDDEN ENGINE OF WORLD GROWTH[6]

by Chrystia Freeland

A quiet revolution is transforming the role of women, particularly in the developed world. Call it capitalist feminism—the powerful alliance between market forces and the talents, ambitions and desires of that 50 per cent of the population which is finally free from many of the legal and social constraints that held it back for repressive millennia.

We tend not to think of capitalism and feminism as natural allies. Conservatives, normally the biggest cheerleaders of American consumer capitalism, become oddly hostile when working women enter the picture. Feminists, meanwhile, have an ambivalent attitude towards what used to be called the capitalist patriarchy.

On the ground, however, the forces of the market economy are doing more than any movement or manifesto to propel women into positions of power—and working women are one of the most important engines of the great burst of economic growth in the postwar era. *The Economist* magazine has dubbed this feminization of global gross domestic product "womenomics" and, in a striking analysis, found that over the past decade or so increased female participation in the paid labor force has contributed more to the growth of the world economy than either booming China or new technology.

Set against centuries of sexism, this transformation has been impressive. The female conquest of the classrooms in the developed world is so complete that educators' big worry is what to do about failing boys. That success carries on to college, with more women than men going to university—in America, 55 per cent of college students under 25 are female.

In America, two-thirds of women of working age have a paid job, double the level in 1950, and not far off the 77 per cent of men in paid work. Women are entrepreneurial, too—one in four Americans now works for a female-owned business.

One driver of capitalist feminism is the business world's discovery that gender diversity makes cents—and dollars, too. It is no accident that Indra Nooyi, PepsiCo's new boss, and several of the other 10 women who head Fortune 500 companies are in the consumer-goods business. Most customers of these companies are female, so it stands to reason that they will do better with some women in charge. Indeed, an oft-cited study by Catalyst, the consultancy, found that companies with more women on top delivered a better financial performance than those with fewer.

Market forces have made the world of work appealing for most women; social forces will have to adapt if we want the nursery to retain its appeal, too. Has anyone noticed that the time men spend on housework increases as their wives' incomes increase, while women spend less time on housework as they earn more?

Quite a difference between this article and Chapter 1's "Would You Believe Men Were Sexists?" —*Y.H.*

WHO AM I?

by Anonymous

I am your constant companion.

I am your greatest helper or heaviest burden.

I will push you onward or drag you down to failure.

I am completely at your command.

Half the things you do might just as well be turned over to me, and I will be able to do them quickly and correctly.

I am easily managed; you must merely be firm with me. Show me exactly how you want something done, and after a few lessons, I will do it automatically.

I am the servant of all great people and of all failures as well.

Those who are great, I have made great.

Those who are failures, I have made failures.

I am not a machine though I work with all the precision of a machine plus the intelligence of a person. You may run me for profit or run me for ruin; it makes no difference to me.

Take me, train me, be firm with me, and I will place the world at your feet. Be easy with me, and I will destroy you.

WHO AM I?

I am HABIT.

Notes

1. Copyright 2009 *Investor's Business Daily*, Inc. Used with permission. All rights reserved.
2. One secret is highlighted and discussed every day on the LEADERS & SUCCESS page at *Investor's Business Daily* Web site, featuring a major success story. Very often, I turn to that page first.
3. Roy H. Williams, the Wizard of Ads®, http://www.MondayMorningMemo.com.
4. Jeffry A. Timmons, Professor of Business at Babson College. Jeffry died April 8, 2008, at the age of 66. *The Entrepreneurial Mind* (Andover, Mass.: Brick House Publishing, 1989).
5. Reprinted with permission of Simon & Schuster, Inc., from *The Spirit of Enterprise* by George Gilder. Copyright 1984 by George Gilder. All rights reserved.
6. Chrystia Freeland is a U.S. Managing Editor at *Financial Times*. Reproduced with permission. All rights reserved, copyright 2008.

CHAPTER 4

WISDOM FOR FUTURE LEADERS

- PERSISTENCE (Calvin Coolidge)
- Fire Them Up: 7 Secrets of Inspiring Leaders (Carmine Gallo)
- Good Fences Make Us Rich (Philip Humbert)
- The Next President's First Task (Robert F. Kennedy Jr.)

High achievers do one thing at a time. They are focused, determined and persistent. But more than anything else, success requires that we are not distracted and that we don't waste our time and energy chasing nonessentials. Most of us do too much of that and wonder why we don't achieve more in life.

—Philip Humbert, founder of Resources for Success

We all have the opportunity to be great leaders throughout life. If you are a parent and are a confident, giving, nonthreatening individual, chances are your children will grow up happy, loving, ambitious, and will have a good shot at being successful in life. You will have made a GIANT DIFFERENCE in their lives, and your children will most likely do likewise with their offspring in future years. Sometimes, when parents have difficulties, children are deprived of the leadership they need and do not get off to as great a start in life as they might.

As a young person growing up with younger siblings, opportunities arise to show leadership by helping younger ones develop. Curbing jealousy and resentment, setting positive examples, and being helpful and caring accomplishes this.

"Fire Them Up!" has seven secrets to help you become an inspiring leader. The previously mentioned quotation, three pages away, is so on the mark that I blew it up to fit a full page and hung it on my wall.

PERSISTENCE

Nothing in this world can take the place of PERSISTENCE. Talent will not; nothing is more common than unsuccessful men with talent. Genius will not; unrewarded genius is almost a proverb. Education alone will not; the world is full of educated derelicts. PERSISTENCE and DETERMINATION alone are omnipotent. The slogan "press on" has solved and always will solve the problems of the human race.

—Calvin Coolidge (1872–1933),
30th U.S. President

■ FIRE THEM UP: 7 SECRETS OF INSPIRING LEADERS[1]

by Carmine Gallo

1. **Demonstrate enthusiasm—constantly**. Inspiring leaders have an abundance of passion for what they do. Once you discover your passion, make sure it's apparent to everyone within your professional circle. Richard Tait created a toy and game company called Cranium. Walk into its Seattle headquarters and you are hit with a wave of fun, excitement, and engagement the likes of which is rarely seen in corporate life. It all started with one man's passion.
2. **Articulate a compelling course of action**. Inspiring leaders craft and deliver a specific, consistent, and memorable vision. A vision is a short (usually 10 words or less), vivid description of what the world will look like if your product or service succeeds. Microsoft had a vision of putting a computer on every desk, in every home. That vision—a computer on every desk, in every home—remains consistent to this day. The power of a vision set everything in motion.
3. **Sell the benefit**. Always remember, it's not about you, it's about them. You need to ask yourself constantly throughout a presentation, meeting, pitch, or any situation where persuasion takes place. Your listeners are asking themselves, what's in this for me? Answer it. Don't make them guess.
4. **Tell more stories**. Inspiring leaders tell memorable stories. Few business leaders appreciate the power of stories to connect with their audiences. Stories connect with people on an emotional level. Tell more of them.
5. **Invite participation**. Inspiring leaders bring employees, customers, and colleagues into the process of building the company or service. This is especially important when trying to motivate young people. Today's managers solicit input, listen for feedback, and actively incorporate what they hear. Employees want more than a paycheck. They want to know that their work is adding up to something meaningful.

6. **Reinforce an optimistic outlook**. Inspiring leaders speak of a better future. Extraordinary leaders throughout history have been more optimistic than the average person. Colin Powell said that optimism was the secret behind Ronald Reagan's charisma. Powell also said that optimism is a force multiplier, meaning it has a ripple effect throughout an organization. Speak in positive, optimistic language. Be a beacon of hope.
7. **Encourage potential**. Inspiring leaders praise people and invest in them emotionally. Richard Branson has said that when you praise people they flourish; criticize them and they shrivel up. Praise is the easiest way to connect with people. When people receive genuine praise, their doubt diminishes and their spirits soar. Encourage people and they'll walk through walls for you.

By inspiring your listeners, you become the kind of person people want to be around. Customers will want to do business with you, employees will want to work with you, and investors will want to back you.

■ GOOD FENCES MAKE US RICH[2]

by Philip Humbert

I've been thinking about the line from Robert Frost that "good fences make good neighbors." I'm convinced that the most overlooked essential for success is the skill of "good boundaries."

High achievers do one thing at a time. They are focused, determined and persistent (a polite word for stubborn). But more than anything else, success requires that we are not distracted, that we don't waste our time and energy chasing non-essentials. Most of us do too much of that and wonder why we don't achieve more in life.

I recently had several conversations that brought this home to me. One friend laughed out loud when I asked him to set limits on his work and "just say no" to outrageous demands. He argued that he would lose customers, that he prides himself on responding to his clients, and that, "I just couldn't do that." As a result, he works long hours doing trivial things that are "urgent" for other people! He's often exhausted and, of course, he is not building his own business.

I was reminded of Michael Gerber's famous dictum to "work on your business rather than in your business." In my friend's case, my fear is that neither his business nor his life will flourish because he spends so much time and energy on his clients' petty interruptions. Highly successful people build tight fences around their work. They define what they do, decide what they won't do, and then stick to it.

A second essential is to "fence out" new opportunities. Yes, you read that right. We live in a world of endless opportunities. You can go to school, start a new business, or buy another house while they're on sale this year. Opportunities abound! Television may be our most common distraction, but I'm convinced having too many opportunities may be our most expensive distraction.

The key to success is to do one thing well. And do a lot of it. And sell it at a price that is a "bargain" for your customers and profitable for you. Failures are always chasing the "next big thing." They are experts at "starting over." Successful people are narrow-minded and they persist. They put good fences around "opportunity."

A final boundary is to put boundaries around our friends and loved ones. This is tough! And, obviously, I'm not talking about putting limits on the *quality* of our relationships. Love and friendship is what life is all about! But, I don't answer my phone every time it rings.

We want to be "nice." We value our relationships, and our friends and family are wonderful people. No wonder we want to "put them first." That's a good thing! But so is doing your work, pursuing your passion and building your business. Balance and boundaries are the key.

Robert Frost observed that "good fences make good neighbors" and I would add that good boundaries make us rich, in every sense of the word. Boundaries are essential to build your business, to create and maintain healthy relationships, and to enjoy the life you truly want. Maintain your boundaries.

■ THE NEXT PRESIDENT'S FIRST TASK (A MANIFESTO)[3]

by Robert F. Kennedy Jr.

The practice of borrowing a billion dollars each day to buy foreign oil has caused the American dollar to implode. More than a trillion dollars in annual subsidies to coal and oil producers have beggared a nation that four decades ago owned half the globe's wealth. Carbon dependence has eroded our economic power, destroyed our moral authority, diminished our international influence and prestige, endangered our national security, and damaged our health and landscapes. It is subverting everything we value.

We know that nations that "decarbonize" their economies reap immediate rewards. Sweden enacted a carbon tax—now up to $150 a ton—and as a result thousands of entrepreneurs rushed to develop new ways of generating energy from wind, the sun, and the tides, and from woodchips, agricultural waste, and garbage. Growth rates climbed to upwards of three times those of the U.S.

Iceland was 80 percent dependent on imported coal and oil in the 1970s and was among the poorest economies in Europe. Today, Iceland is 100 percent energy-independent, with 90 percent of the nation's homes heated by geothermal and its remaining electrical needs met by hydro.

As for solar, according to a study in *Scientific American,* photovoltaic and solar-thermal installations across just 19 percent of the most barren desert land in the Southwest could supply nearly all of our nation's electricity needs without any rooftop installation, even assuming every American owned a plug-in hybrid.

There are a number of things the new president should immediately do to hasten the approaching boom in energy innovation. A carbon cap-and-trade system designed to put downward pressure on carbon emissions is quite simply a no-brainer.

There's a second thing the next president should do, and it would be a strategic masterstroke: push to revamp the nation's antiquated high-voltage power-transmission system so that it can deliver solar, wind, geothermal, and other renewable energy across the country.

The nation urgently needs more investment in its backbone transmission grid, including new direct-current (D.C.) power lines for efficient long-haul transmission.

The federal government needs to work with state authorities to open up the grids, allowing clean-energy innovators to fairly compete for investment, space, and customers. We need open markets where hundreds of local and national power producers can scramble to deliver economic and environmental solutions at the lowest possible price.

The energy sector, in other words, needs an initiative analogous to the 1996 Telecommunications Act, which required open access to all the nation's telephone lines. Marketplace competition among national and local phone companies instantly precipitated the historic explosion in telecom activity.

The benefits to America are beyond measure. We will cut annual trade and budget deficits by hundreds of billions, improve public health and farm production, diminish global warming, and create millions of good jobs. And for the first time in half a century we will live free from Middle Eastern wars and entanglements with petty tyrants who despise democracy and are hated by their own people.

Notes

1. From *Fire Them Up!* by Carmine Gallo. www.Carminegallo.com. Reprinted with permission of John Wiley & Sons, Inc.
2. Written by Dr. Philip E. Humbert, author, speaker and personal success coach. Dr. Humbert has hundreds of tips, tools and articles on his Web site that you can use for YOUR success! It's a great resource! Be sure to sign up for his FREE newsletter! Visit him on the Web at www.philiphumbert.com.
3. Robert F. Kennedy Jr., President of the Waterkeeper Alliance promoting clean water throughout the world. Originally published in *Vanity Fair* (May 2008). www.robertfkennedyjr.com.

CHAPTER 5

UPLIFTING COMMENCEMENT ADDRESSES

- INSPIRATION
- Alan Alda at Connecticut College, 1980
- Famous Graduation Quotes and Advice
- Tia Duer at the Abbingdon Friends School, 2008
- Tony Blair at Yale University, Class Day 2008
- Ray Kurzweil at Worcester Polytechnic Institute, 2005

This is an important chapter for me. If I hadn't gone to my grandson's graduation in June 2008, I might not have written this book. People who give these commencement addresses are hoping to inspire the graduates to "go forth and set the world on fire!" "Go out there and knock 'em dead!" "The world is all yours, go out and conquer it!"

Commencement addresses are usually quite inspirational. What graduation speakers are trying to do is motivate students who have come a long way. The following few sentences were said almost 100 years ago by Darwin P. Kingsley, President of the New York Life Insurance Company.

> You have powers you never dreamed of. You can do things you never thought you could do. There are no limitations in what you can do except the limitations of your own mind.

It was quite true then and still is today; yet, most people go through life only reaching a small fraction of their potential. It's very important that you realize this and work to MAXIMIZE your potential.

INSPIRATION

You have powers you never dreamed of. You can do things you never thought you could do. There are no limitations in what you can do except the limitations in your own mind.

—Darwin P. Kingsley (1857–1932),
President of New York Life

ALAN ALDA AT CONNECTICUT COLLEGE, 1980[1]

by Alan Alda

I want you to be potent, to do good when you can, and to hold your wit and your intelligence like a shield against other people's wantonness. And above all, to laugh and enjoy yourself in a life of your own choosing and in a world of your own making. I want you to be strong and aggressive and tough and resilient and full of feeling. I want you to be everything that's you, deep at the center of your being.

I want you to have chutzpah.

Nothing important was ever accomplished without chutzpah. Columbus had chutzpah. The signers of the Declaration of Independence had chutzpah. Don't ever aim your doubt at yourself. Laugh at yourself, but don't doubt yourself. Whenever you wonder about yourself, look up at the stars swirling around in the heavens and just realize how tiny and puny they are. They're supposed to be gigantic explosions and they're just these insignificant little dots. If you step back from things far enough, you realize how important and powerful you are.

Be bold. Let the strength of your desire give force and moment to your every step. Move with all of yourself. When you embark for strange places don't leave any of yourself safely on shore. They may laugh at you if you don't discover India. Let them laugh. India's already there. You'll come back with a brand new America. Have the nerve to go into unexplored territory. Be brave enough to live life creatively. The creative is the place where no one else has ever been. It is not the previously known. You have to leave the city of your comfort and go into the wilderness of your intuition. You can't get there by bus, only by hard work and risk and by not quite knowing what you're doing, but what you'll discover will be wonderful. What you'll discover will be yourself.

FAMOUS GRADUATION QUOTES AND ADVICE

Graduation day is an important milestone. Many noted people have commented eloquently on how to succeed in life.

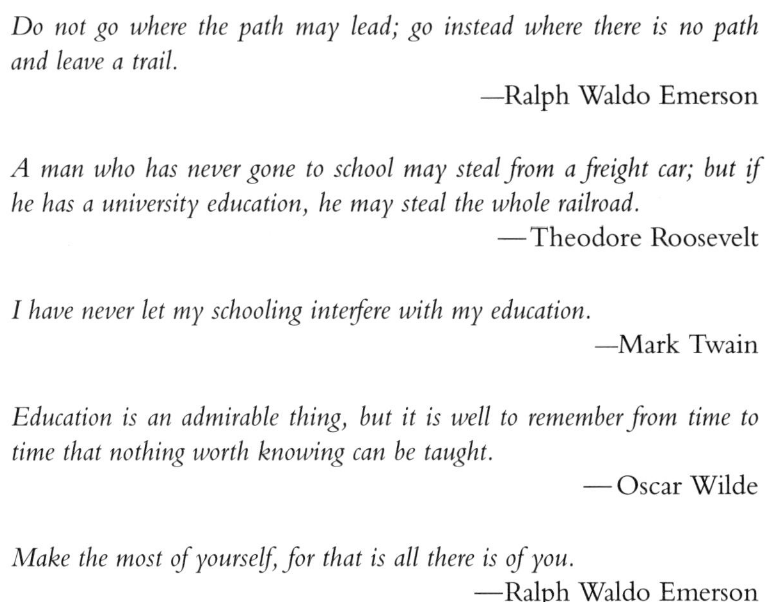

> *Do not go where the path may lead; go instead where there is no path and leave a trail.*
>
> —Ralph Waldo Emerson

> *A man who has never gone to school may steal from a freight car; but if he has a university education, he may steal the whole railroad.*
>
> —Theodore Roosevelt

> *I have never let my schooling interfere with my education.*
>
> —Mark Twain

> *Education is an admirable thing, but it is well to remember from time to time that nothing worth knowing can be taught.*
>
> —Oscar Wilde

> *Make the most of yourself, for that is all there is of you.*
>
> —Ralph Waldo Emerson

Advice You Never Learned in School[2]

Although the following list of eleven useful "rules" you didn't learn in school is typically attributed to Bill Gates, it is actually excerpted from the 1996 book *Dumbing Down Our Kids* by educator Charles J. Sykes.

RULE 1: Life is not fair; get used to it.

RULE 2: The world won't care about your self-esteem. The world will expect you to accomplish something *before* you feel good about yourself.

RULE 3: You will NOT make $60,000 a year right out of high school. You won't be a vice president with a car phone, until you earn both.

RULE 4: If you think your teacher is tough, wait till you get a boss. He doesn't have tenure.

RULE 5: Flipping burgers is not beneath your dignity. Your grandparents had a different word for burger flipping; they called it opportunity.

RULE 6: If you mess up, it's not your parents' fault, so don't whine about your mistakes, learn from them.

RULE 7: Before you were born, your parents weren't as boring as they are now. They got that way from paying your bills; cleaning your clothes and listening to you talk about how cool you are. So before you save the rain forest from the parasites of your parents' generation, try delousing the closet in your own room.

RULE 8: Your school may have done away with winners and losers, but life has not. In some schools they have abolished failing grades; they'll give you as many times as you want to get the right answer. This doesn't bear the slightest resemblance to ANYTHING in real life.

RULE 9: Life is not divided into semesters. You don't get summers off and very few employers are interested in helping you find yourself. Do that on your own time.

RULE 10: Television is NOT real life. In real life people actually have to leave the coffee shop and go to jobs.

RULE 11: Be nice to nerds. Chances are you'll end up working for one.

■ TIA DUER AT THE ABBINGDON FRIENDS SCHOOL, 2008[3]

by Tia Duer (Class of 1967)

Today is an important rite of passage for you. At this moment you're probably feeling relief—and also a great sense of expectation about what lies ahead of you.

Up to now your lives have been quite structured and overseen. From this point on, you'll be more and more independent, and your life will become full of more choices. This is a big threshold you're crossing. From now on you'll be increasingly responsible for shaping your own path, through college and in your life beyond. And in the process you'll be finding yourself and shaping who you are.

As you look ahead many of you are very uncertain as to where your lives will lead. The fact is that very few of us really know! Life is full of serendipity and zigs and zags. In my own case, first I wanted to be a clinical psychologist, then (with activism against the Vietnam War), I wanted to have a bigger social impact. I decided to go to Law School. (My mother: "won't you be bored?") At Yale Law, I took an offbeat course about development and social change that really excited me and led me, through another fluke of fate, to apply to the World Bank—where I've had many roles. Now I lead a program that I created. In short, life doesn't always take a straight course, and that is okay.

Have faith in yourself. Go for what you believe in and where your passions lie. And don't let anyone tell you it can't be done. That's just poverty of imagination.

Now for the important question! Will you make the world a better place? Your experience at American Friends School (AFS) has been all about values—perhaps more than you even realize today.

As you move on in life, you're going to be feeling a lot of pressures to focus on your own individual life, the good job, the good income, the big house, the new car. . . .

In the USA, over the last 40 years or so, our concept of the "good life" has been narrowed down to these material things. The competitive forces in the society and economy certainly *don't support* collective social responsibility—making it hard for us to come together to tackle our big social and environmental challenges.

In my travels, I've seen that many other societies and cultures put greater emphasis ensuring basic services for the whole society, and maintaining social "connectedness." At the macro level, you can see this in Europe, with their strong support for universal health care systems and strong commitment to energy conservation and production of renewable energy. At the micro level you can see this in the strong ethic of community cooperation and mutual assistance all over Asia and Africa, in rural areas of Scandinavia, and parts of Latin America.

The values and commitments developed here at AFS—the deep knowledge that you are part of a world community that depends on your involvement, and that you have a responsibility to contribute to improving the world—are so needed now. We face big challenges:

Climate change is the cause of our time. If we don't act quickly and together, to make the changes that are needed, the effects—for all of us—will be catastrophic. We have to remake the way we live, the way things are produced, reduce the waste we create and the energy we consume. These are not technical issues as much as they're leadership issues—and our joint leadership is critically necessary.

In the USA, the disparity between rich and poor has increased dramatically, and this has only been exacerbated by recent failures in our financial markets and the deindustrialization of the U.S. economy in the recent decades.

Our democracy needs to be rebuilt and reinvigorated, and our collaborative relationships and good will around the world reestablished.

All of these need concerted effort from each of us. And all of our lives will be deeply affected by what happens on these fronts. One can have an impact in a lot of different ways, through different walks of life.

You've already shown that you have strong values and that you act on your sense of social responsibility. When you realized that the T-shirts you sold at Field Day may have come from sweat shops, you took the money and used it to fund a micro-credit project—and presented the problems of sweat shop labor conditions to a school assembly, to sensitize others.

In your senior leadership program, you came together and decided on priorities of what is needed in the school community, and determined to leave a legacy. You had good ideas—but you also understood that the important thing isn't just having good ideas, it's putting them into action and following through, especially when it's difficult.

You're going to find that your experiences in the senior leadership program will be very useful to you. You learned to have patience with each other and to press each other and to engage each other and to negotiate. And perhaps most importantly, you saw each other's strengths and talents and tapped into them to meet your objectives. So much of leadership is about working together, encouraging each other, being engaged, actively listening to each other and working through problems together. You can be very proud of the changes you have made at AFS—in the cafeteria, in mentoring freshmen, in peer tutoring, and in setting a good example for others.

Leadership is not an individual responsibility—it is a collective process. It's about building ways of collaborating, learning how to respect diversity and working together despite differences. It's about learning how to deliberate, to analyze, to propose and engage each other, and to co-create the future.

Committing yourselves to improving our society and the world can be daunting, especially at a time like this, when so much needs to be done, and every system seems to be in decline. But as the environmentalist Paul Hawken said, "the other way to look at it is: 'what a great time to be born. What a great time to be alive.' Because this generation gets to essentially completely change this world."

So find what makes you passionate and pursue it. Act on your values. Be engaged and make a difference. Your time is now!

Though this address was made to particular graduates at a particular school, what she says is valid for all students and graduates and everyone in the world of work and life. Being at my grandson's graduation and hearing this excellent address inspired me to switch focus of this book from "Let's Change the World" to "HOW EACH AND EVERY ONE OF US CAN MAKE A GIANT DIFFERENCE IN OUR FAST-CHANGING WORLD." I am truly grateful to Tia Duer of the World Bank.

—*Y.H.*

■ TONY BLAIR AT YALE UNIVERSITY, CLASS DAY 2008[4]

by Tony Blair

Today, though the land that encompasses Israel and Palestine is small, the conflict symbolizes the wider prospects of the entire vast region of the Middle East and beyond. There, the forces of modernization and moderation battle with those of reaction and extremism. The shadow of Iran looms large.

What is at stake is immense. Will those who believe in peaceful co-existence triumph, matching the growing economic power and wealth with a politics and culture at ease with the 21st Century? Or will the victors be those that seek to use that economic wealth to create a politics and culture more relevant to the feudal Middle Ages?

Thousands of miles from here, this struggle is being played out in the suburbs of Baghdad and Beirut and the Gaza strip. But the impact of its outcome on our security and way of life will register in the core of our well-being.

In fact, if I had to sum up my view of the world, I would say to you: turn your thoughts to the East. Not just to the Middle East, but to the Far East.

For the first time in many centuries, power is moving east. China and India each have populations roughly double those of America and Europe combined.

In the next two decades, these two countries together will undergo industrialization four times the size of the USA's and at five times the speed.

We must be mindful that as these ancient civilizations become somehow younger and more vibrant, our young civilization does not grow old. Most of all we should know that in this new world, we must clear a path to partnership, not stand off against each other, competing for power.

The world in which you, in time to come, will take the reins, cannot afford a return to 20th century struggles for hegemony.

■ RAY KURZWEIL AT WORCESTER POLYTECHNIC INSTITUTE, 2005[5]

by Ray Kurzweil

Three Great Revolutions Coming

It took us 15 years to sequence HIV. We sequenced the SARS virus in 31 days. We'll soon be able to sequence a virus in just a few days' time. We're basically doubling the power of these technologies every year. And that's going to lead to three great revolutions that sometimes go by the letters GNR: GENETICS, NANOTECHNOLOGY, and ROBOTICS.

Genetics, which is really a term for biotechnology, means that we are gaining the tools to actually understand biology as information processes and reprogram them. . . . We're now understanding the information processes underlying disease and aging and getting the tools to reprogram them. We have little software programs inside us called genes, about 23,000 of them. They were designed or evolved tens of thousands of years ago when conditions were quite different. I'll give you just one example. The fat insulin receptor gene says, "Hold on to every calorie because the next hunting season may not work out so well." And that's a gene we'd like to reprogram. It made sense 20,000 years ago when calories were few and far between. What would happen if we blocked that? We have a new technology that can turn genes off called RNA interference. So when that gene was turned off in mice, these mice ate ravenously and yet they remained slim. They got the health benefits of being slim. They didn't get diabetes, didn't get heart disease or cancer. They lived 20 to 25 percent longer while eating ravenously. There are several pharmaceutical companies who have noticed that might be a good human drug. Ten or 15 years from now, which is not that far away, we'll have the maturing of these biotechnology techniques and we'll dramatically overcome the major diseases that we've struggled with for eons and also allow us to slow down, stop and even reverse aging processes.

The next revolution is *Nanotechnology,* where we're applying information technology to matter and energy. We'll be able to overcome major problems that human civilization has struggled with, for example, energy. We have a little bit of sunlight here today. If we captured .03 percent, that's three ten-thousandths of the sunlight that falls on the

Earth, we could meet all of our energy needs. We can't do that today because solar panels are very heavy, expensive and inefficient. New nano-engineered designs, designing them at the molecular level, will enable us to create very inexpensive, very efficient, light-weight solar panels, store the energy in nano-engineered fuel cells, which are highly decentralized, and meet all of our energy needs. The killer APP (Applications Portability Profile) of nanotechnology is something called nanobots, basically little robots the size of blood cells. In regard to the 2020s, these devices will be able to go inside the human body and keep us healthy by destroying pathogens, correcting DNA errors, killing cancer cells and so on and even go into the brain, and interact with our biological neurons.

And finally *Robotics,* which is really artificial intelligence (AI) at the human level, we'll see that in the late 2020s. By that time this exponential growth of computation will provide computer systems that are more powerful than the human brain. We'll have completed the reverse engineering of the human brain to get the software algorithms, the secrets, the principles of operation of how human intelligence works. A side benefit of that is we'll have greater insight into ourselves. We'll know how human intelligence works, how our emotional intelligence works, and what human dysfunction is all about. We'll be able to correct, for example, neurological diseases and also expand human intelligence. And this is not going to be an alien invasion of intelligent machines. We already routinely do things in our civilization that would be impossible without our computer intelligence. If all the artificial intelligence programs embedded in our economic infrastructure were to stop today, our human civilization would grind to a halt. So we're already very integrated with our technology. Computer technology used to be very remote. Now we carry it in our pockets. It'll soon be in our clothing. It's already begun migrating into our bodies and brains. We will become increasingly intimate with our technology.

Notes

1. Copyright 1980 by Alan Alda. All rights reserved. Excerpts are from "The Wilderness of Your Intuition" given at Connecticut College, May 20, 1980. Alan Alda entertained us for 12 years in his memorable role as Hawkeye Pierce on the television series M★A★S★H.
2. Excerpts from *Dumbing Down Our Kids* by Charles J. Sykes. Copyright 1995 by the author, and reprinted by permission of St. Martin's Press, LLC.
3. Excerpts from Tia Duer's speech given June 11, 2008, at the Abington Friends School.
4. Excerpts from Tony Blair's address given at Yale University on May 25, 2008.
5. Ray Kurzweil is the author of *The Singularity Is Near* (2005) and the recipient of 15 Honorary Doctorate degrees. These excerpts were taken from his commencement address given at Worcester Polytechnic Institute May 21, 2005.

CHAPTER 6

FAILURE IS NOT FATAL, IT HAPPENS TO THE BEST

- SUCCESS (Mark Twain)
- Out of the Mouths of "EXPERTS"
- Famous Failures (Joey Green)
- Genius = 1% Inspiration and 99% Perspiration
- Experts Are Never Wrong! Oh Yeah?
- Firstborns vs. Laterborns (Frank J. Sulloway)

Mark Twain's quote on page 75 has always impressed me. When you are growing up and hang around with kids in the neighborhood, just mention that you want to be someone high up in life and most likely many will laugh at you. Their reaction is like saying, "Just who do you think you are?" As in the Twain quote, these are small people! Most

GREAT people do let you know that there are really no barriers, and that you too can go out there and "climb the heights!"

Don't be ashamed of any rejections or failures. If Lincoln, Einstein, Streisand, and Bill Gates suffered failures and still had great successes, so can you. This long list contains names of people who experienced great failures and went on to become great stars in their fields.

Don't be afraid to go up against the "experts!" J.P. Morgan thought the telephone had no commercial value, Thomas Edison felt alternating current was unnecessary and some major names didn't have good things to say about Edison's light bulb. *Business Week* in 1968 didn't feel the Japanese could carve out a decent share of the U.S. auto market. Bill Gates in 1981 may have said 640 kilobytes would be enough memory for anybody at a computer, which he denies he ever said.

Take to heart what Edison said about genius: "It's 1 percent inspiration and 99 percent perspiration." So . . . roll up your sleeves and GET TO WORK!

SUCCESS

Keep away from people who try to belittle your ambitions. Small people always do that, but the really GREAT make you feel that you, too, can become great.

—Mark Twain (1835–1910)

■ OUT OF THE MOUTHS OF "EXPERTS"

Smoking kills. If you're killed, you've lost a very important part of your life.
—Actress Brooke Shields (b. 1965) during an interview to become spokesperson for a federal antismoking campaign

I've never had major knee surgery on any other part of my body.
—Winston Bennett (b. 1965), former University of Kentucky basketball forward

Outside of the killings, Washington has one of the lowest crime rates in the country.
—Marion Barry (b. 1936), former mayor of Washington, D.C.

That lowdown scoundrel deserves to be kicked to death by a jackass, and I'm just the one to do it.
—A congressional candidate in Texas

Half this game is ninety percent mental.
—Danny Ozark (b. 1923), former manager of the Phillys

I love California. I practically grew up in Phoenix.
—Dan Quayle (b. 1947), U.S. Vice-President

It's no exaggeration to say that the undecided could go one-way or another.
—George W. Bush (b. 1946), U.S. President

The word "genius" isn't applicable in football. A genius is a guy like Norman Einstein.
—Joe Theisman (b. 1949), NFL quarterback)

We are ready for an unforeseen event that may or may not occur.
—Al Gore (b. 1948), U.S. Vice-President)

Your food stamps will be stopped effective March 1992 because we received notice that you passed away. May God bless you! You may reapply if there is a change in your circumstances.
—Department of Social Services, Greenville, South Carolina

If somebody has a bad heart, they can plug this jack in at night as they go to bed and it will monitor their heart throughout the night. And the next morning, when they wake up dead, there'll be a record.

—Mark S. Fowler (b. 1941), former Chairman of the Federal Communications Commission

FAMOUS FAILURES[1]

by Joey Green

Never be discouraged by rejections and failures. Many great names were rejected many, many times but persevered and eventually succeeded.

Abraham Lincoln had 12 major failures before winning presidency.

Albert Einstein failed the entrance exams to Swiss Polytechnic Institute.

Barbra Streisand made her debut at 19 in 1961. Show closed in a single night.

Bill Gates, a Harvard dropout, and his first business flopped.

Charles Dickens worked in a factory pasting labels on bottles of shoe polish.

Dick Cheney flunked out of Yale twice.

Edgar Allan Poe was expelled from West Point for "neglect of duty, disobedience."

Frank Sinatra was expelled from high school after 47 days for rowdy behavior.

Fred Astaire's first screen test, "Can't act. Slightly bald. Can dance a little."

George Orwell (author of *1984*) worked as a janitor in a hotel in Paris.

George W. Bush had a straight-C average in college.

Harry Truman, rejected by West Point and Annapolis, went bankrupt in 1922.

Henry Ford's first two automobile companies failed.

Hillary Clinton flunked the Washington, D.C., bar examination.

Humphrey Bogart was dropped by Fox in 1931 after six so-so movies.

J. K. Rowling (author of the Harry Potter series) lived on welfare in a mice-infested apartment.

Jennifer Aniston auditioned for *Saturday Night Live* but wasn't hired.

John Grisham, 16 agents and 12 publishers rejected his first novel.

John McCain graduated 895th of 900 at United States Naval Academy.

Johnny Depp dropped out of high school, sold ink pens over the phone.

Kevin Spacey was expelled from Northridge Military Academy.

Lucille Ball's drama school told her, "You're wasting your time."

Ludwig van Beethoven, "as a composer, he is hopeless," said his teacher.

Marilyn Monroe, dropped from Fox, "unattractive and cannot act."

Martin Luther nailed *95 Theses* to church door, excommunicated by the Pope.

Matt Damon dropped out of Harvard 12 credits short of earning his degree.

Michael Jordan, cut from high school basketball team, went home and cried.

Muhammad Ali graduated 376th from a high school class of 391 students.

Rush Limbaugh flunked two speech classes in his first year of college.

Steve Jobs dropped out of Reed College in his freshman year.

Steven Spielberg, finally finished college, about 30 years later.

The Beatles, turned down by Decca Records ("didn't like their sound").

Theodore Roosevelt ran for mayor of New York City in 1886 and lost.

Thomas Edison, "too stupid to learn anything," said his teacher.

Tom Cruise auditioned for *Fame,* was told he wasn't "pretty enough."

Walt Disney fired from a newspaper: "He lacked imagination."

Whoopi Goldberg worked at a mortuary applying makeup to corpses.

Winston Churchill failed the sixth grade.

GENIUS = 1% INSPIRATION AND 99% PERSPIRATION

So said Thomas Alva Edison (1847–1931). Here are some examples from the life of Abraham Lincoln (1809–1865), the sixteenth U.S. President:

- Failed in business, 1831
- Defeated for legislature, 1832
- Again failed in business, 1833
- Elected to Illinois legislature, 1834
- Defeated in bid to be speaker of the state house, 1838
- Defeated for state elector, 1840
- Defeated for U.S. Congress, 1843
- Elected to U.S. Congress, 1846
- Defeated for U.S. Congress, 1848
- Defeated for U.S. Senate, 1855
- Defeated for Vice-President of the United States, 1858
- Defeated for U.S. Senate, 1858
- Elected President of the United States, 1860

Nothing in the world can take the place of persistence. Talent will not; nothing is more common than unsuccessful men with talent. Genius will not; unrewarded genius is almost a proverb. Education will not; the world is full of educated failures. Persistence and determination alone are omnipotent.

—Calvin Coolidge (1872–1933), 30th U.S. President

I hated every minute of training, but I said, "Don't quit. Suffer now and live the rest of your life like a champion."

—Muhammad Ali (b. 1942), Three-time world heavyweight champ

When you get in a tight place and everything goes against you, till it seems as though you could not hold a minute longer, never give up then, for that is just the place and time that the tide will turn.

—Harriet Beecher Stowe (1811–1896), *Uncle Tom's Cabin*

Let me tell you the secret that has led me to my goal. My strength lies solely in my tenacity.

—Louis Pasteur (1822–1895), French chemist

■ EXPERTS ARE NEVER WRONG! OH YEAH?

I made up a quotation years ago: "What is the greatest lie ever told? Build a better mousetrap and the world will beat a path to your door." Here are some statements by some outstanding individuals about the resistance to innovation.

> *The reasonable man adapts himself to the world; the unreasonable one persists in trying to adapt the world to himself. Therefore, all progress depends upon the unreasonable man.*
>
> —George Bernard Shaw (1856–1950), Irish playwright, *Man and Superman*

> *All human institutions since the dawn of prehistory or earlier had always been designed to prevent change—all of them: family, government, church, army. Change has always been a catastrophic threat to human security.*
>
> —Peter R. Drucker (1909–2005), Management guru

> *At every crossway on the road that leads to the future each progressive spirit is opposed by a thousand men appointed to guard the past.*
>
> —Maurice Maeterlinck (1862–1949), Belgian playwright

> *Invention demands men with fanatic faith in their ideas, men willing to ignore the experts who say it cannot be done, men unafraid to butt heads with authority.*
>
> —Richard Stillerman, coauthor, *The Sources of Invention,* 1959

> *When a distinguished . . . scientist states that something is possible, he is almost certainly right. When he states something is impossible, he is probably wrong.*
>
> —Sir Arthur C. Clarke, British science fiction writer (1917–2008)

Many distinguished "experts" in the past few centuries gave thumbs down to innovations, which later revolutionized the world. Here are some of their (unverified) authoritative pronouncements:

1486 *So many centuries after the Creation, it is unlikely that anyone could find hitherto unknown lands of any value."*

—Spanish Royal Commission, rejecting Christopher Columbus's proposal to sail west

1530 *The multitude of books is a great evil. There is no limit to this fever for writing.*

—Martin Luther (1483–1546), German theologian

1800 *What, sir, would you make a ship sail against the wind and currents by lighting a bonfire under her deck? I pray you, excuse me; I have not the time to listen to such nonsense.*

—Napoleon Bonaparte (1769–1821), when told of Robert Fulton's steamboat

1825 *What can be more palpably absurd than the prospect held out of locomotives traveling twice as fast as stagecoaches?*

—*The Quarterly Review*

1830 *Rail travel at high speeds is not possible because passengers, unable to breathe, would die of asphyxia.*

—Dionysius Lardner (1793–1859), Professor of Natural Philosophy and Astronomy at University College, London

1842 *I watched his countenance closely, to see if he was not deranged, and I was assured by other senators, after he left the room, that they had no confidence in it.*

—Oliver H. Smith (1794–1859), U.S. Senator, after a demonstration of Samuel Morse's telegraph

1844 *The advancement of the arts from year to year taxes our credulity and seems to presage the arrival of that period when further improvements must end.*

—Henry L. Ellsworth (1791–1858), First U.S. Commissioner of Patents

1864 *No one will pay good money to get from Berlin to Potsdam in one hour when he can ride his horse there in one day for free.*

—Prussian King William I (1861–1888) on railroads

1865 *Well-informed people know it is impossible to transmit the voice over wires and that were it possible to do so, the thing would be of no practical value.*

—Boston Post

1872 *It's a great invention but who would want to use it anyway?*

—Rutherford B. Hayes, 19th U.S. President, after a demonstration of Alexander Bell's telephone

1872 *Louis Pasteur's theory of germs is ridiculous fiction.*

—Pierre Pachet, professor of physiology at Toulouse

1873 *The abdomen, the chest, and the brain will forever be shut from the intrusion of the wise and humane surgeon.*

—Sir John Eric Ericksen, surgeon to Queen Victoria

1876 *This "telephone" has too many shortcomings to be seriously considered as a means of communication. The device is inherently of no value to us.*

—Western Union Co. memo

1877 *Mr. Bell, after careful consideration of your invention, while it is a very interesting novelty, we have come to the conclusion it has no commercial possibilities.*

—J. P. Morgan to Alexander G. Bell

1878 *The Americans have need of the telephone, but we do not. We have plenty of messenger boys.*

—Sir William Preece, Chief Engineer, British Post Office

1878 *Good enough for our transatlantic friends . . . but unworthy of the attention of practical or scientific men.*

—Parliamentary Committee, on Edison's lightbulb

1880 *Such startling announcements as these should be deprecated as being unworthy of science and mischievous to its true progress.*

—Sir William Siemens, on Edison's lightbulb

1880 *Everyone acquainted with the subject will recognize it as a conspicuous failure.*

—Henry Morton, president of the Stevens Institute of Technology, on Edison's lightbulb

1889 *My personal desire would be to prohibit entirely the use of alternating currents. They are unnecessary as they are dangerous.*

—Thomas Alva Edison

1895 *Heavier-than-air flying machines are impossible.*

—Lord Kelvin, Pres. Royal Society

1897 *Radio has no future.*

—Lord Kelvin, Pres. Royal Society

1899 *Everything that can be invented has been invented.*

—Charles H. Duell, Commissioner, U.S. Office of Patents

1899 *The ordinary "horseless carriage" is at present a luxury for the wealthy; and although its price will probably fall in the future, it will never, of course, come into as common use as the bicycle.*

—*Literary Digest*

1902 *The actual building of roads devoted to motorcars is not for the near future in spite of rumors to that effect.*

—*Harper's Weekly*

1902 *Flight by machines heavier than air is unpractical and insignificant, if not utterly impossible.*

—Simon Newcomb, Canadian-born American astronomer

1904 *Airplanes are interesting toys but of no military value.*

—Marechal Ferdinand Foch, Professor of Strategy, Ecole Superieure de Guerre

1919 *Taking the best left-handed pitcher in baseball and converting him into a right fielder is one of the dumbest things I ever heard.*

—Tris Speaker, baseball expert, on Babe Ruth.

1922 *The radio craze will die out in time.*

—Thomas Alva Edison

1926 *While theoretically television may be feasible, commercially and financially I consider it an impossibility, a development of which we need waste little time dreaming.*

—Lee de Forest (1873–1961), radio pioneer

1927 *Who the hell wants to hear actors talk?*

—H. M. Warner, Warner Brothers

1928 *There is no likelihood that man can ever tap the power of the atom. The glib supposition of utilizing atomic energy when our coal has run out is a completely unscientific Utopian dream, a childish bug-a-boo.*

—Robert Millikan

1929 *Stocks have reached what looks like a permanently high plateau.*

—Irving Fisher, Professor of Economics, Yale University

1936 *A rocket will never be able to leave the earth's atmosphere.*

—*New York Times*

1939 *Atomic energy might be as good as our present-day explosives, but it is unlikely to produce anything very much more dangerous.*

—Winston Churchill

1942 *The Americans are good about making fancy cars and refrigerators, but that doesn't mean they are any good at making aircraft. They are bluffing. They are excellent at bluffing.*

—Hermann Goering, Commander-in-Chief of the Luftwaffe

1943 *I think there is a world market for maybe five computers.*

—Tom Watson, IBM

1945 *That is the biggest fool thing we have ever done . . . the [atom] bomb will never go off, and I speak as an expert in explosives."*

—Admiral William Leahy to President Truman

1946 *Television won't last because people will soon get tired of staring at a plywood box every night.*

—Darryl Zanuck (1902–1979), motion picture mogul

1949 *Computers in the future may weigh no more than 1.5 tons.*

—*Popular Mechanics*

1956 *Space travel is utter bilge.*

—Dr. Richard van der Reit Wooley (1906–1986), space advisor to the British government

1957 *Space travel is bunk.*

—Sir Harold Spencer Jones, Astronomer Royal

1957 *I have traveled the length and breadth of this country and talked with the best people, and I can assure you that data processing is a fad that won't last out the year.*

—The editor in charge of business books for Prentice Hall

1958 *We will bury you.*

—Nikita Khrushchev to the United States

1962 *We don't like their sound. We don't think they will do anything in their market. Guitar groups are on their way out.*

—Decca on declining to sign the Beatles

1962 *Transmission of documents via telephone wires is possible in principle, but the apparatus required is so expensive that it will never become a practical proposition.*

—Dennis Gabor (1900–1979), 1971 Nobel Prize in physics

1966 *The concept is interesting and well formed, but in order to earn better than a "C," the idea must be feasible.*

—Yale University management professor in response to FedEx's Fred Smith after submitting a paper proposing overnight delivery service

1968 *With over fifteen types of foreign cars already on sale here, the Japanese auto industry isn't likely to carve out a big share of the market.*

—*BusinessWeek*

1968 *But what is it good for?*
—Engineer at Advanced Computing Systems Division of IBM, on the idea of microchips

1977 *There is no reason for any individual to have a computer in his home.*
—Ken Olsen (b. 1926), President, Digital Equipment Corp.

1981 *640K ought to be enough for anybody.*
—Bill Gates (b. 1955), Microsoft CEO (Mr. Gates denies ever making this statement.—Y.H.)

■ FIRSTBORNS VS. LATERBORNS[2]

by Frank J. Sulloway

These are excerpts from one of the most interesting books I have ever read. Mr. Sulloway spent two decades employing evolutionary theory to understand how family dynamics affect personality development. Likely the world's authority on "Birth Order Factor." The Clintons, Bill and Hillary, and Winston Churchill were firstborns; Bill Gates and Warren Buffett were laterborns. **Birth order isn't fatal.** —*Y.H.*

Laterborns are more likely to identify with the underdog and to challenge the established order. Because they identify with parents and authority, firstborns are more likely to defend the status quo.

During the earliest stages of radical revolutions in science, laterborns have been 17 times more likely than firstborns to adopt a revolutionary point of view.

Firstborns covet status and power. They specialize in strategies designed to subordinate rivals. . . . Firstborns tend to be dominant, aggressive, ambitious, jealous, and conservative.

The first rule of the sibling road is to be different from one's brothers and sisters, especially if one happens to be a laterborn. . . . Siblings go out of their way to be different because it is in their Darwinian interests to do so. Diversity reduces competition for scarce resources.

In American history, the most radical women reformers have tended to be younger siblings. Firstborn women have tended to reject radical reforms and have generally confined their own reforming efforts to improving the system, not to overthrowing it.

When a youngest son like Benjamin Franklin is descended from four previous generations of youngest sons, he is usually a rebel.

Owing to sibling differences, there will always be social conservatives yearning for a return to hereditary rank, class, distinctions, and other markers of social standing. Birth order, age gaps between siblings, parent–offspring conflict, temperament, and other attributes of family niches all help to shape social attitudes.

Reading Malthus's *Essay on the Principle of Population,* Darwin was led to reflect on the relentless struggle for existence that arises owing to overpopulation. This struggle is largely carried out through the agency of sibling competition, the continuous competition among rivals for scarce resources. He called this process natural selection. . . . Thomas Robert Malthus was the youngest son of a middleborn and a lastborn, both of whom nurtured his liberal inclinations. . . . Sibling differences, compounded across the generations, build relentlessly toward radical change.

By their early thirties, the majority of firstborns have already aligned themselves with the scientific status quo. Thereafter, they tend to oppose heterodox (not in agreement with accepted beliefs) innovations with their usual degree of erudite zeal.

During the Protestant Reformation, laterborns were 48 times more likely than firstborns to suffer martyrdom for this reform effort.

Notes

1. "Famous Failures" by Joey Green, reprinted from *Famous Failures: Hundreds of Hot Shots Who Got Rejected, Flunked Out, Worked Lousy Jobs, Goofed Up, or Did Time in Jail Before Achieving Phenomenal Success* (Los Angeles: Lunatic Press, 2007). Copyright 2009 by Joey Green. All right reserved. Reprinted with permission.
2. From *Born to Rebel* by Frank J. Sulloway, copyright 1996 by Frank J. Sulloway. Used by permission of Pantheon Books, a division of Random House, Inc.

CHAPTER 7

RELAX! YOU ARE ABOUT TO BE MOTIVATED

- UNLIMITED CAPACITIES
- Alexis de Tocqueville: Seer Extraordinaire
- An Ode to America (Cornel Nistorescu)
- Beauty Is in the Soul (Sam Levenson)
- Children Learn What They Live (Dorothy L. Nolte)
- Footprints on the Sands of Time
- I Cannot Exist without You (John Keats)
- Six Lessons for Life (Marian Wright Edelman)
- The People Who Make a Difference!

If you are still not convinced that YOU can make a GIANT difference, then take a look at what American steel magnate Charles M. Schwab had to say about 100 years ago, "Everyone's got it in them, if they only make up their minds and stick to it," he observed. "There's no limit possible to the expansion of each one of us."

This same message is the focus of a song I wrote for a musical:

Each of us is a special person
Everyone of us is unique
Yes, each of us has unlimited potential
To achieve whatever we may seek
There's no end to the possibilities
There's no end to the heights you can climb
You can be anything you want to be
And leave your FOOTPRINTS ON THE SANDS OF TIME

One of the most inspiring one-pagers ever written is *Children Learn What They Live*. It should be on the wall of **EVERY** home in the world! And Tocqueville's *Democracy in America,* written in 1831, is still amazing!

UNLIMITED CAPACITIES

Everyone's got it in them, if they only make up their minds and stick to it. None of us are born with a stop-valve on our powers or with a set limit to our capacities. There's no limit possible to the expansion of each one of us.

—Charles M. Schwab (1862–1939),
founder of Bethlehem Steel

■ ALEXIS DE TOCQUEVILLE: SEER EXTRAORDINAIRE[1]

A young Frenchman, 27 years old, spent nine months studying the United States back in 1831. What he subsequently wrote about us in *Democracy in America* in 1835 still amazes 174 years later. How could someone so young and from a foreign shore sense the USA would subsequently become the leading capitalist nation in the world, with almost one-third of the world's GDP?

> Two great nations in the world, starting from different points, seem to be advancing toward the same goal: the Russians and the Anglo-Americans. Both have grown in obscurity, and while the world's attention was occupied elsewhere, they have suddenly taken their place among the leading nations, making the world take note of their birth and of their greatness almost at the same instant. All other peoples seem to have nearly reached their natural limits and need nothing but to preserve them; but these two are growing. . . . The American fights against natural obstacles; the Russian is at grips with men. The former combats the wilderness and barbarism; the latter, civilization with all its arms. America's conquests are made with the plowshare, Russia's with the sword. To attain their aims the former relies on personal interest and gives free scope to the unguided strength and common sense of individuals. The latter in a sense concentrates the whole power of society in one man. One has freedom as the principal means of action; the other has servitude. Their point of departure is different and their paths diverse; nevertheless, each seems called by some secret design of Providence one day to hold in its hands the destinies of half the world.

It still boggles the mind that a French visitor to the United States in 1831 could have been so prescient about us. More of his prescient observations:

> *As one digs deeper into the national character of the Americans, one sees that they have sought the value of everything in this world only in the answer to this single question: how much money will it bring in?*

I think the chief cause of the extraordinary prosperity and growing power of this nation . . . is due to the superiority of their women.

One finds that love of money is either the chief or a secondary motive at the bottom of everything the Americans do.

America is great because America is good. If America ever ceases to be good it will cease to be great.

Americans believe that their chief business is to secure for themselves a government, which will allow them to acquire the things they covet, and which will not debar them from the peaceful enjoyment of those possessions, which they have acquired.

■ AN ODE TO AMERICA[2]

by Cornel Nistorescu

Why are Americans so united? They don't resemble one another even if you paint them! They speak all the languages of the world and form an astonishing mixture of civilizations. Some of them are nearly extinct; others are incompatible with one another, and in matters of religious beliefs, not even God can count how many they are.

Still, the American tragedy turned three hundred million people into a hand put on the heart. Nobody rushed to accuse the White House, the army, and the secret services that they are only a bunch of losers. Nobody rushed to empty their bank accounts. Nobody rushed on the streets nearby to gape about.

The Americans volunteered to donate blood and to give a helping hand. After the first moments of panic, they raised the flag on the smoking ruins, putting on T-shirts, caps and ties in the colors of the national flag. They placed flags on buildings and cars as if in every place and on every car a minister or the president was passing. On every occasion they started singing their traditional song: "God Bless America!"

Silent as a rock, I watched the charity concert broadcast on Saturday once, twice, three times, on different TV channels. There were Clint Eastwood, Willie Nelson, Robert De Niro, Julia Roberts, Cassius Clay, Jack Nicholson, Bruce Springsteen, Sylvester Stallone, James Wood, and many others whom no film or producers could ever bring together. The American's solidarity spirit turned them into a choir. Actually, choir is not the word.

What you could hear was the heavy artillery of the American soul. What neither George W. Bush, nor Bill Clinton, nor Colin Powell could say without facing the risk of stumbling over words and sounds, was being heard in a great and unmistakable way in this charity concert.

I don't know how it happened that all this obsessive singing of America didn't sound croaky, nationalist, or ostentatious! It made you green with envy because you weren't able to sing for your country without running the risk of being considered chauvinist, ridiculous, or suspected of who-knows-what mean interests.

I watched the live broadcast and the rerun of its rerun for hours listening to the story of the guy who went down one hundred floors with a woman in a wheelchair without knowing who she was, or of the Californian hockey player, who fought with the terrorists and prevented the plane from hitting a target that would have killed other hundreds or thousands of people.

How on earth were they able to bow before a fellow human?

Imperceptibly, with every word and musical note, the memory of some turned into a modern myth of tragic heroes. And with every phone call, millions and millions of dollars were put in a collection aimed at rewarding not a man or a family, but a spirit, which nothing can buy.

What on earth can unite the Americans in such a way: their land, their galloping history, their economic power, and money? I tried for hours to find an answer, humming songs and murmuring phrases, which risk of sounding like commonplaces. I thought things over, but I reached only one conclusion: Only freedom can work such miracles!

Cornel Nistorescu, the editor of the Romanian newspaper *Daily Event,* wrote and published this beautiful evocation on September 24, 2001, shortly after 9/11. —*Y.H.*

■ BEAUTY IS IN THE SOUL[3]

by Sam Levenson

Actress Audrey Hepburn was regarded as one of the world's most beautiful women. When asked for her secrets, she responded with this poem by the humorist Sam Levenson. He wrote it for his grandchild, even though it is often credited to Ms. Hepburn. She read it to her children on the very last Christmas Eve she spent with us on Earth. —*Y.H.*

For attractive lips,
Speak words of kindness.

For lovely eyes,
Seek out the good in people.

For a slim figure,
Share your food with the hungry.

For beautiful hair,
Let a child run his or her fingers through it once a day.

For poise,
Walk with the knowledge you'll never walk alone.

People, even more than things, have to be restored, renewed,
revived, reclaimed, and redeemed; Never throw out anybody.

Remember, if you ever need a helping hand,
you'll find one at the end of your arm.

As you grow older, you will discover that you have two hands,
one for helping yourself, the other for helping others.

The beauty of a woman is not in the clothes she wears, the figure that she carries, or the way she combs her hair. The beauty of a woman must be seen from in her eyes, because that is the doorway to her heart, the place where love resides.

The beauty of a woman is not in a facial mole, but true beauty in a woman is reflected in her soul. It is the caring that she lovingly gives, the passion that she shows, and the beauty of a woman with passing years only grows!

CHILDREN LEARN WHAT THEY LIVE[4]

by Dorothy L. Nolte

If children live with ***criticism,*** they learn to condemn.

If children live with ***hostility,*** they learn to fight.

If children live with ***fear,*** they learn to be apprehensive.

If children live with ***pity,*** they learn to feel sorry for themselves.

If children live with ***ridicule,*** they learn to be shy.

If children live with ***jealousy,*** they learn to feel envy.

If children live with ***shame,*** they learn to feel guilty.

BUT,

If children live with ***encouragement,*** they learn confidence.

If children live with ***tolerance,*** they learn patience.

If children live with ***praise,*** they learn appreciation.

If children live with ***acceptance,*** they learn to love.

If children live with ***approval,*** they learn to like themselves.

If children live with ***recognition,*** they learn it is good to have a goal.

If children live with ***sharing,*** they learn generosity.

If children live with ***honesty,*** they learn truthfulness.

If children live with ***fairness,*** they learn justice.

If children live with ***kindness*** and ***consideration,*** they learn respect.

If children live with ***security,*** they learn to have faith in themselves and in those about them.

If children live with ***friendliness,*** they learn the world is a nice place in which to live.

With what are your children living? —*Y.H.*

■ FOOTPRINTS ON THE SANDS OF TIME[5]

by Yale Hirsch

This is from a musical I wrote about the Elephant Man, *Merrick & Melissa.* It is in production at this writing. This lyric applies to *every* human being on Earth, *including* YOU.

Each of us is a special person
Every one of us is unique
Yes, each of us has unlimited potential
To achieve whatever we may seek
There's no end to the possibilities
There's no end to the heights you can climb
You can be anything you want to be
And leave your **FOOTPRINTS ON THE SANDS OF TIME**
In each of us there's a sleeping giant
All-powerful, at your command
Make your dreams come true, wake that giant up within you
And you'll hold a miracle in your hands
There's no end to the possibilities
Seize the moment, while you're young, in your prime
You can be most anything you want to be
And leave your **FOOTPRINTS ON THE SANDS OF TIME**
On this planet Earth, we can each make a difference
Help to make our world a much better place
And all it takes is a little love and caring
From each of us to enrich the human race
There's no end to the possibilities
There's no end to the heights we can climb
Let's be what we can be and live free in harmony
And leave our **FOOTPRINTS ON THE SANDS OF TIME**

■ I CANNOT EXIST WITHOUT YOU[6]

John Keats (1795–1821) to Fanny Brawne

I cannot exist without you
I am forgetful of every thing
But seeing you again
My Life seems to stop there
I see no further.
You have absorbed me.
I have a sensation at the present moment
As though I were dissolving
. . . .
I have been astonished that Men
could die Martyrs for religion
I have shudder'd at it
I shudder no more
I could be martyr'd for my Religion
Love is my religion
I could die for that
I could die for you.
My creed is Love
And you are its only tenet
You have ravished me away
By a Power I cannot resist.

Love is so powerful . . . may it happen to you! —*Y.H.*

■ SIX LESSONS FOR LIFE[7]

by Marian Wright Edelman

The first lesson: There is no free lunch in life. Please don't feel entitled to anything you don't sweat and struggle for. You've got to work your way up hard and continuously, pay attention to detail, take great care and pride in your work and don't ever stop learning and improving your mind, if you do you're going to be left behind.

The second lesson: Assign yourself. Don't wait around for your boss or your friends or teachers to direct you to do what you're able to figure out and do for yourself. And don't do just as little as you can to get by. Initiative and persistence are still the non-magic carpets to success for most of us.

The third quick lesson: Never work just for money. Money alone won't save your soul or build a decent family life or help you sleep at night. So don't ever confuse wealth or fame with character. And don't give anybody the proxy for your conscience.

The fourth lesson: Don't be afraid of taking risks or of being criticized. Don't be afraid of failing, it is the way you learn to do things right. Don't be afraid of falling down; just keep getting up. And don't wait for everybody to come along to get something done. It's always a few people who get things done and keep things going.

Fifth lesson: Listen to the sound of the genuine in yourself. It is the only true guide you will ever have, if you cannot hear it in yourself, you will spend all of your life on the end of strings that somebody else pulls.

Last lesson: Never think life is not worth living or that you can't make a difference. Never give up. Harriet Beecher Stowe said, "when you get into a tight place and everything goes against you, till it seems as though you cannot hold on a minute longer, never give up, for that is just the place and time that the tide will turn."

I hope you will dream a new world, I hope you will believe you can achieve it, I hope you will have faith in yourself, I hope you will struggle to make sure that this is a world where everyone can succeed as you have.

■ THE PEOPLE WHO MAKE A DIFFERENCE!

by Anonymous

Now I see why powerful people often wear sunglasses—the spotlight blinds them to reality. They suffer from a delusion that power means something (it doesn't). They suffer from the misconception that titles make a difference (they don't). They are under the impression that earthly authority will make a heavenly difference (it won't).

Can I prove my point? Take this quiz:

- Name the ten wealthiest people in the world.
- Name the last ten Heisman trophy winners.
- Name the last ten winners of the Miss America contest.
- Name eight people who have won the Nobel or Pulitzer Prize.
- How about the last ten Academy Award winners for best picture or the last decade's worth of World Series winners?

How did you do? I didn't do well, either. With the exception of a few trivia hounds, none of us remember the headliners of yesterday too well.

Surprising how quickly we forget, isn't it? And what I've mentioned above are no second-rate achievements. These are the best in their fields. But the applause dies. Awards tarnish. Achievements are forgotten. Accolades and certificates are buried with their owners.

Here's another quiz. See how you do on this one:

- Think of three people you enjoy spending time with.
- Name ten people who have taught you something worthwhile.
- Name five friends who have helped you in a difficult time.
- List a few teachers who have aided your journey through school.
- Name half-a-dozen heroes whose stories have inspired you.

Easier? It was for me, too. The lesson? The people who make a difference are not the ones with the credentials, but the ones who show concern.

Notes

1. Alexis de Tocqueville, *Democracy in America* (1835).
2. Cornel Nistorescu, "Cîntarea Americii" [Ode to America], *Evenimentul Zilei* [The Daily Event], September 24, 2001.
3. Sam Levinson, *In One Era and Out the Other* (New York: Simon & Schuster, 1973). Reprinted by permissions of SLL/Sterling Lord Literistic, Inc. Copyright by Samuel Levenson.
4. This poem by Dorothy Law Nolte has appeared in various versions over the years. I like this version best.
5. Yale Hirsch, *Merrick & Melissa,* 2009.
6. John Keats in a letter to his fiancé Fanny Brawne, 1818.
7. *The Measure of Our Success* by Marian Wright Edelman. Copyright 1992 by Marian Wright Edelman. Reprinted by permission of Beacon Press, Boston.

CHAPTER 8

NO LIMIT TO HOW HIGH YOU CAN CLIMB

- CONTRARINESS (Arnold M. Ludwig, M.D.)
- Achieving Personal Excellence (Steve Brunkhorst)
- Awaken the Giant Within! (Tony Robbins)
- Ayn Rand's Anthem (Ayn Rand)
- How to Live on 24 Hours a Day (Arnold Bennett)
- It's Not What You Do Its How You Do It That Determines Your Success (Paul Kearley)
- Make Each and Every Moment of Your Life a Moment to Remember (Anonymous)
- Must Thinking (Paul Kearley)
- There's No Limit to How High You Can Climb (Masami Saionji)
- You Are the Creator of Your Life (James Allen)

If you still have any doubt that you can make it to the top in any profession you choose, have you noticed who is now President of the United States of America? A few years ago most people would be willing to bet any amount of money and give odds of 30/1 or even 50/1 that we wouldn't see an African American become president of the United States, especially with the name Barack Hussein Obama.

All the great talents I have selected for this chapter have tried in the past, or are currently trying, to get people to realize the enormous potential each and every one of us has. As Masami Saionji tells us: "Every human being is a creator: whatever your country, whatever your religion, whatever your culture, each of us is in the process of creating ourselves . . . you must put an end to your self-doubt. Believing in yourself is your first step."

Don't waste another minute! Get started NOW!

CONTRARINESS[1]

People destined for greatness tend to have difficulty working within the framework of existing paradigms in their fields.

To create new schools of thought, blaze new trails, make major discoveries, or promote new products, they must show irreverence toward established authority and readiness to discard prevalent views.

They have an attitude set that is oppositional in nature. This antagonism to traditional beliefs and practice assumes many forms.

They are most likely to resent authority, including the authority of their parents.

—Arnold M. Ludwig, M.D. (b. 1933),
professor of psychiatry

ACHIEVING PERSONAL EXCELLENCE[2]

by Steve Brunkhorst

The expectations we have for ourselves contribute greatly to the degree of excellence we achieve. Through our expectations, we define the boundaries inside towards which we are willing to strive.

Excellence, however, is not a state of perfection; it is a personal vision and guiding principle to live with daily. By striving for excellence, we continue to learn and improve throughout our lives.

A vision of excellence, consistently kept in mind, builds resolve and deepens involvement in each task before us. It allows every small action, even the most routine ones, to glow with the creative joy needed to produce achievements of outstanding value.

Each individual will define excellence in a deeply personal way. Consider these five questions while envisioning the quality that you desire for your life and career:

1. What would your vision of excellence look like if it had no restrictions, and you knew that you could achieve it?
2. In what areas of your life are you tolerating and expecting less than the best that you desire?
3. What, if any, are the challenges that repeatedly block you from performing at your highest potential?
4. What resources could you mobilize to help create the most abundance for the future?
5. What must happen next for you to move closer to your personal vision of excellence?

Your answers will help to clarify and strengthen your vision of the excellence that you seek.

■ AWAKEN THE GIANT WITHIN![3]

by Anthony Robbins

We all have dreams. We all want to believe deep down in our souls that we have a special gift, that we can make a difference, that we can touch others in a special way, and that we can make the world a better place. At one time in our lives, we all had a vision for the quality of life that we desire and deserve. Yet, for many of us, those dreams have become so shrouded in the frustrations and routines of daily life that we no longer even make an effort to accomplish them. For far too many, the dream has dissipated—and with it, so has the will to shape our destinies. Many have lost that sense of certainty that creates the winner's edge. My life's quest has been to restore the dream and to make it real, to get each of us to remember and use the unlimited power that lies sleeping within us.

I learned to harness the principle I now call *concentration of power.* Most people have no idea of the giant capacity we can immediately command when we focus all of our resources on mastering a single area of our lives. Controlled focus is like a laser beam that can cut through anything that seems to be stopping you. When we focus consistently on improvement in any area, we develop unique distinctions on how to make that area better. One reason so few of us achieve what we truly want is that we never direct our focus; we never concentrate our power. Most people dabble their way through life, never deciding to master anything in particular.

I truly believe we all have a **SLEEPING GIANT** within us. Each of us has a talent, a gift, our own bit of genius just waiting to be tapped. . . . I continue to recognize the power individuals have to change virtually anything and everything in their lives *in an instant.* I've learned that the resources we need to turn our dreams into reality are within us, merely waiting for the day when we decide to wake up and claim our birthright.

My whole life changed in just one day—the day I determined not just what I'd like to have in my life or what I wanted to become, but when I *decided who and what I was committed to having and being in my life.* . . . If you truly decide to, you can do almost anything. So if you don't like the current relationship you're in, make the decision now to change it. If you don't like your current job, change it. If you don't like the way you feel about yourself, change it. In a moment you can seize the same power that has shaped history.

The most exciting thing about this force, this power, is that you already possess it. The explosive impetus of decision is not something reserved for a select few with the right credentials or money or family background. It's available to the common laborer as well as the king. In the very next moment you can muster the courage to claim it. Will today be the day you finally *decide* that who you are as a person is much more than you've been demonstrating? Will today be the day you *decide* once and for all to make your life consistent with the quality of your spirit?

AYN RAND'S *ANTHEM*[4]

This is an excerpt from Anthem, a wonderful novella written by Ayn Rand (1905–1982), author of *The Fountainhead* and *Atlas Shrugged.* It is a futuristic story, published in 1938, of a society where the pronoun "I" has been forbidden. The leading character refuses to follow the stringent rules of this closed society and breaks away. —*Y.H.*

I stand here on the summit of the mountain. I lift my head and I spread my arms. This, my body and spirit, this is the end of the quest. I wished to know the meaning of things. I am the meaning. I wished to find a warrant for being. I need no warrant for being, and no word of sanction upon my being. I am the warrant and the sanction.

It is my eyes which see, and the sight of my eyes grants beauty to the earth. It is my ears which hear, and the hearing of my ears gives its song to the world. It is my mind which thinks, and the judgment of my mind is the only searchlight that can find the truth. It is my will which chooses, and the choice of my will is the only edict I must respect. Many words have been granted me, and some are wise, and some are false, but only three are holy: "I will it!"

Whatever road I take, the guiding star is within me; the guiding star and the loadstone which point the way. They point in but one direction. They point to me.

I know not if this earth on which I stand is the core of the universe or if it is but a speck of dust lost in eternity. I know not and I care not. For I know what happiness is possible to me on earth. And my happiness needs no higher aim to vindicate it. My happiness is not the means to any end. It is the end. It is its own goal. It is its own purpose.

Neither am I the means to any end others may wish to accomplish. I am not a tool for their use. I am not a servant of their needs. I am not a bandage for their wounds. I am not a sacrifice on their altars.

I am a man. This miracle of me is mine to own and keep, and mine to guard, and mine to use, and mine to kneel before!

I do not surrender my treasures, nor do I share them. The fortune of my spirit is not to be blown into coins of brass and flung to the winds as alms for the poor of the spirit. I guard my treasures: my thought, my will, my freedom. And the greatest of these is freedom.

I owe nothing to my brothers, nor do I gather debts from them. I ask none to live for me, nor do I live for any others. I covet no man's soul, nor is my soul theirs to covet.

I am neither foe nor friend to my brothers, but such as each of them shall deserve of me. And to earn my love, my brothers must do more than to have been born. I do not grant my love without reason, nor to any chance passer-by who may wish to claim it. I honor men with my love. But honor is a thing to be earned.

I shall choose friends among men, but neither slaves nor masters. And I shall choose only such as please me, and them I shall love and respect, but neither command nor obey. And we shall join our hands when we wish, or walk alone when we so desire. For in the temple of his spirit, each man is alone. Let each man keep his temple untouched and undefiled. Then let him join hands with others if he wishes, but only beyond his holy threshold.

For the word "We" must never be spoken, save by one's choice and as a second thought. This word must never be placed first within man's soul, else it becomes a monster, the root of all the evils on earth, the root of man's torture by men, and of an unspeakable lie.

The word "We" is as lime poured over men, which sets and hardens to stone, and crushes all beneath it, and that which is white and that which is black are lost equally in the grey of it. It is the word by which the depraved steal the virtue of the good, by which the weak steal the might of the strong, by which the fools steal the wisdom of the sages.

What is my joy if all hands, even the unclean, can reach into it? What is my wisdom, if even the fools can dictate to me? What is my freedom, if all creatures, even the botched and the impotent, are my masters? What is my life, if I am but to bow, to agree and to obey?

But I am done with this creed of corruption.

I am done with the monster of "We," the word of serfdom, of plunder, of misery, falsehood and shame.

And now I see the face of god, and I raise this god over the earth, this god whom men have sought since men came into being, this god who will grant them joy and peace and pride. This god, this one word: "I."

HOW TO LIVE ON 24 HOURS A DAY[5]

by Arnold Bennett

Some notes I underlined when I read them years ago. —*Y.H.*

THE TIME ELEMENT. In the realm of time there is no aristocracy of wealth, and no aristocracy of intellect. There is an equal distribution of time to all. Some kill it, some idly watch it go by, some wade through it and others enslave it. It depends upon the individual. Putting something off until you have more time is misleading because you never have any more time.

BEGINNING. The sense of uneasy waiting for something to start, which has not started, disturbs the peace of the soul. You are constantly haunted by a suppressed dissatisfaction with the arrangement of your daily life. "How do I begin?" Dear Sir, you simply begin. There is no magic method of beginning

PRECAUTION. A warning! Ardor is a misleading thing. It isn't content till it perspires. Too often, when it feels the perspiration on its brow, it wearies all of a sudden and dies. BEWARE of undertaking too much at the start. Also, a failure or so doesn't matter.

CONTROLLING THE MIND. Without the power to concentrate, to dictate to the brain its task and to ensure obedience, true life is impossible. Mind control is the first element of a full existence. It can be done thusly: The first business of the day should be to put the mind through its paces. Cultivate your mind in the street, on the train, wherever. Upon leaving the house, concentrate your mind on a subject. In no time at all, it will have wandered off to another subject. Bring it back by the scruff of the neck. You will have brought it back 40 times until you reach your destination. Don't despair. Continue. You will succeed. By regular concentration you can tyrannize over your mind every hour of the day, no matter where you are.

CAUSE AND EFFECT. The most important of all perceptions is cause and effect. When one has thoroughly gotten imbued into one's head, the leading truth that nothing happens without cause, one grows not only large-minded, but also large-hearted. One loses that absurd air which so many people have of always being shocked and pained by the curiousness of LIFE. Such people live amid human nature as if it were a foreign country full of awful foreign customs. The study of cause and effect, while it lessens the painfulness of life, adds to life's picturesqueness. The whole field of daily habit and scene is waiting to satisfy that curiosity, which means life, and the satisfaction of which means an understanding heart.

SELF-IMPROVEMENT. Why not devote 90 minutes a night for three nights a week for self-improvement by study and serious reading on various subjects. Think as well as read! Unless you give at least 45 minutes to careful, fatiguing reflection upon what you are reading, your 90 minutes a night are wasted.

DANGERS TO AVOID. Becoming that most odious and least supportable of persons—a PRIG. A prig is a pert fellow who gives himself airs of wisdom: a pompous fool who has lost his sense of humor: a tedious individual who, having made a discovery, is so impressed by his discovery that he is capable of being highly displeased because the entire world is not also impressed by it. It is well not to chatter too much about what one is doing and not to betray a too-pained sadness at the spectacle of a whole world out there deliberately wasting so many hours out of every day, and therefore not really living. *It will be found ultimately, that in taking care of one's self, one has quite all one can do.*

IT'S NOT WHAT YOU DO, IT'S HOW YOU DO IT THAT DETERMINES YOUR SUCCESS[6]

by Paul Kearley

There are way too many people in school or the workplace who are just getting by, doing the minimum amount of work required to get a job done, who try to make poor workmanship standard practice. These are also the people who try to franchise this idea to everyone they are associated with so they don't look bad.

Whatever you do, you must do it to the best of your ability, with what you have, wherever you are. What you are doing right now may not be what you promised yourself you would be doing in earlier days, but that doesn't mean it is a life sentence. You can become better no matter what the circumstances are or seem to be. This may simply be a temporary learning experience you needed to go through to enable you to press on and become more.

Just because where you are may not be where you wanted to be, is that any reason to quit? Of course not! You're better that that.

Have you ever noticed that those who do things to the best of their ability always seem to be the ones who get further in life? They don't criticize, condemn or complain, they don't worry that someone else will make them look bad, they simply put their head down and work to the best of their ability and they expect others to do the same: They know that being the best means doing their best.

What about you? Has the realization that you are not where you wanted to be been driving the quality of your work? Has the lure of fitting in without rocking the boat been causing you to hold back your best work? Have you simply resigned yourself that things will never change so why bother?

You can become better. You must simply choose to, and who cares what the others say; they don't live under your skin and they don't share your dreams of becoming more.

If you truly want to create the life you want, you must first determine just what that life will look like. Write it down, create powerful pictures, and use positive words. Then, when you have engineered the picture, you must get into action. Do at least one thing each and every day that will move you in a positive direction toward your picture.

Make this week the launching point for the rest of your life. Refuse to be one of the "crowd" who is just waiting for time; focus on who you will be, keep that picture in your mind and then act as if you are already that person, and when you do, you will soon see opportunities that once seemed distant, becoming reality.

■ MUST THINKING[7]

by Paul Kearley

You are probably tired of hearing the same old things about achieving goals and reaching success. I must have visited thousands of Web sites, read through hundreds of books and spoke to dozens of people, all with the intention of discovering "When your back is against the wall, and you MUST get something done, what do you do?"

If you knew that you already had the power to predict where your life will go, what goals would you set? What actions would you take?

You do, you know, have the power to predict your future, and I have discovered how to release that power so that you can access it. Imagine having the audacity to predict your own success, and then actually achieving it? Want to know how? It's all in my e-book *"MUST Thinking: An easy four step guide for creating the results you want."*

Here's just some of what you'll find in *Must Thinking*:

- 8 ways to overcome your "Giants"
- How to predict your future with accuracy
- How to make decisions easier with less anxiety
- The M.U.S.T. strategy for creating what you want in your life and how to make it work for you every time
- How to make change and opportunity work for you
- How to get out of procrastination and into action
- How to conquer convenient excuses
- Create a discipline of success
- Understanding how words can impact your results
- Unlock your hidden creativity
- How to set the "success hook"
- Breaking the barrier to commitment
- How to be unstoppable
- What to do when you don't know what to do
- How to create a blueprint for success
- Discover the three truths that create momentum
- An easy problem solving method for getting faster results.
- Knowing what you must have before you can have what you want
- The true secret for creating your own success

■ MAKE EACH AND EVERY MOMENT OF YOUR LIFE A MOMENT TO REMEMBER

You can find the words that follow all over the Internet. Parts of this poem can be found in the works of Wayne Dyer (*Pulling Your Own Strings* and *Your Erroneous Zones*) and a large number of lines are attributed to Susan Polis Schutz from her *Creeds to Live By, Dreams to Follow* as well. —*Y.H.*

Be a person who likes virtually everything about life—
who is comfortable doing just about anything,

and who wastes no time complaining

or wishing that things were otherwise.
Be enthusiastic about life,

and want all you can get out of it.
Refuse to worry, and keep yourself free

from the anxiety that accompanies worry.
Live now, rather than in the past or the future.
Be strikingly independent.
Treasure your own freedom from expectations,
and want those you love to be independent,
to make their own choices,

and to live their lives for themselves.

Know how to laugh, and how to create laughter.
Accept yourself without complaint.
Appreciate the natural world.
Enjoy being outdoors in nature

and tripping around all that is unspoiled and original.
Have insight into the behavior of others, and into yourself, too.
Treat your body well. Be honest.
Have little concern with order, organization,

or systems in your life.
Be creative.

Love life and all the activities in it.
Search for more to learn each and every present moment of your life.
Do not be afraid to fail; in fact, welcome it!
Accept others as they are,

and work at changing events that you dislike.
View all people as human,

and place no one above yourself in importance.
Don't chase after happiness; live and happiness is your payoff.

THERE'S NO LIMIT TO HOW HIGH YOU CAN CLIMB[8]

by Masami Saionji

All human beings, without exception, are continually creating themselves with the life-energy that is constantly flowing within them. To create is our life's mission, and without it there would be no life. For better or worse, we continue to live because we continue to create.

What do you create? How do you create it? What is your purpose in this world? At each moment, your present self is created by the way in which you proceed toward your fundamental goal. As you progress toward this goal, from moment to moment, you exert your creativity to fashion the self that you imagine yourself to be.

Every human being is a creator: whatever your country, whatever your religion, whatever your culture, each of us is in the process of creating ourselves.

How can you rise above a negative way of living? First and foremost, you must put an end to your self-doubt. Believing in yourself is your first step—your point of departure.

All those who lead unhappy lives are people who doubt themselves. All those who lead happy lives are people who believe in themselves. To believe in oneself is to live with dignity, confidence, and courage.

Why do people doubt themselves? It is because they do not truly know themselves, and are not actively trying to know themselves. If you really wish to be happy, you must sever your fondness for doubt. Doubt cannot create anything bright or new. Doubt only destroys. Doubt only attracts darkness. If doubt creeps into your mind, you must never allow it to run about on its own. Confront your doubt immediately, and confirm whether or not it is rooted in reality. Once you know the facts, you can turn your attention toward the positive.

The important thing is to cherish your heartfelt goal and hold it close to you each day. As the saying goes, many drops of water make a river. Little by little, what you create each day will grow into something bigger, until you accomplish your purpose in this world.

There is no need to create anything grand at the beginning, but it is important to set your sights high. As you continue to create yourself, you can be sure that what you are aiming for will appear. Your future is waiting to be created.

If you wish to draw bright, harmonious conditions into this world, the best thing you can do is to think only good thoughts in your mind and speak only good words with your voice. You must give expression to your brightest hopes and wishes. You must say things like: "I can do it, for sure. Everything is possible. Everything will come together perfectly. Everything will change for the better. All ills will be resolved. All needs will be filled. Everything will find harmony. I will develop my talents. I will build wonderful friendships. I will have a splendid marriage" and so on. You must give voice to your most cherished aspirations.

The process of creating a new, expansive self will bring you untold bliss. If you choose to follow this road, you will surely recognize the pointlessness of continuing to create negative thoughts, words, and emotions.

It is up to you to create what you wish to create. You create it by using your own life force—your creativity—as you move toward your chosen goals.

How important it is for you to set your own goals! Once you decide what kind of life you wish to lead, or what kind of person you wish to become, your creative power acts upon your wish, and your life takes shape in this world.

We human beings freely create our own personalities, our own habits, our own situations, and our own futures. If you wish, you can create your life with shining, positive goals. Or, if you choose, you can mold your life in the shape of conflict, misery, and illness.

Again, first and foremost, to rise above a negative way of living you must put an end to your self-doubt. Believing in yourself is your first step—your point of departure.

People who doubt themselves lead unhappy lives. People who believe in themselves lead happy lives. TO BELIEVE IN *YOU* IS TO LIVE WITH DIGNITY, CONFIDENCE, AND COURAGE.

If you have any doubt that you will have a very happy and successful life, this book will erase that doubt. —*Y.H.*

YOU ARE THE CREATOR OF YOUR LIFE[9]

by James Allen

What you *are* so is your world. Everything in the universe is resolved into your own inward experience. It matters little what is without, for it is all a reflection of your own state of consciousness. It matters everything what you are within, for everything without will be mirrored and colored accordingly.

Your own thoughts, desires, and aspirations comprise your world, and, to you, all that there is in the universe of beauty and joy and bliss, or of ugliness and sorrow and pain, is contained within yourself. By your own thoughts you make or mar your life, your world, your universe. As you build within by the power of thought, so will your outward life and circumstances shape themselves accordingly. Whatsoever you harbor in the inmost chambers of your heart will, sooner or later by the inevitable law of reaction, shape itself in your outward life.

The soul that is impure, sordid and selfish is gravitating with unerring precision toward misfortune and catastrophe; the soul that is pure, unselfish, and noble is gravitating with equal precision toward happiness and prosperity. Every soul attracts its own, and nothing can possibly come to it that does not belong to it. To realize this is to recognize the universality of Divine Law.

The incidents of every human life, which both make and mar, are drawn to it by the quality and power of its own inner thought-life. Every soul is a complex combination of gathered experiences and thoughts, and the body is but an improvised vehicle for its manifestation. What, therefore, your thoughts are, that is your real self; and the world around, both animate and inanimate, wears the aspect with which your thoughts clothe it.

It therefore follows that if people are happy, it is because they dwell in happy thoughts; if miserable, because they dwell in despondent and debilitating thoughts. Whether one is fearful or fearless, foolish or wise, troubled or serene, within that soul lies the cause of its own state or states, and never without.

And now you may ask, "But do you really mean to say that outward circumstances do not affect my mind?" I do not say that, but I say this, and know it to be an infallible truth, that circumstances can only affect you in so far as you allow them to do so. You are swayed by circumstances because you have not a right understanding of the nature, use, and power of thought.

You believe (and upon this little word *belief* hang all our sorrows and joys) that outward things have the power to make or mar your life; by so doing you submit to those outward things, confess that you are their slave, and they your unconditional master; by so doing, you invest them with a power which they do not, of themselves, possess, and you succumb, in reality, not to the mere circumstances, but to the gloom or gladness, the fear or hope, the strength or weakness, which your thought-sphere has thrown around them.

If circumstances had the power to bless or harm, they would bless and harm all people alike, but the fact that the same circumstances will be alike good and bad to different souls proves that the good or bad is not in the circumstance, but only in the minds of those who encounter it.

When you begin to realize this you will begin to control your thoughts, to regulate and discipline your mind, and to rebuild the inward temple of your soul, eliminating all useless and superfluous material, and incorporating into your being thoughts alone of joy and serenity, of strength and life, of compassion and love, of beauty and immortality; and as you do this you will become joyful and serene, strong and healthy, compassionate and loving, and beautiful with the beauty of immortality.

Notes

1. Reprinted with permission of The Guilford Press from Arnold M. Ludwig, M.D., *The Price of Greatness.* Copyright 1995.
2. Copyright by Steve Brunkhorst. Steve is a life strategies coach, inspirational writer, and the editor of *Achieve! 60-Second Nuggets of Inspiration* at www.AchieveEzine.com.
3. Reprinted with the permission of Simon & Schuster, Inc., from *Awaken the Giant Within* by Anthony Robbins. Copyright 1991 by Anthony Robbins. All rights reserved. Robbins (b. 1960) is a self-help writer and speaker.
4. Excerpted from Ayn Rand's *Anthem* (New York: Caxton Press, 1966), 94–97.
5. Arnold Bennett's *How to Live on 24 Hours a Day* was first published in 1908, and it's still poignant today.
6. Paul Kearley, President, Personal Best Training Solutions, Dale Carnegie Business Group. www.mustthinking.com.
7. Paul Kearley, President, Personal Best Training Solutions, Dale Carnegie Business Group. www.mustthinking.com.
8. Excerpted from Masami Saionji, *Vision for the 21st Century* (Tokyo: Byakko Press, 2009). Ms. Saionji is chairperson of Goi Peace Foundation (www.goipeace.or.jp), World Peace Prayer Society.
9. James Allen had a gigantic talent over a century ago. These excerpts are from *The Path to Prosperity,* which can be read in its entirety at the James Allen Free Library, http://james-allen.in1woord.nl.

CHAPTER 9

STRATEGIES FOR CLIMBING THE LADDER OF SUCCESS

- EXERCISE (Christopher Crowley and Henry S. Lodge)
- 10 Creative Myths (Jeffrey Baumgartner)
- 10 Steps for Boosting Creativity (Jeffrey Baumgartner)
- 16 Rules Bob Parsons Tries to Live by (Bob Parsons)
- 18 Important Thoughts to Consider (Steve Brunkhorst)
- Top 10 Reasons to Keep a Journal (Philip Humbert)
- Top 10 Secrets of Getting Rich! (Philip Humbert)
- Top 10 Steps to Set and Achieve Your Goals (Philip Humbert)
- Top 10 Things to Think about if You Want to Change the World (Michael Angier)
- Two Ideas to Guide You on Your Life Journey (Chuck Gallozzi)
- What I Wished I Learned in School (Guy Kawasaki)

Notice I seem to have "thrown the kitchen sink" into this chapter. Any one of these 10 sets of "steps" or "rules" or "secrets" could change one's life. They could help you jumpstart your life and dramatically speed up the process toward greater achievement and success. Yes! You can do it!

Most people are well aware that their ambitions conflict with their lifestyles. Many people are content to stay the way they are despite their faults and foibles. Apply the advice in these rules to yourself, and with consistent effort you will be on the fast track to a successful future.

What inspires people to speed up the process of self-change? Understanding parents, great teachers, and supportive friends are important contributors to your development through the years. As you mature, finding that special person with whom you will spend the rest of your life is a great bonus.

Younger Next Year is one of the best books on exercise that I have ever read. Don't be too surprised that I put this bold statement on physical exercise here and in the poster quote. Strengthening the mind is not too different from developing the body's muscles. People can excel in anything their minds (or bodies) concentrate on. The old standby is still the same: ***PRACTICE, PRACTICE, and PRACTICE*** **if you wish to make a GIANT difference!**

EXERCISE

Every time you work out and sweat, you stress your muscles, draining them of energy stores; you actually injure them a little bit. It's not enough to do long-term damage, but enough to stimulate repair and growth and to make muscles a little stronger. Enzymes and proteins from those muscles enter your blood stream, where they start a powerful chain reaction of inflammation, or decay, then repair, and finally growth.

—Christopher Crowley (b. 1934) and Henry S. Lodge, M.D. (b. 1958)[1]

■ 10 CREATIVE MYTHS[2]

by Jeffrey Baumgartner

Over the years, I have heard a lot of people say a lot of daft things about creativity. Some of those things, I hear again and again. What's worse, a lot of these daft notions—or myths—about creativity are detrimental to the creative process. So, let's end this once and for all. Below are 10 creative myths. If you share these with everyone in the world, these myths will go away.

1. **I am not creative.**
   I have heard a lot of people say precisely that: "I am not creative." The truth, of course, is that we are all creative. That's what differentiates us from Parrots who can say clever things but couldn't have a creative idea if their lives depended upon it. And while some people are naturally more creative than others, we can all have very creative ideas. The problem is, as we grow older, most of us learn to inhibit our creativity for reasons relating to work, acceptable behavior and just the notion of being a grown-up.
2. **That's a stupid [or daft, or silly, or ridiculous] idea.**
   People say this kind of thing to colleagues, family and even to themselves. Indeed, this is one reason why people believe they are not creative: they have got into such a habit of censoring their creative ideas, by telling themselves that their ideas are stupid, that they no longer feel creative. Next time you have an idea you think is stupid, don't censor it. Rather, ask yourself how you could improve the idea.
3. **Creative people always have great ideas.**
   Rubbish! Creative people always have ideas. Whether they like it or not, they are having ideas and sharing those ideas (often with people who tell them their ideas are stupid, no less!) every waking hour of the day. Of those ideas, a precious few are great. Many are good, many are mediocre and a precious few really are stupid ideas. Over time, we tend to forget creative people's weak ideas and remember their great ideas.
4. **Constructive criticism will help my colleague improve her idea.**
   Yeah, and tripping a child when she is learning to walk will help her improve her walking skills. Nonsense! Criticism, whether

constructive or destructive (as most criticism truly is) squelches creative thinking and teaches your colleague to keep her ideas to herself. Likewise, other colleagues will see what happens when ideas are shared and will also learn to keep their ideas to themselves. Fresh ideas are fragile. They need nurturing, not kicking. Instead of criticizing a colleague's new idea, challenge her to improve the idea by asking her how she could get over the idea's weakness.

5. **We need some new marketing ideas for the upcoming product launch. Let's get the marketing people together and brainstorm ideas.**
   This is a sure recipe for coming up with the same kind of marketing ideas you have had in the past: i.e., uncreative. Brainstorming, as well as ideas campaigns and other group ideation events get the most creative results with the widest variety of participants. Want marketing ideas? Then bring in sales, accounting, human resources, financial, administrative, production, design, research, legal and other people into the brainstorming event. Such a wide range of knowledge, experience and backgrounds will encourage a wide range of ideas. And that results in more creative ideas.
6. **In order for our innovation strategy to be a success, we need a system of review processes for screening ideas and determining which ideas to implement.**
   In fact, the review process is very often about eroding creativity by removing risk from ideas. The most important component for corporate innovation is a method of soliciting and capturing focused business ideas. The ideas campaign approach—where you challenge employees to submit ideas on specific business issues, such as "in what ways might we improve product X?" is the best way to focus innovation. A transparent tool that allows employees to submit, read and collaborate on ideas is the best way to focus creative thinking. And, framing your challenges effectively is arguably one of the most important aspects of successful corporate innovation. Yes, reviewing ideas is important. But first you need to be generating the creative ideas so that they may be reviewed.
7. **That's a good idea. Let's run with it.**
   When we are looking for ideas, we have a tendency to stop looking and start implementing with the first good idea that comes to mind. Unfortunately, that means that any great ideas

you might have had, had you spent more time thinking, are lost. Moreover, good ideas can often be developed into significantly better ideas with a little creative thought. So, don't think of a good idea as an end—rather, think of it as a beginning of the second stage of creative thought.

8. **Drugs will help me be more creative.**
   The 1960s drug culture and glamour of musicians and artists getting high and being creative led to this myth. A lot of drugs or alcohol will alter your mind and may very likely make you believe you are being more creative. But to people watching you, you will just seem like someone who is very high.
9. **If it ain't broke, don't fix it.**
   Just the other day I was at a workshop where some people were complaining about a colleague who always had ideas. Worse, he wanted to use those ideas to change processes that were working perfectly well. Sadly, too many of us (but not you, of course) are like the complainers. If something works well as it is, whether it is a machine or a process, we often feel there is no need to change the way it works. Fortunately, Dr. Hans von Ohain and Sir Frank Whittle didn't think like that—or we'd still be flying in propeller airplanes. Bear in mind that propeller airplanes were working perfectly fine when the two gentlemen in question individually invented the jet engine.
10. **I don't need a notebook. I always remember my ideas.**
   Maybe. But I doubt it. When we are inspired by an idea, that idea is very often out of context with what we are doing. Perhaps a dream we had upon waking inspires us with the solution to a problem. But, then we wake up, get the children up, have breakfast, run through in our minds an important presentation we'll be giving in the morning, panic that the kids will miss their bus, run for the train, flirt with an attractive young thing on the train, etc.—until late afternoon when you finally have time to think about the problem. How likely are you really to remember the idea you had upon wakening?

10 STEPS FOR BOOSTING CREATIVITY[3]

by Jeffrey Baumgartner

1. Listen to music by Johann Sebastian Bach. If Bach doesn't make you more creative, you should probably see your doctor—or your brain surgeon if you are also troubled by headaches, hallucinations or strange urges in the middle of the night.
2. Brainstorm. If properly carried out, brainstorming can help you not only come up with sacks full of new ideas, but can help you decide which is best.
3. Always carry a small notebook and a pen or pencil around with you. That way, if you are struck by an idea, you can quickly note it down. Upon rereading your notes, you may discover about 90% of your ideas are daft. Don't worry, that's normal. What's important are the 10% that are brilliant.
4. If you're stuck for an idea, open a dictionary, randomly select a word and then try to formulate ideas incorporating this word. You'd be surprised how well this works. The concept is based on a simple but little known truth: freedom inhibits creativity. There are nothing like restrictions to get you thinking.
5. Define your problem. Grab a sheet of paper, electronic notebook, computer or whatever you use to make notes, and define your problem in detail. You'll probably find ideas positively spewing out once you've done this.
6. If you can't think, go for a walk. A change of atmosphere is good for you and gentle exercise helps shake up the brain cells.
7. Don't watch TV. Experiments performed by the *JPB Creative Laboratory* show that watching TV causes your brain to slowly trickle out your ears and/or nose. It's not pretty, but it happens.
8. Don't do drugs. People on drugs think they are creative. To everyone else, they seem like people on drugs.
9. Read as much as you can about everything possible. Books exercise your brain, provide inspiration and fill you with information that allows you to make creative connections easily.

10. Exercise your brain. Brains, like bodies, need exercise to keep fit. If you don't exercise your brain, it will get flabby and useless. Exercise your brain by reading a lot, talking to clever people and disagreeing with people—arguing can be a terrific way to give your brain cells a workout. But note, arguing about politics or film directors is good for you; bickering over who should clean the dishes is not.

16 RULES BOB PARSONS TRIES TO LIVE BY[4]

by Bob Parsons

1. **Get out and stay out of your comfort zone.** I believe that not much happens of any significance when we're in our comfort zone. I hear people say, "But I'm concerned about security." My response to that is simple: "Security is for cadavers."
2. **Never give up.** Almost nothing works the first time it's attempted. Just because what you're doing does not seem to be working, doesn't mean it won't work. It just means that it might not work the way you're doing it. If it was easy, everyone would be doing it, and you wouldn't have an opportunity.
3. **When you're ready to quit, you're closer than you think.** There's an old Chinese saying that I just love, and I believe it is so true. "The temptation to quit will be greatest just before you are about to succeed."
4. **With regard to whatever worries you, not only accept the worst thing that could happen, but make it a point to quantify what the worst thing could be.** Very seldom will the worst consequence be anywhere near as bad as a cloud of "undefined consequences." My father would tell me early on, when I was struggling and losing my shirt trying to get Parsons Technology going, "Well, Robert, if it doesn't work, they can't eat you."
5. **Focus on what you want to have happen.** Remember that old saying, "As you think, so shall you be."
6. **Take things a day at a time.** No matter how difficult your situation is, you can get through it if you don't look too far into the future, and focus on the present moment. You can get through anything one day at a time.
7. **Always be moving forward.** Never stop investing. Never stop improving. Never stop doing something new. The moment you stop improving your organization, it starts to die. Make it your goal to be better each and every day, in some small way. Remember the Japanese concept of Kaizen. Small daily improvements eventually result in huge advantages.

8. **Be quick to decide.** Remember what the Union Civil War general, Tecumseh Sherman said: "A good plan violently executed today is far and away better than a perfect plan tomorrow." (Also attributed to General George S. Patton.)
9. **Measure everything of significance**. I swear this is true. Anything that is measured and watched, improves.
10. **Anything that is not managed will deteriorate.** If you want to uncover problems you don't know about, take a few moments and look closely at the areas you haven't examined for a while. I guarantee you problems will be there.
11. **Pay attention to your competitors, but pay more attention to what you're doing.** When you look at your competitors, remember that everything looks perfect at a distance. Even the planet Earth, if you get far enough into space, looks like a peaceful place.
12. **Never let anybody push you around.** In our society, with our laws and even playing field, you have just as much right to what you're doing as anyone else, provided that what you're doing is legal.
13. **Never expect life to be fair.** Life isn't fair. You make your own breaks. You'll be doing good if the only meaning fair has to you, is something that you pay when you get on a bus (i.e., fare).
14. **Solve your own problems.** You'll find that by coming up with your own solutions, you'll develop a competitive edge. Masura Ibuka, the co-founder of SONY, said it best: "You never succeed in technology, business, or anything by following the others." There's also an old Asian saying that I remind myself of frequently. It goes like this: "A wise man keeps his own counsel."
15. **Don't take yourself too seriously.** Lighten up. Often, at least half of what we accomplish is due to luck. None of us are in control as much as we like to think we are.
16. **There's always a reason to smile. Find it.** After all, you're really lucky just to be alive. Life is short. More and more, I agree with my little brother. He always reminds me: "We're not here for a long time; we're here for a good time."

18 IMPORTANT THOUGHTS TO CONSIDER[5]

by Steve Brunkhorst

1. The greatest inventions and accomplishments began as the flicker of an idea. This tiny flame was then fueled by desire and faith. Watch out for those tiny little ideas. You have the potential to turn them into great things.
2. Look ahead; envision the beautiful blessings waiting on your distant shores. If you follow your personal stepping-stones with joy, love, faith and gratitude, the swiftest currents will not impede your journey.
3. Other people cannot really motivate you, and it isn't the books you read that make you successful. People and books can light your fire if there's a passion and a motive already inside you. They can guide you and awaken valuable insights. But it's your choice to move or stay where you are.
4. There is more to success than reaching goals. Success must also include a joyful appreciation of living—an authentic joy that pulls us toward the next episode of our life's purpose.
5. Persistence is a common foundation beneath the achievements of every successful man and woman.
6. It is more naive to risk nothing and gain nothing than to risk failure and gain experience.
7. Setbacks are included in the price tag of success; they teach tenacity and provide experiences that let us achieve our goals with compassion and dignity.
8. If you have made a positive difference in one individual's life, you have succeeded in making a positive difference for many!
9. Winning is not a true measure of success. Success for its own sake or winning to acquire trophies and awards overlooks true success that can only be measured by inner growth.
10. Within each storm of life is hidden a key that will unlock another door that you were meant to walk through.
11. Every waking moment we see our legacies in their current state of being. The term "living legacy" might be more accurate

because it is now that our quality of life will determine what we leave behind.

12. Life is not defined by what happens to us; it is defined by how we use our circumstances to make this a better world. Our destinations are not determined by the trails we inherit but by those we create.
13. Give life the best you have, and life will give its best back to you.
14. The day you stop making excuses and accept personal responsibility for yourself and your results will be the day you will step onto a winning path where you will attract the most cherished dreams of your life.
15. People waste precious years while believing that there will be more time tomorrow than there is today. Today is the perfect day to accept and develop our gifts and talents.
16. Pick a big dream, a once-in-a-lifetime dream, a song-in-your-heart dream, a gift-to- mankind dream, a purpose-filling dream. Then run with it and persevere!
17. Intention reflects an unstoppable resolve. It gives an energetic feeling that says, "This will be done, and I'm *not* going to quit!"
18. We must nurture our own well being to attract trusting relationships. We attract qualities in others that we first develop in ourselves.

■ TOP 10 REASONS TO KEEP A JOURNAL[6]

by Philip Humbert

In earlier generations it was common to keep a diary or personal journal. Today few people do it, and very few recognize the value and astonishing power of keeping a journal. If you can read and write, you have access to the most amazing source of personal power and magic! Try it for 30 days and watch it transform your life! Clients periodically tell me they couldn't possibly find the time. I ask them to try it for 30 days. Then clients often tell me they couldn't possibly live without the power of their journals. Here are my TOP 10 REASONS to keep a journal.

1. **Clarifies your goals.** As you write a few thoughts each day, your ideas about what is important, what is worthy of your life and your time will become much clearer. You'll automatically discover what you really want in life.
2. **Simplifies your life.** Spending as little as 10 minutes with pen and paper describing your values, noting your achievements and giving thanks for the joys of life, will make you less tolerant of life's distractions. Things become much simpler when you write them down.
3. **Strengthens your relationships.** It will give you time and the words to express your feelings, it will help you understand and be patient with your loved one's peccadilloes, and it will teach you to love more powerfully.
4. **Makes you more attractive.** Socrates said, "Know thyself." Keeping a journal will help you know yourself and express yourself more clearly, and that is amazingly attractive!
5. **Empowers you.** Thinking with pen and paper forces you to eliminate fuzzy or confusing images and "laser" in on precisely the right word, the most powerful image to express yourself. Keeping a journal will make you a much better communicator, and that can make you rich!
6. **Eliminates temptation.** Some ideas sound great in our imagination, but when written on paper they just aren't the same! It's easy to blurt out "I hate my job!" but writing about what it means to quit, change careers and start over will quickly result in one of

two things: The temptation will go away, or you'll start generating actual plans to make your life better. Either way, you win!

7. **Affirms the reality of your life.** Writing about life adds meaning and power. Journal your child's first steps or first tooth, starting school, her first date and high school graduation adds substance to these things. A friend of mine just became a grandfather for the first time and gave his son, the proud father, a fat three-ring binder of notes he'd written as he'd watched his baby boy grow 25 years ago. Together they cried and laughed at the reality that life is a sacred, wonderful thing.
8. **Helps you be quiet.** Journalizing has been called a form of meditation. It has a similar power to quiet the mind and focus your thoughts. It even has the power to turn off the TV! It can heal anxiety, change your breathing and make you smile. What more could you ask?
9. **Helps you speak out.** Many of my articles, letters to the local paper, and letters to friends began as notes in my journal. A journal helps ideas become words, and it provides a nursery for words to grow into sentences and paragraphs, until finally they need a stage on which to express themselves. Sometimes that "stage" is a candle-lit dinner; other times it's a protest sign or a letter to an old friend. Whatever form it takes, many of those messages would never have been born without the safety of a journal in which to grow.
10. **Finally, a journal just feels good!** Using quality paper and a fountain pen or other beautiful instrument with just the right "heft" and feel is a wonderfully sensuous, delightful experience. It will cheer you up, reduce your stress, make you smile, and add to your life.

TOP 10 SECRETS OF GETTING RICH![7]

by Philip Humbert

As many people have observed, "Success leaves clues." If you want to achieve extraordinary success in the coming year, study the experts, do what they do, and modify their techniques to suit your particular situation. It's easy!

Well, maybe not easy, but there are basic fundamentals. In the belief that we all need to be reminded of them regularly, here are some of the secrets that have helped my clients and me over the years:

1. **Focus on values.** I've known people who made some money, but I've never known anyone who got rich without examining their own values, priorities and beliefs. Start by writing down a list of things you value, things you believe, what you want, and what you plan to do with this incredible life you have. Start with your values.
2. **Get a life.** Before you can handle great wealth, you must make room for it. This is the old, "if you build it, they will come" model. Trying to squeeze success, wealth, fame or fortune into a small life won't work. Create a life first; the lifestyle of your dreams will follow.
3. **Eliminate clutter.** Trying to create success and achieve wealth while your life's a mess won't work. Success requires clear priorities and a passionate commitment. Simplify your life. Eliminate the excuses. Clean up everything that distracts you from reaching your most important goals.
4. **Specify your results.** Nobody can hit a target they can't see. Define your outcomes and set clear, achievable results in advance. Know what "success" looks like! Have measurable, specific outcomes and determine that you will achieve them!
5. **Burn your ships.** There's an ancient story about a Greek general who landed his troops on an enemy shore, then burned his ships. He wanted to make it very clear: Retreat and failure were not an option! Leave no room for failure.
6. **Put in more than you take out.** No one will pay you more than your services are worth! Get clear about that! You just can't fool people very long. Your services and your results must be far

more valuable than the small fee you charge. Some people will rip you off; the rest will make you rich!

7. **Live below your means.** Rich people know this. Wealth is accumulated, reinvested, used wisely and given away. It is never spent! Let the millionaire athletes and folks who win lotteries buy the fancy cars and flashy jewelry. If you want to achieve great wealth, live simply, invest wisely, enjoy it all!
8. **Get rich slowly.** The key to great wealth is to minimize income, while maximizing your assets. Income is taxed. Income gets spent—think about all the cars, boats, diamonds and houses people with huge incomes like to buy! Investing in assets that are hard to spend (buildings, stocks and bonds, collectible art, etc) creates wealth that is not taxed, and isn't spent on a casual impulse.
9. **Pay lots of taxes.** No, I'm not talking about paying more than you owe, but pay every cent the law requires. Rich folks don't haggle over nickels and dimes, they invest to make millions! If you can legally avoid taxes, do so! Use the law to your advantage when you can. But juggling the books to hide income or save a few bucks, wastes your time, wastes your energy, creates fear of getting caught, and makes you cheap. Don't do it!
10. **Give it away.** You can't take it with you when you die, and money is not attracted to the selfish, the miserly or the mean. If you would attract money to your life, be clear about what you want to do with it. Contribute to charities that will use it for good. Make the world a better, richer place and you'll create wealth that will last for generations to come. Your children will thank you!

■ TOP 10 STEPS TO SET AND ACHIEVE YOUR GOALS[8]

by Philip Humbert

It's been said that everyone has goals, whether we know it or not. We have goals to keep our current job, or to get a different one. We have goals to save for the future, or to travel, take a vacation, or purchase the things we need and want to make our lives more enjoyable. An important distinction, however, is that top achievers are very intentional and focused on their goals, while many of the rest of us are not.

Top achievers know that the wording, structure, timing and format of a goal can make it's achievement much easier—or far more difficult. Top achievers understand the basic skills for setting and reaching their goals, every time! They know how to design goals that create success. Here are the 10 most important steps to set and achieve your goals:

1. Reachable goals are **SPECIFIC**. Top achievers know that to reach their goals, the brain must know exactly, precisely, what they are trying to accomplish. Never word a goal with vague terms like "some" or "a little bit," or "more." Be specific! If you want to lose 8 pounds and reach a weight of 175, specify those exact numbers. If you want to save $200 this month, be exact. Your brain can help you accomplish almost anything if it knows precisely what you are aiming for.
2. Reachable goals are **SIMPLE**. Many people describe their goals in complex terms of retiring on the beach in Hawaii, with nice cars and lots of money, and. . . . Their list goes on and on. Any ONE of those things is a great goal, but the combination becomes over whelming and the brain gets confused. If you want to retire in Hawaii, just say so! If you want to increase your sales by 10% this month, say so! Keep your goals simple, clear, and focused.
3. Reachable goals are **SIGNIFICANT**. No one can muster the enthusiasm, hard work and courage to reach a goal they don't really care about. A reachable goal is one you really, really, REALLY want! It's something that will change your life, enhance your health or wealth, and make you proud. It gets your juices flowing, gets you up in the morning, and keeps you going all

day long, because it is important! Set goals that are worth achieving!

4. Reachable goals are **STRATEGIC**. High achievers know that the best goals accomplish many great outcomes, all at one time. Running a 10K race will almost certainly: (1) feel great! (2) help you lose weight. (3) lower your cholesterol level (4) strengthen your heart (5) lower you risk of heart disease (6) increase your energy and stamina, and (7) improve your outlook. Design your goals to strategically impact as many areas of your life as possible. You'll have more reasons to reach your goal and more excitement when you do!
5. Reachable goals are **MEASURABLE**. A goal without a measurable outcome is just a pipe dream. You can't achieve a pound of "happiness" or 6 inches of "self-esteem," but you CAN get a new job. You CAN run a mile in under 7 minutes, or do 100 sit-ups. Someone has wisely observed that, "What gets measured, gets done." Define your goals in terms of height, weight, dollars, inches, or hours. Then measure your progress until you achieve your desired outcome.
6. Reachable goals are **RATIONAL**. To reach your goal, you will need a plan, a path, and a vehicle for getting there. Your goals must make sense! When you explain them to friends and family, your goals should create excitement and draw support and encouragement. Your goals should be just out of reach, but not out of sight! You want to stretch to be your best, not strain after impossible dreams. Set goals you CAN and WILL achieve!
7. Reachable goals are **TANGIBLE**. Choose goals that you can see, hear, smell or touch. Go for things you will enjoy and that you can clearly visualize. The brain has a hard time going for "financial security," but it can visualize a bank statement with nice, large numbers on it! Define your goals in terms that excite the senses, and then go for it with all your heart!
8. Reachable goals are **WRITTEN**. High achievers always know precisely what they want, because they've written it down. Often, they write a short description of their goals every single morning, as a personal reminder of their priorities and their objectives. The act of writing your goals down vastly increases your chance of success. Write it down! Then, keep your notes where you can see and read them every day.

9. Reachable goals are **SHARED**. We are far more likely to stick to our plan and reach our goals if we know our friends and family support us. Being part of a team increases our determination, our stamina, and our courage. Caution: Never share your goals with anyone who may ridicule, tease or discourage you! The world is full of doubters and you have no time for them. But find a support team, a group of cheerleaders, and a coach who will encourage you every step of the way. High achievers count on and work with other winners!
10. Reachable goals are **CONSISTENT WITH YOUR VALUES**. One of the biggest reasons people fail to achieve their goals is that they have conflict between their behavior and their values. However, when your values and your goals are in agreement, there is no stopping you! Clarify your values first, then set simple, specific, measurable, tangible, written goals that are consistent with those values. You will achieve them, every single time!

TOP 10 THINGS TO THINK ABOUT IF YOU WANT TO CHANGE THE WORLD[9]

by Michael Angier

1. Know that all significant change throughout history has occurred not because of nations, armies, governments and certainly not committees. They happened as a result of the courage and commitment of individuals. People like Joan of Arc, Albert Einstein, Clara Barton, Abraham Lincoln, Thomas Edison and Rosa Parks. They might not have done it alone, but they were, without question, the change makers.
2. Believe that you have a unique purpose and potential in the world. It's not so much something to create as to be discovered. And it's up to you to discover it. Believe that you can and will make a difference.
3. Recognize that everything you do, every step you take, every sentence you write, every word you speak—or DON'T speak—counts. Nothing is trivial. The world may be big, but there are no small things. Everything matters.
4. To be the change you want to see in the world, you don't have to be loud. You don't have to be eloquent. You don't have to be elected. You don't even have to be particularly smart or well educated. You do, however, have to be committed.
5. Take personal responsibility. Never think "it's not my job." It's a cop-out to say, "What can I do, I'm only one person." You don't need everyone's cooperation or anyone's permission to make changes. Remember this little gem, "If it's to be, it's up to me."
6. Don't get caught up in the how of things. If you're clear on what you want to change and why you want to change it, the how will come. Many significant things have been left undone because someone let the problem solving interfere with the decision-making.
7. Don't wait for things to be right in order to begin. Change is messy. Things will never be just right. Follow Teddy Roosevelt's timeless advice, "Do what you can, with what you have, where you are."

8. The genesis for change is awareness. We cannot change what we don't acknowledge. Most of the time, we aren't aware of what's wrong or what's not working. We don't see what could be. By becoming more aware, we begin the process of change.
9. Take to heart these words from Albert Einstein—arguably one of the smartest change masters who ever lived: "All meaningful and lasting change starts first in your imagination and then works its way out. Imagination is more important than knowledge."
10. In order for things to change, YOU have to change. We can't change others; we can only change ourselves. However, when WE change, it changes everything. And in doing so, we truly can be the change we want to see in the world.

■ TWO IDEAS TO GUIDE YOU ON YOUR LIFE JOURNEY[10]

by Chuck Gallozzi

1. **The Adventure of a Lifetime**

Whether you're in high school or college, congratulations! You have embarked on the adventure of a lifetime. *Your* lifetime! Your life and adventure are one and the same. You probably have already discovered that life *is* an adventure. Yet, your understanding should be at the deepest level possible. This simple idea should become a part of you, a guiding principle. When you welcome this notion into your heart, you will find that every day can be an exciting one. This principle will also help you overcome difficulties and lead you down the path to happiness and success. If you're ready to learn more, read on.

Is your life an adventure or a misadventure? This question is an important one because the view we take colors everything we experience. Our attitude or perspective either works for us, or against us. So, now and then we need to pause and examine which way our life is headed, to determine if we need to make a change of direction.

If you believe life is a misadventure or struggle, you will live with resentment, distrust, and fear. You will also feel that life is unfair and a form of punishment. Yet, one's view of life is a choice we all make. If you don't like what you see, you can change the channel just the way you do on a TV set. Are you getting tired of seeing nothing but violence and suffering? Well, then, simply ***CHANGE THE CHANNEL!***

Remember that YOU can choose what you pay attention to. When you shift your attention from the negative to the positive, you begin to see the world in a new way. This change of perspective will cause you to act differently. And by acting differently, life itself will become different in a positive way for you.

The secret of life is realizing that it is a great adventure. Missing this simple point can have disastrous effects. For example, imagine you and some primitive man are strapped in a roller coaster. He was plucked out of a South American jungle and knows nothing about modern life. At the end of the ride, how will his experience differ from yours? In his eyes, the ride was a devilish form of torture. During the entire trip he was in a state of bewilderment and fear. And you? You enjoyed every thrilling moment!

Can you see how the failure to understand the nature of a roller coaster prevented this primitive individual from enjoying the ride? It is no different with life. Those who have yet to learn that life is an adventure mistakenly believe they are victims of circumstances, condemned to a life of suffering.

Yet, once the nature of life is understood, everything changes. Can a roller coaster be exciting without steep falls and sharp twists and turns? Neither can life be exhilarating unless there are challenges to face, hurdles to overcome, and problems to solve. Adventurers understand that, so they don't fight and struggle with events, but choose to go with the flow. True, the flow may be as turbulent as white-water rafting, but isn't that part of the adventure?

Life invites us to become adventurers. It invites us to stop whining and start shining, to stop being a victim and start being a victor. It invites us to journey on our quest to discover, uncover, and recover our potential. It invites us to become the hero in our life story by living courageously. It invites us to lead powerful lives in which we make an important difference to many others in the world.

Life is not a war to wage, but a gift to cherish. You will realize this as soon as you shift your attention from what you lack to what you have. Your feeling of gratitude and sense of appreciation releases energy, which will then help you to continue tirelessly in your adventure.

Adventurers don't repress or hide their emotions. Like rainbows, they burst into color as they feel and express a full range of feelings. Fear, anger, disgust, joy, pity, loneliness, surprise, elation, enthusiasm, passion, embarrassment, pain, sorrow, happiness, awe, calmness, and confusion are just a few of the emotions they experience. Unlike the numbness of the living dead, adventurers are alive with vibrant feelings. They feel life, soak it in, sense it, taste it, and fully express it.

Another characteristic of adventurers is their willingness to welcome change and uncertainty. Why shouldn't you? For change and uncertainty are just other words for surprise. No wonder adventurers believe life is a celebration; after all, they spend their entire lives in a surprise party. They love dueling with the unexpected because it keeps them on their toes. Our lives don't have to be boring; they can be as exciting as that of any swashbuckler. All one has to do is accept life's offer; it's just asking you to jump in and join in the fun.

If you want to become a heroic adventurer, how do you get from where you are to where we want to be? The best way to begin is with an inspiring dream. Pick a dream that is worthy of a hero. For as Robert Fritz, author of *The Path of Least Resistance,* wrote, "If you limit your choices only to what seems possible or reasonable, you disconnect yourself from what you truly want, and all that is left is compromise."

Another thing you can do is open your eyes and see. See what? See what Jawaharlal Nehru, first Prime Minister of India, spoke about, "We live in a wonderful world that is full of beauty, charm and adventure. There is no end to the adventures that we can have if only we seek them with our eyes open." Every crossroad you come to is a choice between following the path of adventure or the road to boredom. Which will it be? As long as you awaken from your sleep, and look for the right path, you will find it. When you open your heart, mind, and eyes to what the world offers, a flood of riches awaits you, so remain alert.

2. The Power of Self-Discipline

Most people sense that happiness and freedom are linked, but only in an imperfect way. For instance, you may think the freedom to give up study or work and the ability to do anything you please will bring happiness. But here is the paradox: when you seek freedom, you become a prisoner, but when you seek self-discipline, you really discover freedom. You then become free to achieve your dreams.

How can we apply this principle to our lives? Well, let's look at an example of a day in the life of someone named Johnny. I don't know about you, but Johnny likes to believe that Sunday is a day to relax, a day in which he can do anything he pleases. But, his conscience was reminding him that an exam was approaching and he should be preparing for it. Being Sunday, he didn't feel like studying. But he realized it isn't necessary for us to enjoy EVERYTHING we do. Enjoy it or not, we should do whatever needs to be done. So, Johnny packed his bags and headed for the library where he wouldn't be distracted.

Despite not being in the mood to study, Johnny was at the library doing just that. You see, he suspected we have the power to do even those things we don't feel like doing. About two-and-a-half hours later, he was growing restless and wondering if he should return home and continue studying there. No, he thought, that idea might be just a temptation to take a break. He also felt he'd better return his attention to his studies and get it done as soon as possible. Johnny's behavior reminds me of something someone once said, "Self-discipline is when your conscience tells you to do something and you don't talk back." Johnny got the message and he didn't talk back. As a result, five hours later, he understood the material and felt comfortable with it. Johnny left the library with a broad grin on his face. While returning home, he thought about what happened. Here's what he discovered:

- We have the power to do what we don't feel like doing. It is our responsibility, duty, or obligation that is important, not our feelings.
- We cannot think of two things at the same time, so once we dive into work or study, that's all we can think about. All thoughts about whether it is pleasant or not fade from our mind. And as we get involved with what we are doing, it grows increasingly interesting.
- So, the "pain" of doing something we don't feel like doing doesn't last very long. Real effort is only needed in the beginning. What we need to remember is pain is never permanent. Besides, pain is nothing more than breaking the shell that imprisons us. Our freedom to succeed and get the most from life is worth the effort.
- After finishing an important task that we didn't feel like doing, there is a feeling of excitement. We feel proud of our accomplishment and delighted to learn we have the self-discipline to take charge of our life. So, what we thought would be painful turns out to be pleasurable.

- Also, as we experience this truth, we come to welcome discomfort because of the pleasure conquering it will bring. Not only pleasure, but also power. For when we master self-discipline, we can be, do, or have anything we want. A little effort is a small price to pay for the treasures of success and happiness.
- When you do what you don't feel like doing because it needs to be done, you develop self-confidence and a strong sense of responsibility, two critical keys to success.
- To avoid missing out on success, you mustn't be tricked into avoiding responsibility by indulging in some momentary pleasure. After all, if you were to do so, you will find the "pleasure" (such as watching TV) is pleasure in name only. For as you waste valuable time, you will be troubled by guilt, greatly reducing your "pleasure." And even if you did experience pleasure, it would later be followed by stress and regret.
- When you carefully consider these facts, you will discover that what you usually think of as pleasurable ends up being painful, and what you first believe is painful, turns out to be pleasurable. The lesson, then, is you have to think before you act, for the price of living irresponsibly and neglecting your duties is loss of happiness. On the other hand, the result of being self-disciplined and living up to your responsibilities is happiness.

American businessman, author, speaker, and philosopher Jim Rohn said, "We must all suffer one of two things: the pain of discipline or the pain of regret or disappointment." Which will it be for you?

As you step out into the world armed with the knowledge that life is a great adventure and protected by the shield of self-discipline, you are destined to succeed. So, enjoy what awaits you. True, as you move forward, you will occasionally trip, stumble or fall, as we all do, but just pick yourself up, dust yourself off, and move on. After all, you are in great hands—your own!

WHAT I WISHED I LEARNED IN SCHOOL[11]

by Guy Kawasaki

How to talk to your boss. In school, you're supposed to bring problems to your teachers during office hours. In the real world, you're supposed to bring solutions to your boss in an email, in the hall, or in a five-minute conversation.

How to survive a meeting that's poorly run. Focus on what you want to accomplish in the meeting and ignore everything else. Once you get what you want, take yourself "out of your body," sit back, and enjoy the show. Vow to yourself that someday you'll start a company, and your meetings won't work like this.

How to run a meeting. The primary purpose of a business meeting is to make a decision. It is not to share experiences or feel warm and fuzzy. (1) Start on time; (2) Invite the fewest people possible; (3) Set an agenda; (4) End on time; (5) Send an email to all participants that confirms decisions and reviews action items.

How to figure out anything on your own. Armed with Google, PDFs of manuals, and self-reliance, force yourself to learn how to figure out just about anything on your own. There are no office hours, no teaching assistants, and study groups in the real world.

How to negotiate. The only method that works in the real world involves: (1) Prepare for the negotiation by knowing your facts; (2) Figure out what you really want, what you don't care about, and what the other party really wants; and (3) Create a win-win outcome to ensure that everyone is happy.

How to have a conversation. Generally, if you listen more than you talk, you will (ironically) be considered not only a good conversationalist but also smart. Yes, life is mysterious sometimes.

How to explain something in thirty seconds. Think mantra (three words), not mission statements (sixty words). Think time, not money, is the most important commodity. If you can't explain enough in thirty seconds to incite interest, you're going to have a long, boring career.

How to write a one-page report. The best reports in the real world are one page or less.

How to write a five-sentence email. All you should do is explain who you are, what you want, why you should get it, and when you need it by.

How to get along with co-workers. What becomes more and more important is the ability to work with / through / besides and sometimes around others. Most importantly: Share the credit with others because a rising tide floats all boats.

How to use PowerPoint. Limit yourself to 10 slides, 20 minutes, and a 30-point font.

How to leave a voicemail. The purpose of a voicemail is to make progress along a continuum whose end is getting what you want. The optimal length of a voicemail is fifteen seconds.

Notes

1. Excerpted from the book *Younger Next Year.* Copyright 2004, 2005 by Christopher Crowley and Henry S. Lodge. Used by permission of Workman Publishing Co., Inc., New York. All rights reserved.
2. By Jeffrey Baumgartner (www.jpb.com), business services entrepreneur.
3. See note 2.
4. The article is included with the permission of Bob Parsons. www.bobparsons.com. Copyright 2005 by Bob Parsons. All rights reserved.
5. Copyright by Steve Brunkhorst. Steve is a life strategies coach, inspirational writer, and the editor of *Achieve! 60-Second Nuggets of Inspiration* at www.AchieveEzine.com.
6. Written by Dr. Philip E. Humbert, author, speaker and personal success coach. Dr Humbert has hundreds of tips, tools and articles on his web site that you can use for YOUR success! It's a great resource! And, be sure to sign up for his free newsletter! Visit him on the Web at www.philiphumbert.com.
7. See note 6.
8. See note 6.
9. Used with permission of SuccessNet.org and founder Michael E. Angier.
10. Copyright Chuck Gallozzi, Chuck.Gallozzi@rogers.com, http://www.personal-development.com/chuck. Mr. Gallozzi is a personal development author of over 300 articles.
11. Guy Kawasaki, managing director of Garage Technologies Ventures and author of eight books. More information available at www.alltop.com.

CHAPTER 10

TEACHERS CAN MAKE A HUGE DIFFERENCE

- TEACHER'S CREDO (Haim G. Ginott)
- UNITY
- What Do Teachers Make? (Taylor Mali)
- Quotes about Teachers
- Great Movies about Great Teachers
- Stand up to Bullying and Change Our World (SuEllen Fried)

"What do teachers make?" is a thoughtful question I must have read it dozens of times. Teachers help you understand that you can succeed in life if you work hard and follow your heart and use the gifts you were given. They can and do ***MAKE A DIFFERENCE!***

The learning process is a lifelong endeavor. Many people in our lives will be teachers to us, besides those in schools. People we usually don't think of as teachers often help us gain important knowledge: parents, friends, grandparents, coworkers, a boss, an aunt, an uncle, or a neighbor.

They teach by example, direct instruction, and by being supportive and encouraging. President Obama could turn out to be a fine role model for youngsters around the world.

Ever stop to think about how difficult it is to be a teacher? What about you? What kind of student are you in life? How open are you to learning and what kind of energy do you put into the process? Is it all up to the teacher? How about your responsibility?

Teachers CAN and DO make a difference and help us grow and change for the better, often overcoming strong resistance from the student. It does take some time, though many great movies about teachers accomplish a great deal in just 120 minutes, given the talents of Sidney Poitier, Michelle Pfeiffer, Robin Williams, and Hillary Swank.

TEACHER'S CREDO

I have come to the frightening conclusion that I am the decisive element in the classroom. My personal approach creates the climate. My daily mood makes the weather.

As a teacher, I possess a tremendous power to make a child's life miserable or joyous. I can be a tool of torture or an instrument of inspiration. I can humiliate or humor, hurt or heal.

In all situations, it is my response that decides whether a crisis will be escalated or de-escalated and a child will be humanized or dehumanized.

—Haim G. Ginott (1922–1973), teacher, child psychologist, and psychotherapist, adapted from Johann Wolfgang von Goethe (1749—1832), German poet, dramatist, novelist, philosopher, and scientist

■ UNITY

by Anonymous

I dreamt I stood in a studio and watched two sculptors there.

The clay they used was a young child's mind and they fashioned it with care.

One was a teacher; the tools she used were books and music and art;

One was a parent with a guiding hand and a gentle loving heart.

Day after day the teacher toiled, with a touch that was deft and sure, while the parent labored by her side and polished and smoothed it over.

And when at last their work was done, they were proud of what they had wrought, for the things they had molded into the child, could neither be sold or bought.

And each agreed they would have failed if each had worked alone. For behind the parent stood the school, and behind the teacher, the home.

■ WHAT DO TEACHERS MAKE?[1]

Taylor Mali

The dinner guests were sitting around the table discussing life. One man, a CEO, decided to explain the problem with education. He argued, "What's a kid going to learn from someone who decided his best option in life was to become a teacher?" He reminded the other dinner guests what they say about teachers: "Those who can, do. Those who can't, teach." To stress his point he said to another guest; "You're a teacher, Bonnie. Be honest. What do you make?" Bonnie, who had a reputation for honesty and frankness replied, "You want to know what I make?" (She paused for a second, then began.)

"Well, I make kids work harder than they ever thought they could. I make a C+ feel like the Congressional Medal of Honor. I make kids sit through forty minutes of class time when their parents can't make them sit for five without an iPod, Game Cube, or movie rental. You want to know what I make?" (She paused again and looked at each and every person at the table.)

"I make kids wonder. I make them question. I make them criticize. I make them apologize and mean it. I make them have respect and take responsibility for their actions. I teach them to write and then I make them write. I make them read, read, read. I make them show all their work in math. I make my students from other countries learn everything they need to know in English while preserving their unique cultural identity.

"I make my classroom a place where all my students feel safe. I make my students stand to say the Pledge of Allegiance to the Flag, because we live in the United States of America. Finally, I make them understand that if they use the gifts they were given, work hard, and follow their hearts, they can succeed in life." (Bonnie paused one last time then continued.) "Then, when people try to judge me by what I make, I can hold my head up high and pay no attention because they are ignorant. You want to know what I make?

I MAKE A DIFFERENCE! What do you make?"

QUOTES ABOUT TEACHERS

In a completely rational society, the best of us would be teachers and the rest of us would have to settle for something less.

—Lee Iacocca (b. 1924), former Chrysler CEO

We have lots of heroes today—sportsmen, supermodels, media personalities. They come, they have their 15 minutes of fame, and they go. But the influence of good teachers stays with us. They are the people who really shape our life.

—Sir Jonathan Sacks (b. 1948) Chief Rabbi of the United Hebrew Congregations of the British Commonwealth

Teachers are expected to reach unattainable goals with inadequate tools. The miracle is that at times they accomplish this impossible task.

—Haim G. Ginot (1922–1973), teacher, child psychologist, and psychotherapist

One looks with appreciation to the brilliant teachers, but with gratitude to those who touched our human feelings. The curriculum is so much necessary raw material, but warmth is the vital element for the growing plant and for the soul of the child.

—Carl Jung (1875–1961, Swiss psychiatrist)

As we look at the 21st century, we recognize that societies all around the world are changing dramatically, and therefore I think teachers will make a tremendous difference in the lives of individuals, the lives of communities, and the lives of nations.

—Mary Hatwood Futrell (b. 1940), educator

Better than a thousand days of diligent study is one day with a great teacher.

—Japanese proverb

The dream begins, most of the time, with a teacher who believes in you, who tugs and pushes and leads you on to the next plateau, sometimes poking you with a sharp stick called truth.

—Dan Rather (b. 1931), former CBS News anchor

When the uncapped potential of a student meets the liberating art of a teacher, a miracle unfolds.

—Mary Hatwood Futrell (b. 1940), educator

■ GREAT MOVIES ABOUT GREAT TEACHERS[2]

Last year, *Teacher Magazine* reported that members of the Teacher Leaders Network did a survey of teachers to find the ten best movies about teachers. Here they are, with year of release, and actor in the leading role.

1. ***Mr. Holland's Opus (1995)***, Richard Dreyfuss
2. ***Stand and Deliver (1988)***, Edward James Olmos
3. ***October Sky (1999)***, Jake Gyllenhaal
4. ***Dangerous Minds (1995)***, Michelle Pfeiffer
5. ***Freedom Writers (2007)***, Hillary Swank
6. ***Chalk (2006),*** Troy Schremmer
7. ***To Sir, with Love*** (1967), Sidney Poitier
8. ***Dead Poets Society*** (1989), Robin Williams
9. ***Remember the Titans (2000)***, Denzel Washington
10. ***Teachers (1984)***, Nick Nolte

Many great movies show how teachers change many lives. We see youngsters lifting themselves up and realizing their enormous potential.

- ***Mr. Holland's Opus (1995)***. When the music program at his school is canceled, a music teacher wonders what he has accomplished in his life. Successful students from the past appear and tell him what a huge difference he has made to them.
- ***Stand and Deliver (1988)***. Dedicated teacher inspires his dropout-prone students to learn calculus to build up their self-esteem. When they do very well, they surprise everybody and some people even suspect them of cheating.
- ***Freedom Writers (2007)***. In this more recent film, a group of ghetto youngsters are made to feel proud of their accomplishments and are inspired to climb higher in life. *Dangerous Minds* (1995), *To Sir, with Love* (1967), and *Blackboard Jungle* (1955) all have a similar theme.

Other teacher movies that you can rent for home viewing include: *Goodbye Mr. Chips* (1939), *Up the Down Staircase* (1967), *Kindergarten Cop* (1990), *Good Will Hunting* (1997), *Born Yesterday* (1950), *Music of the*

Heart (1999), and *Miracle Worker* (1962). According to *Martha Alderson* of BlockbusterPlots.com, in each of these films "the protagonist undergoes a major transformation. The climax . . . is where protagonists are able to do something they were unable to do at the beginning of the movie, showing true power having undergone the transformation."

STAND UP TO BULLYING AND CHANGE THE WORLD[3]

by SuEllen Fried

It used to be people believed that bullying was a part of child's play, "boys will be boys" kind of stuff. It wasn't playful to children on the receiving end, but adults just wouldn't take it seriously. The tragic shootings at Columbine in 1999 changed all of that.

Fast forward and let's look at what we know today. We know that when children experience pain it collects and can turn to rage. When enough rage accumulates, it can provoke revenge. The revenge causes pain and the cycle continues. Or the pain can lead to depression, which can lead to suicide. Either way, pain is powerful. The pain, rage, revenge cycle escalates from the schoolyard battlefield to the battlefields between countries, regions, tribes and religions. If we could work together to stop pain whenever possible, could we ultimately change the world?

For many children the pain begins at home where children experience or observe bullying behaviors in their family. For these children, teachers offer a crucial alternative role model. Teachers who reach out to students who are a challenge, who nurture their neediness and believe in their possibilities, can make a profound difference in a child's life.

One way to engage the classroom to create a culture of compassion is to initiate a discussion about the FIVE kinds of bullying:

- PHYSICAL (any action involving body contact)
- VERBAL (the use of language to inflict pain)
- EMOTIONAL (body language, sign language, rejection, isolation)
- SEXUAL (inappropriate touching, harassment, gender discrimination, sexual language)
- CYBER (use of technology to threaten, torment, embarrass, expose)

Research indicates that 29.9% of students engage in one or more of these bullying activities as a bully, a target or both. That means 70% of students are not engaged in these behaviors. This large majority of students could assert their power and use their ingenuity to respond to students in pain (who can be both bullies and targets). Mobilizing student witnesses is such an important element to a bullying prevention strategy.

When it becomes "cool to be kind" instead of "cool to be cruel" it can be transformational.

Witnesses can also take action to report bullying situations to adults. Too often, targets are concerned about retaliation, if they divulge the name of their bully. Consequently, adults who could intervene never receive the info. Another approach is for teachers to guarantee confidentiality and encourage targets to self- report to an adult they trust.

Once when I was working with a class, a boy publicly apologized to Katie, a girl with Tourette syndrome who was taunted by everyone in the school. Later all of the students in her class apologized and then became her buffers and protectors. Soon everyone in the school stopped tormenting Katie. Her teacher maintains that it wasn't only Katie's life that was changed, it was all of her classmates who developed confidence in their ability to dramatically affect the atmosphere of their school.

Notes

1. Many versions of this work have been posted on the Web without attribution. This version is based on the work of Taylor Mali, teacher, poet, and performer, who claims to be its originator. You can visit his Web site at www.taylormali.com.
2. *Plots for Kids and Teens,* http://plothelpforyoungreadersandwriters.blogspot.com.
3. SuEllen Fried, Founder of BullySafeUSA, www.bullysafeusa.com.

CHAPTER 11

WE MUST CURE THE WORLD'S ADDICTION TO OIL AND COAL!

- SOLAR ENERGY (Thomas Alva Edison)
- End Our Oil and Coal Addiction NOW! (Richard Holbrooke)
- Quotes about Free Energy
- A Hydrogen Economy in Our Future? (Jeremy Rifkin)
- Set America Free! A Blueprint for U.S. Energy Security
- Future Energy Possibilities
- Ted Turner's Eleven Voluntary Initiatives
- What Jules Verne Said in 1874

Half the people alive today are already living in what we would consider intolerable conditions. One-sixth don't have access to clean drinking water; one-fifth live on less

> than a dollar a day; half the women in the world don't have equal rights with men; the forests are shrinking; the temperature's rising, and the oceans are rising, because of the melting of the ice cap."
>
> —Ted Turner (b. 1938), founder of CNN

In Chapter 1, we saw how horses and wagons a century ago posed a giant pollution problem and how lucky we were to change over to the automotive age. Now, we are experiencing a far greater problem for Planet Earth, which can be devastating in the coming years—POLLUTION. There is no other solution but to end the coal and oil age. We MUST! The whole world MUST rapidly switch over to ways of providing power for transportation and heating without the use of coal and oil.

There were many different electric cars a hundred years ago but great oil discoveries and getting rid of the hand cranking of engines made the gasoline cars more affordable. For example, gasoline powered cars in 1912 cost about $650, while electric cars cost about $1,750. As the dollar then had 25 times more purchasing power, the two cars today would sell for $16,250 versus $43,750. See these Web sites for additional interesting data:

- *GreenHybrid.com,* http://greenhybrid.com
- *Pure Energy Systems,* "Congress: Top 100 Technologies," http://peswiki.com/energy/Congress:Top_100_Technologies_—_RD
- *Now on PBS,* "Electric Car Timeline," http://www.pbs.org/now/shows/223/electric-car-timeline.html
- *Electric-Cars-Are-for-Girls.com,* "The Electric Car's History," http://www.electric-cars-are-for-girls.com/history.html

Opportunities!

SOLAR ENERGY

We are like tenant farmers chopping down the fence around our house for fuel when we should be using nature's inexhaustible sources of energy—sun, wind and tide. I'd put my money on the sun and solar energy. What a source of power! I hope we don't have to wait until oil and coal run out before we tackle that.

—Thomas Alva Edison
(1847–1931), inventor

■ END OUR OIL ADDICTION NOW![1]

by Richard Holbrooke

The following paragraphs are from an article by the former U.S. ambassador to the United Nations, Richard Holbrooke (b. 1941), from the September–October 2008 edition of the very interesting *Foreign Affairs* magazine. Holbrooke is now the Special Representative for Afghanistan and Pakistan.

Consider the following, from the noted oil expert Daniel Yergin: the United States consumes more than 20 million barrels of oil a day, about 12 million of which are imported. Based on prices from the first half of 2008, that means the United States is transferring about $1.3 billion to the oil-producing countries every day—$475 billion a year. (At the June 2008 price, $147 for a barrel of crude, the amount was far greater.) The other major consumers, including China, the European Union, India, and Japan, are sending even greater portions of their wealth to the producing countries, for a total annual transfer of well over $2.2 trillion. These figures are climbing.

Suppose high oil prices continue for, say, another decade—a gloomy but not unreasonable scenario given the long lead-time required to wean the consuming nations off their expensive habit. The wealth now accumulating in the producing nations will lead over time not only to even greater economic muscle but also to greater political power. Some of these producing nations have very different political agendas from those of the United States, Europe, and Japan. Groupings of oil-rich nations with goals opposed to those of the United States and its European allies will become more common and act more boldly.

The world economic downturn has caused a dramatic drop in gasoline prices. This will cause the oil nations to cut production to get prices back up. Despite lower prices, it is full speed ahead on the many fronts to knock out or cut down the use of gasoline in motor vehicles. —*Y.H.*

QUOTES ABOUT FREE ENERGY

Electric power is everywhere present in unlimited quantities and can drive the world's machinery without the need of coal, oil, gas, or any other common fuels.

—Nikola Tesla (1856–1943), "father" of alternating current

Presently, only 1% of the U.S. energy supply comes from renewable sources, including solar, wind and hydro. If we applied the $400 billion that has been spent in the Iraq war toward installing wind turbines on non-farmable lands in North and South Dakota, we could power the U.S., and become independent of imported oil.

—Jim Dunn, Center for Technology Commercialization, November 19, 2006

Considering the many productive uses of petroleum, burning it for fuel is like burning a Picasso for heat.

—Anonymous

I can now state that I have succeeded in operating a motive device by means of [cosmic rays]. I will tell you in the most general way, the cosmic ray ionizes the air, setting free many charges, ions and electrons. These charges are captured in a condenser, which is made to discharge through the circuit of the motor.

—Nikola Tesla (1856–1943), *Brooklyn Eagle*, July 10, 1932

I have no doubt that we will be successful in harnessing the sun's energy. If sunbeams were weapons of war, we would have had solar energy centuries ago.

—Sir George Porter (1920–2002,) Shared Nobel Prize in Chemistry in 1967

When one "fringe" free energy technology finally goes commercial, it will open a floodgate of interest in all the other technologies that science said were 'impossible.' Free energy *will promulgate a forward leap in human progress akin to the discovery of fire. It will bring the dawn of an entirely new civilization—one based on freedom and abundance.*

—Sterling D. Allan (b. 1963), CEO, Founder PES Network and New Energy Congress

■ A HYDROGEN ECONOMY IN OUR FUTURE?[2]

by Jeremy Rifkin

I don't know if we will ever be able to completely switch over to such an economy but much of the data in the book *The Hydrogen Economy,* by Jeremy Rifkin, is quite compelling. Here are some excerpts.

- The average American uses 8,000 pounds of oil, 4,700 pounds of natural gas, 5,150 pounds of coal, and one-tenth of a pound of uranium each year. Walter Youngquist, author *GeoDestinies,* 1997
- If we purchased the energy in a barrel of oil at the same price we pay for human labor ($5/hr), it would cost us over $45,000. Walter Youngquist, author *GeoDestinies,* 1997
- The popular conception is that Rome collapsed because of the decadence of its ruling class, the corruption of its leaders, the exploitation of its servants and slaves, and the superior military tactics of invading barbarian hordes. . . . The deeper cause of Rome's collapse lies in the declining fertility of its soil and the decrease in agricultural yields.
- Nearly half of the human race—more than 2.5 billion people—still rely on wood, animal manure, and crop residue for their fuels. Clive Ponting, *A Green History of the World,* 1991
- In 1850, a single farm produced enough food to feed four people. By 1982, a single farmer produced enough food to feed 78 people. *Scientific American,* September 1982
- Nitrate pollution from fertilizer runoff now accounts for half of our water pollution and two-thirds of our sold-waste pollution.
- The single most important question now facing human civilization is whether or not a new energy regime can be found and harnessed in time to replace fossil fuels and meet the needs of a growing human population on Earth in the coming century.
- Water decomposed into its primitive elements and decomposed doubtless, by electricity, which will then have become a powerful and manageable force. . . . Yes my friends, I believe that water will one day be employed as fuel, that hydrogen and oxygen which constitute it, used singly or together, will furnish an inexhaustible

source of heat and light, of an intensity of which coal is not capable. Jules Verne, *The Mysterious Island,* 1874

- In the 21st century coal, oil, and natural gas, the great fossil fuels that had propelled the world into the industrial era, would give way to a revolutionary regime based on hydrogen and that Shell Oil had already committed up to a billion dollars to making the transition into a renewable resource economy. A prediction by Phil Watts, Chairman, Royal Dutch Shell, October 2001
- Hydrogen is the most abundant element in the universe. It makes up 75% of the mass of the universe and 90% of its molecules. *Columbia Encyclopedia*
- Electricity generated from fuel cells now costs $3,000 to $4,000 per kilowatt [to build], whereas electricity generated from a typical gas-fired central power plant runs between $500 and $1,000 per kilowatt. Alan C. Lloyd, *Scientific American,* July 1999
- I believe fuel cells will finally end the 100-year reign of the internal combustion engine. Bill Ford, Chairman, Ford Motor Company (Quoted by Steve Silberman in *Wired*), July 2001
- 65% of the human population has never made a single telephone call, and one-third of the human race has no access to electricity. Steven E. Miller, *Civilizing Cyberspace,* 1996
- By 2010, 1.4 billion people will live without clean water and sanitation. Barbara Crossette, Foreign correspondent *New York Times,* June 3, 1996
- Lack of access to energy, and especially electricity, is a key factor in perpetuating poverty around the world. Conversely, access to energy means more economic opportunity. Electric Power Research Institute, July 1999
- To achieve universal global electrification by 2050 . . . a new 1,000-megawatt power plant would have to be brought on line every 48 hours for the next 50 years. Electric Power Research Institute, July 1999
- The larger hydrogen fuel cells have the additional advantage of producing pure drinking water as a byproduct, a not-insignificant consideration in village communities around the world where access to clean water is often a critical concern.
- Only by freeing themselves from dependence on foreign oil and gas imports can Third World countries get out from under and improve the economic conditions of their populations.

SET AMERICA FREE! A BLUEPRINT FOR U.S. ENERGY SECURITY[3]

Introduction

Historically, the United States has pursued a three-pronged strategy for minimizing the vulnerabilities associated with its dependency on oil from unstable and/or hostile nations: diversifying sources of oil, managing inventory in a strategic petroleum reserve and increasing the efficiency of the transportation sector's energy consumption. In recent years, the focus has been principally on finding new and larger sources of petroleum globally.

Rapidly growing worldwide demand for oil, however, has had the effect of largely neutralizing this initiative, depleting existing reserves faster than new, economically exploitable deposits are being brought on line. Under these circumstances, diversification among such sources is but a stopgap solution that can, at best, have a temporary effect on oil supply and, hence, on national security. Conservation can help, but with oil consumption expected to grow by 60% over the next 25 years, conservation alone will not be a sufficient solution.

The Set America Free Project

Long-term security and economic prosperity requires the creation of a fourth pillar—technological transformation of the transportation sector through what might be called "fuel choice." By leading a multinational effort rooted in the following principles, the United States can *immediately* begin to introduce a global economy based on next-generation fuels and vehicles that can utilize them:

- **Fuel diversification:** Today, consumers can choose among various octanes of gasoline, which accounts for 45% of U.S. oil consumption, or diesel, which accounts for almost another fifth. To these choices we can and should promptly add other fuels that are domestically produced, where possible from waste products, and that are clean and affordable.
- **Real world solutions:** We have no time to wait for commercialization of immature technologies. The United States should

implement technologies **that exist today and are ready for widespread use.**

- **Using existing infrastructure:** The focus should be on utilizing competitive technologies that do not require prohibitive or, if possible, even significant investment in changing our transportation sector's infrastructure. Instead, "fuel choice" should permit the maximum possible use of the existing refueling and automotive infrastructure.
- **Domestic resource utilization:** The United States is no longer rich in oil or natural gas. It has, however, a wealth of other energy sources from which transportation fuel can be safely, affordably and cleanly generated. Among them: hundreds of years worth of coal reserves, 25% of the world's total (especially promising with Integrated Gasification and Combined Cycle technologies); billions of tons a year of biomass, and billions of tons of agricultural and municipal waste. Vehicles that meet consumer needs (e.g., "plug-in" hybrids), can also tap America's electrical grid to supply energy for transportation, making more efficient use of such clean sources of electricity as solar, wind, geothermal, hydroelectric and nuclear power.
- **Environmentally sensible choices:** The technologies adopted should improve public safety and respond to the public's environmental and health concerns.

Key Elements of the Set America Free Project

Vehicles

Hybrid electric vehicles: There are already thousands of vehicles on America's roads that combine hybrid engines powered in an integrated fashion by liquid fuel-powered motors and battery-powered ones. Such vehicles increase gas-consumption efficiency by 30–40%.

Ultra light materials: At least two-thirds of fuel use by a typical consumer vehicle is caused by its weight. Thanks to advances in both metals and plastics, ultra light vehicles can be affordably manufactured with today's technologies and can roughly halve fuel consumption without compromising safety, performance or cost effectiveness.

"Plug-in" hybrid electric vehicles: Plug-in hybrid electric vehicles are also powered by a combination of electricity and liquid fuel. Unlike standard hybrids, however, plug-ins draw charge not only from the engine and captured braking energy, but also directly from the electrical grid by being plugged into standard electric outlets when not in use. Plug-in hybrids have liquid fuel tanks and internal combustion engines, so they do not face the range limitation posed by electric-only cars. Since fifty-percent of cars on the road in the United States are driven 20 miles a day or less, a plug-in with a 20-mile range battery would reduce fuel consumption by, on average, 85%. **Plug-in hybrid electric vehicles can reach fuel economy levels of 100 miles per gallon of gasoline consumed.**

Flexible fuel vehicles (FFVs): FFVs are designed to burn on alcohol, gasoline, or any mixture of the two. About 4 million FFV's have been manufactured since 1996. The only difference between a conventional car and a flexible fuel vehicle is that the latter is equipped with a different control chip and some different fittings in the fuel line to accommodate the characteristics of alcohol. The marginal additional cost associated with such FFV-associated changes is currently under $100 per vehicle. That cost would be reduced further as volume of FFVs increases, particularly if flexible fuel designs were to become the industry standard.

Flexible fuel/plug-in hybrid electric vehicles: If the two technologies are combined, such vehicles can be powered by blends of alcohol fuels, gasoline, and electricity. If a plug-in vehicle is also a FFV fueled with 80% alcohol and 20% gasoline, fuel economy could reach ***500 miles per gallon*** of gasoline. **If by 2025, all cars on the road are hybrids and half are plug-in hybrid vehicles, U.S. oil imports would drop by 8 million barrels per day (mbd). Today, the United States imports 10 mbd and it is projected to import almost 20 mbd by 2025. If all of these cars were also flexible fuel vehicles, U.S. oil imports would drop by as much as 12 mbd.**

Fuels

- **Fuel additives:** Fuel additives can enhance combustion efficiency by up to 25%. They can be blended into gasoline, diesel and bunker fuel.
- **Electricity as a fuel:** Less than 2% of U.S. electricity is generated from oil, so using electricity as a transportation fuel would greatly reduce dependence on imported petroleum. Plug-in hybrid vehicles

would be charged at night in home garages—a time-interval during which electric utilities have significant excess capacity. **The Electric Power Research Institute estimates that up to 30% of market penetration for plug-in hybrid electric vehicles with 20-mile electric range can be achieved without a need to install additional electricity-generating capacity.**

- **Alcohol fuels: ethanol, methanol and other blends:**

Ethanol (also known as grain alcohol) is currently produced in the U.S. from corn. The industry currently has a capacity of 3.3 billion gallons a year and has increased on the average of 25% per year over the past three years. Upping production would be achieved by continuing to advance the corn-based ethanol industry and by commercializing the production of ethanol from biomass waste and dedicated energy crops. *P-Series* fuel (approved by the Department of Energy in 1999) is a more energy-efficient blend of ethanol, natural gas liquids and ether made from biomass waste. *(I hope we stop using corn, which drives up food prices. —Y.H.)*

Methanol (also known as wood alcohol) is today for the most part produced from natural gas. Expanding domestic production can be achieved by producing methanol from coal, a resource with which the U.S. is abundantly endowed. The commercial feasibility of coal-to-methanol technology was demonstrated as part of the DOE's "clean coal" technology effort. Currently, methanol is being cleanly produced from coal for under 50 cents a gallon. It only costs about $60,000 to add a fuel pump that serves one of the above fuels to an existing refueling station.

- **Non-oil based diesel:** Biodiesel is commercially produced from soybean and other vegetable oils. Diesel can also be made from waste products such as tires and animal byproducts, and is currently commercially produced from turkey offal. Diesel is also commercially produced from coal.

Policy Recommendations:

- Provide incentives to auto manufacturers to produce and consumers to purchase, hybrid vehicles, plug-in hybrid electric vehicles and FFVs across all vehicle models.

- Provide incentives for auto manufacturers to increase fuel efficiency of existing, non-FFV auto models.
- Conduct extensive testing of next-generation fuels across the vehicle spectrum to meet auto warranty and EPA emission standards.
- Mandate substantial incorporation of plug-ins and FFVs into federal, state, municipal and covered fleets.
- Provide investment tax incentives for corporate fleets and taxi fleets to switch to plug-ins, hybrids and FFVs.
- Encourage gasoline distributors to blend combustion enhancers into the fuel.
- Provide incentives for existing fueling stations to install pumps that serve all liquid fuels that can be used in the existing transportation infrastructure, and mandate that all new gas stations be so equipped.
- Provide incentives to enable new players, such as utilities, to enter the transportation fuel market, and for the development of environmentally sound exploitation of non-traditional petroleum deposits from stable areas (such as Canadian tar sands).
- Provide incentives for the construction of plants that generate liquid transportation fuels from domestic energy resources, particularly from waste, that can be used in the existing infrastructure.
- Allocate funds for commercial scale demonstration plants that produce next-generation transportation fuels, particularly from waste products.
- Implement federal, state, and local policies to encourage mass transit and reduce vehicle-miles traveled.
- Work with other oil-consuming countries towards distribution of the above-mentioned technologies and overall reduction of reliance on petroleum, particularly from hostile and potentially unstable regions of the world.

A New National Project

In 1942, President Roosevelt launched the Manhattan Project to build an atomic weapon to be ready by 1945 because of threats to America, and to explore the future of nuclear fission. The cost in today's prices was $20 billion. The outcome was an end to the war with Japan, and the beginning of a wide new array of nuclear-based technologies in energy, medical treatment, and other fields.

In 1962, President Kennedy launched the Man to the Moon Project to be achieved by 1969 because of mounting threats to U.S. and international security posed by Soviet space-dominance and to explore outer space. The cost of the *Apollo* program in today's prices would be well over $100 billion. The outcome was an extraordinary strategic and technological success for the United States. It engendered a wide array of spin-offs that improved virtually every aspect of modern life, including but not limited to transportation, communications, health care, medical treatment, food production and other fields.

The security of the United States, and the world, is no less threatened by oil supply disruptions, price instabilities and shortages. It is imperative that America provide needed leadership by immediately beginning to dramatically reduce its dependence on imported oil. This can be done by embracing the concepts outlined above with a focus on fuel choice, combined with concerted efforts at improving energy efficiency and the increased availability of energy from renewable sources.

The estimated cost of the "Set America Free" plan over the next 4 years is $12 billion. This would be applied in the following way: $2 billion for automotive manufacturers to cover one-half the costs of building FFV-capability into their new production cars (i.e., roughly 40 million cars at $50 per unit); $1 billion to pay for at least one out of every four existing gas stations to add at least one pump to supply alcohol fuels (an estimated incentive of $20,000 per pump, new pumps costing approximately $60,000 per unit); $2 billion in consumer tax incentives to procure hybrid cars; $2 billion for automotive manufacturers to commercialize plug-in hybrid electric vehicles; $3 billion to construct commercial-scale demonstration plants to produce nonpetroleum-based liquid fuels (utilizing public-private cost sharing partnerships to build roughly 25 plants in order to demonstrate the feasibility of various approaches to perform efficiently at full-scale production); and $2 billion to continue work on commercializing fuel cell technology.

Since no major, new scientific advances are necessary to launch this program, such funds can be applied toward increasing the efficiencies of the involved processes. The resulting return-on-investment—in terms of enhanced energy and national security, economic growth, quality of life and environmental protection—should more than pay for the seed money required.

■ FUTURE ENERGY POSSIBILITIES[4]

- Covering just 9 percent (92 square miles) of Nevada with solar power systems could generate enough electric power for the entire country (U.S. Department of Energy).
- Wind could provide 5,800 quads of energy each year. That's about 15 times the current global energy demand (U.S. Department of Energy).
- Over 100 million quads of geothermal energy are accessible worldwide. We consume only 400 quads (according to the Massachusetts Institute of Technology).
- Wave energy along the U.S. coastline is estimated at 2,100 TWh (terawatt hours) per year. That's just half of the total U.S. consumption of electricity (Electric Power Research Institute).
- If all cars on the road were hybrids, and half were PHEVs (plug-in hybrid electric vehicles), by 2025, U.S. oil imports could be reduced by 8 million barrels per day (Set America Free Coalition of the Institute for the Analysis of Global Security).

■ TED TURNER'S ELEVEN VOLUNTARY INITIATIVES[5]

I recently read *Call Me Ted,* the autobiography of Ted Turner, and found it interesting and informative. Despite experiencing a number of tragedies, Ted went on to have a great career, most notably creating Cable News Network (CNN). Here are some rules that the environmentalist Turner tries to live by:

1. I promise to care for planet Earth and all living things thereon, especially my fellow human beings.
2. I promise to treat all persons everywhere with dignity, respect and friendliness.
3. I promise to have no more than one or two children.
4. I promise to use my best efforts to help save what is left of our natural world in its undisturbed state, and to restore degraded areas.
5. I promise to use as little of our non-renewable resources as possible.
6. I promise to minimize my use of toxic chemicals, pesticides and other poisons, and to encourage others to do the same.
7. I promise to contribute to those less fortunate, to help them become self-sufficient and enjoy the benefits of a decent life, including clean air and water, adequate food, health care, housing, education and individual rights.
8. I reject the use of force, in particular military force, and I respect the United Nations arbitration of international disputes.
9. I support the total elimination of all nuclear, chemical and biological weapons, and ultimately the elimination of all weapons of mass destruction.
10. I support the United Nations and its efforts to improve the condition of the planet.
11. I support renewable energy and feel we should move rapidly to contain greenhouse gases.

■ WHAT JULES VERNE SAID IN 1874

Many people in the world are currently trying to do what Jules Verne (1828–1905) wrote as fiction in his 1874 novel, *The Mysterious Island:*

> Water decomposed into its primitive elements, and decomposed doubtless by electricity, which will then have become a powerful and manageable force. Yes, my friends, I believe that water will one day be employed as a fuel, that hydrogen and oxygen which constitute it, used singly or together, will furnish an inexhaustible source of heat and light, of an intensity of which coal is not capable.

Notes

1. Richard Holbrooke, "The Next President: Mastering a Daunting Agenda,"*Foreign Affairs,* September–October 2008. The full text may be purchased and read at http://www.foreignaffairs.org/20080901faessay87501/richard-holbrooke/the-next-president.html.
2. Jeremy Rifkin, *The Hydrogen Economy* (New York: Penguin Putnam, 2002).
3. Permission to reproduce granted by www.SetAmericaFree.org.
4. Technology Innovation Office, Bonneville Power Administration, *Renewable Energy Technology Roadmap (Wind, Ocean Wave, In-Stream Tidal & Solar Photovoltaic),* http://www.bpa.gov/corporate/business/innovation/docs/2008/RM-08_Renewables_Updated.pdf.
5. Excerpts from Ted Turner, *Call Me Ted* (New York: Grand Central, 2008). Copyright 2008. By permission of Grand Central Publishing.

CHAPTER 12

YOU CAN DO IT! YES YOU CAN!

- WHAT DOES IT TAKE TO BE AN ENTREPRENEUR? (*Entrepreneur* magazine)
- Who Am I to Be Brilliant, Gorgeous, Talented? (Marianne Williamson)
- Invictus (William Ernest Henley)
- The Optimist Creed (Christian D. Larson)
- The Man Who Thinks He Can (Walter D. Wintle)
- What Will Matter (Michael Josephson)
- Goals Are Only Achieved with Action (ThinkTQ.com)
- The "Real" Seven Wonders of the World
- Can't (Edgar Guest)
- The Path of Least Resistance (Robert Fritz)
- Triumph over Troubles (Philip Humbert)

No matter who you are, where you come from, or who your parents are, there are no limits to how far you can go and how much you can achieve in life. The vast majority of people rarely accomplish more than 5 or 10 percent of their potential. As was stated earlier, Inside each of us are POWERS so strong, TREASURES so rich, POSSIBILITIES so endless, that if I command them all to action I could make a GIANT DIFFERENCE to millions of people in the world."

Life can be great and fulfilling, and you can take a big bite out of it. All that's needed is to believe in yourself and start moving onward and upward. And no one out there can stop you, except yourself. As you are reading these words right NOW, it means YOU! Yes, YOU! Make a vow to yourself that from this day forward you will not place any limits on how far you can go. You can be more emphatic by writing down somewhere, even on these pages, FROM NOW ON . . . I AM IN CHARGE OF MY FUTURE!

WHAT DOES IT TAKE TO BE AN ENTREPRENEUR?

Hard work. Dedication.
Eating, breathing and
living your dreams,
every day.
Pushing harder.
Taking risks
when others won't.
Never stopping.
Never surrendering
Being fearless.
Being a leader.
Inspiring yourself.
Inspiring those
around you,
every day.

—*Entrepreneur* magazine[1]

■ WHO AM I TO BE BRILLIANT, GORGEOUS, AND TALENTED?[2]

by Marianne Williamson

This poem is often erroneously attributed to Nelson Mandela.

Our deepest fear is not that we are inadequate.
Our deepest fear is that we are powerful beyond measure.
It is our light, not our darkness that most frightens us.
We ask ourselves,
Who am I to be *brilliant, gorgeous, talented, fabulous*?
Actually, who are you *not* to be?
You are a child of God.
Your playing small does not serve the world.
There is nothing enlightened about shrinking
so that other people won't feel insecure around you.
We are all meant to shine, as children do.
We were born to make manifest
the glory of God that is within us.
It's not just in some of us; it's in everyone.
And as we let our own light shine,
we unconsciously give other people
permission to do the same.
As we are liberated from our own fear,
our presence automatically liberates others.

INVICTUS[3]

by William Ernest Henley

Out of the night that covers me,
Black as the Pit from pole to pole,
I thank whatever gods may be
For my unconquerable soul.
In the fell clutch of Circumstance
I have not winced nor cried aloud.
Under the bludgeonings of Chance
My head is bloody, but unbowed.
Beyond this place of wrath and tears
Looms but the Horror of the shade,
And yet the menace of the years
Finds, and shall find me, unafraid.
It matters not how strait the gate,
How charged with punishments the scroll,
I am the master of my fate:
I am the captain of my soul.

Henley contracted tuberculosis of the bone at the age of 12. In spite of his illness, in 1867 he successfully passed the Oxford local examination as a senior student. His diseased foot had been amputated directly below the knee, and physicians advised that the only way to save his life was to amputate the other. Henley persevered and survived with one foot intact. He was discharged in 1875, and was able to lead an active life for nearly 30 years despite his disability. With an artificial foot, he lived until the age of 54. "Invictus" (unconquered in Latin) was written from a hospital bed.

Now, what were you complaining about yesterday? —*Y.H.*

■ THE OPTIMIST CREED[4]

by Christian D. Larson

Promise yourself
To be so strong that nothing can
disturb your peace of mind.
To talk health, happiness, and prosperity
to every person you meet.
To make all your friends feel
they are unique and special people.
To look at the sunny side of everything
and make your optimism come true.
To think only of the best, to work only
for the best, and expect only the best.
To be just as enthusiastic about the success
of others as you are about your own.
To forget the mistakes of the past and press on
to the greater achievements of the future.
To wear a cheerful countenance at all times
and give every creature you meet a smile.
To give so much time to the improvement
of yourself, you have no time to criticize others.
To be too large for worry, too noble for anger,
too strong for fear and too happy to permit
the presence of trouble.

■ THE MAN WHO THINKS HE CAN[5]

by Walter D. Wintle

If you think you are beaten, you are.
If you think you dare not, you don't
If you like to win but think you can't,
It's almost a cinch you won't.

If you think you'll lose, you're lost.
For out in the world we find
Success begins with a fellow's will.
It's all in the state of mind.

If you think you are outclassed, you are.
You've got to think high to rise.
You've got to be sure of yourself before
You can ever win the prize.

Life's battles don't always go
To the stronger or faster man.
But sooner or later, the man who wins
Is the man who thinks he can.

WHAT WILL MATTER[6]

by Michael Josephson

Ready or not, some day it will all come to an end.
There will be no more sunrises, no minutes, hours or days.

All the things you collected, whether treasured or forgotten

will pass to someone else.
Your wealth, fame and temporal power will shrivel to irrelevance.

It will not matter what you owned or what you were owed.
Your grudges, resentments, frustrations and jealousies

will finally disappear.

So too, your hopes, ambitions, plans and to do lists will expire.
The wins and losses that once seemed so important will fade away.
It won't matter where you came from or what side of the tracks

you lived on at the end.
It won't matter whether you were beautiful or brilliant.

Even your gender and skin color will be irrelevant.
So what will matter? How will the value of your days be measured?

- What will matter is not what you **bought** but what you **built,** not what you **got** but what you **gave**.
- What will matter is not your **success** but your **significance**.
- What will matter is not what you **learned** but what you **taught**.
- What will matter is every act of **integrity**, **compassion**, **courage**, **or sacrifice** that **enriched, empowered or encouraged** others to emulate your example.
- What will matter is not your **competence** but your **character**.
- What will matter is **not how many people you knew**, but how many will feel a lasting loss when you're gone.

- What will matter is **not your memories but the memories that live in those who loved you**.
- **What will matter is how long you will be remembered, by whom and for what.**

Living a life that matters doesn't happen by accident. It's not a matter of circumstance but of choice.

Choose to live a life that matters.

GOALS ARE ACHIEVED ONLY WITH ACTION[7]

Here are ten steps to achieve your goals, from *ThinkTQ.com:*

1. Make all your dreams real by first identifying and then focusing on specific, tangible targets for what you want.
2. Maintain at least one clearly defined goal for every major interest and role in your life.
3. Set your goals so they are directly aligned with your life's mission.
4. Create goals high enough to ignite your spirit and inspire you to take action.
5. Write down all your goals in specific, measurable detail with declared target dates.
6. Absolutely, unconditionally commit to hitting each of your targets.
7. Share your goals with others for mutual accomplishment.
8. Set a whole series of related daily, weekly and long-term goals, complete with starting times and completion dates.
9. Take time every day to imagine how terrific it will feel when your goals are actually realized.
10. Take an action step toward the attainment of at least one goal every day.

In the spirit of these 10 steps are three apt quotes by psychologist Fitzhugh Dodson (1923–1993):

1. Without goals, and plans to reach them, you are like a ship that has set sail with no destination.
2. First you write down your goal; your second job is to break down your goal into a series of steps, beginning with steps which are absurdly easy.
3. Some people, in working towards a goal, find themselves seized by inertia when it comes time for action. If this should happen to you, despite the small graduated steps, then it is time to re examine your goal. Consider how important it actually is and then either discard the goal and replace it with a more suitable one or continue the steps with a renewed sense of the value of achieving it.

THE "REAL" SEVEN WONDERS OF THE WORLD

by Anonymous

Junior high school students in Chicago were studying the Seven Wonders of the World. At the end of the lesson, the students were asked to list what they considered to be the Seven Wonders of the World. Though there was some disagreement, the following seven received the most votes:

1. Egypt's Great Pyramids
2. The Taj Mahal in India
3. The Grand Canyon in Arizona
4. The Panama Canal
5. The Empire State Building
6. St. Peter's Basilica
7. China's Great Wall

While gathering the votes, the teacher noted that one student, a quiet girl, hadn't turned in her paper yet. So she asked the girl if she was having trouble with her list. The quiet girl replied, "Yes, a little. I couldn't quite make up my mind because there were so many." The teacher said, "Well, tell us what you have, and maybe we can help."

The girl hesitated, then read, "I think the Seven Wonders of the World are:

1. To touch
2. To taste
3. To see
4. To hear

She hesitated a little, and then added:

5. To feel
6. To laugh . . . and
7. To love

The room was so quiet you could have heard a pin drop.

May this story serve as a gentle reminder to all of us that the things we overlook as simple and ordinary are often the most wonderful—and we don't have to travel anywhere special to experience them. Enjoy your gifts!

■ CAN'T[8]

by Edgar Guest

Can't is the worst word that's written or spoken;
Doing more harm here than slander and lies;
On it is many a strong spirit broken,
And with it many a good purpose dies.
It springs from the lips of the thoughtless each morning
And robs us of courage we need through the day;
It rings in our ears like a timely sent warning
And laughs when we falter and fall by the way.
Can't is the father of feeble endeavor,
The parent of terror and halfhearted work;
It weakens the efforts of artisans clever,
And makes of the toiler an indolent shirk.
It poisons the soul of the man with a vision,
It stifles in infancy many a plan;
It greets honest toiling with open derision
And mocks at the hopes and the dreams of a man.
Can't is a word none should speak without blushing;
To utter it should be a symbol of shame;
Ambition and courage it daily is crushing;
It blights a man's purpose and shortens his aim.
Despise it with all of your hatred of error;
Refuse it the lodgement it seeks in your brain;
Arm against it as a creature of terror,
And all that you dream of you someday shall gain.
Can't is the word that is foe to ambition
An enemy ambushed to shatter your will;

Its prey is forever the man with a mission
And bows but to courage and patience and skill.
Hate it, with hatred that's deep and undying,
For once it is welcomed 'twill break any man;
Whatever the goal you are seeking, keep trying
And answer this demon by saying: "I can."

■ THE PATH OF LEAST RESISTANCE[9]

by Robert Fritz

We may not know it, but most of us long to create something in our lives. It may not be a painting, a novel, or a musical composition, the products we usually associate with "creativity." It may be a beautiful, functional kitchen, a computer program, or good health. Yet achieving these end results requires the same skills that the painter, novelist, or musician would use in completing their masterpieces.

The Path of Least Resistance (Fawcett Books) contains Robert Fritz's revolutionary program for creating anything, based not on pop psychology, but on the tradition of the arts and sciences. You will learn:

- The steps of creating—from conceiving the result to taking action to building momentum
- The importance of creating what you truly love
- The creative cycle—germination, assimilation, and completion—and how to make the most of each stage as you travel through it
- Why manipulating will power, affirmations, positive thinking, and other human potential programs don't work
- The difference between making fundamental, primary, and secondary choices in your life, and how making each kind of choice will affect you ability to create what you want
- The importance of having a firm grip on both current reality and future vision—and how to focus the creative process to move from where you are to where you want to be

Fritz's most astounding finding is that once an individual makes a conscious choice to be the predominant creative force in his or her own life, that life is changed forever: possibilities open up, projects are born from other projects, and the practice of being true to yourself, your project, your vision of life, becomes more and more effortless. Most important, he dispels the idea that you have to be born "creative"; creativity is a skill that can be learned, practiced and mastered.

TRIUMPH OVER TROUBLES[10]

by Philip Humbert

In the face of life's uncertainties, high achievers maintain an attitude of optimism, humor, strength and determination. They know that as they become more and more successful, the size and complexity of their problems will grow. How could it be otherwise? Here are seven keys to solving problems:

1. **Expect difficulty!** This is no surprise; it is not "unfair" or unusual. Life is complicated. Get good at it.
2. **Keep a buffer** around the edges of your life. Maintain a "reserve" of extra time, savings in the bank, and a bit of energy to handle the unexpected.
3. **Optimism and enthusiasm** are essential. Fear and pessimism will never inspire greatness.
4. **Words matter!** View difficulties as "challenges" rather than as problems. How we talk about our difficulties makes a huge difference in how we handle them.
5. **"We get by with a little help from our friends."** Have a team of cheerleaders, experts and colleagues to help you analyze and over-come any problem.
6. **Be proactive.** Take care of problems while they are small. Preventive maintenance is good for your car, your relationships, and your life.
7. **Choose new problems!** Learn from every experience and (try) not to have the same problems twice. Learn from difficulties, make changes, and move on. Pay the tuition once, then never repeat the same life-lesson! Understanding challenges are how we learn and grow. Success is the result of solving problems and moving forward in the face of difficulty, so expect "interesting" situations. Taking them in stride builds your confidence. Never fear trouble; triumph over it!

Notes

1. *Entrepreneur* magazine.
2. Marianne Williamson, *A Return to Love: Reflections on the Principles of a Course in Miracles* (New York: HarperCollins, 1992).
3. William Ernest Henley, 1875.
4. Christian D. Larson was a highly-influential New Thought leader. These words are from *Your Forces and How to Use Them* (1912). Used with permission of Optimist International.
5. Walter D. Wintle, 1905. There is little information available on Wintle. This same poem, with the different title, "The Victor," is sometimes credited to C. W. Longnecker.
6. Reprinted with permission of the Josephson Institute. Copyright© 2008. Its mission is to improve the ethical quality of society by changing personal and organizational decision making and behavior. Please visit them at www.CharacterCounts.org.
7. Reprinted with permission of ThinkTQ.com.
8. Edgar Guest originally published this poem *A Heap o' Livin'* (Chicago: Reilly & Lee, 1916).
9. Robert Fritz, *The Path of Least Resistance* (New York: Ballantine, 1989). Robert Fritz is founder of Technologies for Creating Inc., www.robertfritz.com.
10. Dr. Philip E. Humbert is an author, speaker, and personal success coach. He has hundreds of tips, tools, and articles on his Web site that you can use for YOUR success! It's a great resource! And, be sure to sign up for his FREE newsletter! Visit him on the Web at www.philiphumbert.com.

CHAPTER 13

A GOOD SENSE OF HUMOR IS PRICELESS

- GRADUATION (Robert Orben)
- A Doctor's Sense of Humor Never Hurts
- Puns to Put a Smile on Your Face
- Nice to Be Amusing, to Tell a Joke or Two

One day a guy hears his doorbell ring and goes to answer the door. He doesn't see anybody there, but looking down he sees a snail creeping along the welcome mat. He picks it up and tosses it far across the lawn. Two years pass. The doorbell rings. The guy goes to open the door. The snail looks up from the doormat and says, "What was *that* all about?"

Two guys are walking down the street when a mugger approaches them and demands their money. They both grudgingly pull out their wallets and begin taking out their

> cash. Just then one guy turns to the other and hands him a bill and says, "Here's that $20 I owe you."
>
> I went to a restaurant with a sign that said they served breakfast at any time. So I ordered French toast during the Renaissance.
>
> —Steven Wright

Having a good sense of humor can be very valuable as you go through life. Some people with excellent memories can hold on to a number of humorous bits and tell them at a moment's notice. One thing that helped me was to type out a number of them on a single sheet of paper and fold it to fit in my wallet. So, whenever the occasion arose, I was prepared.

According to Communications Coach Cheryl Stephens, "the psychological benefits of humor are amazing. . . . People store negative emotions, such as anger, sadness and fear, rather than expressing them. Laughter provides a way for these emotions to be harmlessly released. Laughter is cathartic. That's why some people who are upset or stressed out go to a funny movie or a comedy club, so they can laugh the negative emotions away."[1]

GRADUATION

A graduation ceremony is an event where the commencement speaker tells thousands of students, dressed in identical caps and gowns, that "individuality" is the key to success.

—Robert Orben (b. 1927), magician, comedy writer

A DOCTOR'S SENSE OF HUMOR NEVER HURTS

This is why it's sometimes hard to build new hospitals. When the staff doctors were told to make a contribution:

- **Allergists** voted to scratch it.
- **Anesthesiologists** thought the whole idea was a gas.
- **Audiologists** were deaf to the idea.
- **Cardiologists** didn't have the heart to say no.
- **Dermatologists** preferred no rash moves.
- **Gastroenterologists** had a gut feeling about it.
- **Internists** thought it was a hard pill to swallow.
- **Micro surgeons** were thinking along the same vein.
- **Neurologists** thought the administration "had a lot of nerve."
- **Obstetricians** stated they were laboring under a misconception.
- **Ophthalmologists** considered the idea short-sighted.
- **Orthopedists** issued a joint resolution.
- **Parasitologists** said, "Well, if you encyst."
- **Pathologists** yelled, "Over my dead body!"
- **Pediatricians** said, "Grow up!"
- **Physiotherapists** thought they were being manipulated.
- **Plastic surgeons** said, "This puts a whole new face on the matter."
- **Podiatrists** thought it was a big step forward.
- **Proctologists** said, "We are in arrears."
- **Psychiatrists** thought it was madness.
- **Radiologists** could see right through it.
- **Urologists** felt the scheme wouldn't hold water.
- Finally, **Surgeons** decided to wash their hands of the whole thing.

Here's some more wordplay:

- An invisible man marries an invisible woman. The kids were nothing to look at, either.
- A short fortuneteller who escaped from a prison: a small medium at large.
- A group of chess enthusiasts checked into a hotel and were standing in the lobby discussing their recent tournament victories. After about an hour, the manager came out of the office and asked them to disperse. "But why," they asked, as they moved off. "Because," he said, "I can't stand chess-nuts boasting in an open foyer."

PUNS TO PUT A SMILE ON YOUR FACE

- A backwards poet writes inverse.
- Sea captains don't like crew cuts.
- Without geometry, life is pointless.
- A hangover is the wrath of grapes.
- Does the name Pavlov ring a bell?
- Every calendar's days are numbered.
- Dijon vu—the same mustard as before.
- Corduroy pillows are making headlines.
- Santa's helpers are subordinate clauses.
- When two egotists meet, it's an I for an I.
- A boiled egg in the morning is hard to beat.
- A pessimist's blood type is always b-negative.
- Marriage is the mourning after the knot before.
- Reading while sunbathing makes you well-red.
- I used to work in a blanket factory, but it folded.
- Those who jump off a Paris bridge are in Seine.
- A chicken crossing the road is poultry in motion.
- Energizer Bunny arrested—charged with battery.
- A gossip is someone with a great sense of rumor.
- You feel stuck with your debt if you can't budge it.
- When a clock is hungry, it goes back four seconds.
- If you don't pay your exorcist, you get repossessed.
- A successful diet is the triumph of mind over platter.
- A bicycle can't stand on its own because it is two-tired.
- A lot of money is tainted. It t'aint yours and it t'aint mine.
- He had a photographic memory that was never developed.
- Marathon runners with bad footwear suffer the agony of defeat.
- When you dream in color, it's a pigment of your imagination.
- In democracy your vote counts. In feudalism your Count votes.
- The man who fell into an upholstery machine is fully recovered.
- What's the definition of a will? (Come on, it's a dead giveaway!).
- A grenade thrown into a kitchen in France would result in Linoleum Blown apart.
- Mahatma Gandhi walked barefoot in India most of the time, which produced an impressive set of calluses on his feet. He also ate very little, which made him rather frail and, with his odd diet, he suffered from bad breath. This made him (Are you ready?) a super calloused fragile mystic hexed by halitosis.

NICE TO BE AMUSING, TO TELL A JOKE OR TWO

In Italy, for thirty years under the Borgias, they had warfare, terror, murder and bloodshed, but they produced Michelangelo, Leonardo da Vinci and the Renaissance. In Switzerland, they had brotherly love, they had five hundred years of democracy and peace—and what did that produce? The cuckoo clock.

—The Third Man, *1949*

If you don't go to other people's funerals, they won't go to yours.

—Yogi Berra (b. 1925)

Advice to give a nervous friend who has to speak in front of the whole class: "Just imagine that everyone in the audience is naked."

—Anonymous

Too bad the only people who know how to run the country are busy driving cabs and cutting hair.

—George Burns, Actor, comedian (1896–1996)

When I die, I want to go peacefully like my Grandfather did, in his sleep—not screaming, like the passengers in his car.

—Steven Wright (b. 1955), American comedian

It's been a rough day. I got up this morning, put on a shirt and a button fell off. I picked up my briefcase and the handle came off. I'm afraid to go to the bathroom.

—Rodney Dangerfield (1921–2004), American comedian

My Grandmother started walking five miles a day when she was sixty. She's ninety-five now, and we don't know where the heck she is.

—Ellen Degeneres (b. 1958-), American comedienne

When somebody tells you nothing is impossible, ask him to dribble a football.

—Anonymous

If at first you don't succeed, skydiving is not for you.

—Anonymous

English is a language in which double negatives are a no-no.

—Anonymous

If you steal from one another, it's plagiarism; if you steal from many, it's research.

—Wilson Mizner (1876–1933), American writer

The trouble with some women is that they get all excited about nothing – and then marry him.

—Cher (b 1946), born Cherilyn Sarkisian, American singer, songwriter, and actor

Never test the depth of the water with both feet.

—Anonymous

Notes

1. Cheryl Stephens, www.cherylstephens.com.

CHAPTER 14

INFORMATION TO PUT THINGS INTO PERSPECTIVE

- MONEY (Anthony Sampson)
- Annual Average Consumer Price Index
- Broadband Subscribers per 100 Inhabitants, 2001–2007
- Casualties in Principal U.S. Wars
- Countries Ranked by Population, 2008
- *Forbes* Counts 793 Billionaires in 2009
- *Forbes* 100 Most Powerful Women (Top 35)
- Freedom House Country Rankings, 2008 (1.0 to 7.0)
- Freedom House Country Rankings (since 1973)
- Global Gender Gap Index, 2008 Rankings
- How Can Anyone Have So Many Ancestors?
- Useful Web Sites
- Billionaires Ranked by Country, 2008
- Millionaire Households: Top 15 Countries, 2008
- Millionaires Ranked by Numbers, per 10,000
- The Beauty of Math
- U.S. Census since 1790 by Decades
- Wonders of the Human Body
- Gross Domestic Product by Country (Ranked)
- World Population and Fact Sheet

I always like to see important data at a glance. Many categories of interesting data are presented in this chapter. Enjoy!

MONEY

Money had taken over many attributes of a religion. Like a religion it binds together different parts of the world, providing the means by which people and nations judge each other. Like a religion it demands great faith, a huge priesthood with rituals and incantations that few ordinary people understand. Like missionaries, the bankers and brokers travel the still unconverted parts of the world, bringing the deserts and jungles into the same system of values, seeking to convert still more tribes to their own faith in credit, interest rates, and the sacred bottom line.

—Anthony Sampson (1926–2004),
British writer, journalist

ANNUAL AVERAGE CONSUMER PRICE INDEX (CPI)

CPI 1982–1984 = 100

Year	CPI	% Chg	Year	CPI	% Chg	Year	CPI	% Chg
1889	8.9	−3.3	1929	17.1	0.0	1969	36.7	5.5
1890	8.8	0.1	1930	16.7	−2.3	1970	38.8	5.7
1891	8.8	0.0	1931	15.2	−9.0	1971	40.5	4.4
1892	8.8	0.0	1932	13.7	−9.9	1973	44.4	6.2
1893	8.7	−0.1	1933	13.0	−5.1	1972	41.8	3.2
1894	8.3	−4.6	1934	13.4	3.1	1974	49.3	11.0
1895	8.1	−2.4	1935	13.7	2.2	1975	53.8	9.1
1896	8.1	0.0	1936	13.9	1.5	1976	56.9	5.8
1897	8.0	−1.2	1937	14.4	3.6	1977	60.6	6.5
1898	8.0	0.0	1938	14.1	−2.1	1978	65.2	7.6
1899	8.0	0.0	1939	13.9	−1.4	1979	72.6	11.3
1900	8.1	1.2	1940	14.0	0.7	1980	82.4	13.5
1901	8.2	1.2	1941	14.7	5.0	1981	90.9	10.3
1902	8.3	1.2	1942	16.3	10.9	1982	96.5	6.2
1903	8.5	2.4	1943	17.3	6.1	1983	99.6	3.2
1904	8.6	1.2	1944	17.6	1.7	1984	103.9	4.3
1905	8.5	−1.2	1945	18.0	2.3	1985	107.6	3.6
1906	8.7	2.4	1946	19.5	8.3	1986	109.6	1.9
1907	9.1	4.6	1947	22.3	14.4	1987	113.6	3.6

1908	8.9	2.2	1948	24.1	8.1	1988	118.3	4.1
1909	8.8	−1.1	1949	23.8	−1.2	1989	124.0	4.8
1910	9.2	4.5	1950	24.1	1.3	1990	130.7	5.4
1911	9.2	0.0	1951	26.0	7.9	1991	136.2	4.2
1912	9.4	2.2	1952	26.5	1.9	1992	140.3	3.0
1913	9.9	5.3	1953	26.7	0.8	1993	144.5	3.0
1914	10.0	1.0	1954	26.9	0.7	1994	148.2	2.6
1915	10.1	1.0	1955	26.8	−0.4	1995	152.4	2.8
1916	10.9	7.9	1956	27.2	1.5	1996	156.9	3.0
1917	12.8	17.4	1957	28.1	3.3	1997	160.5	2.3
1918	15.1	18.0	1958	28.9	2.8	1998	163.0	1.6
1919	17.3	14.6	1959	29.1	0.7	1999	166.6	2.2
1920	20.0	15.6	1960	29.6	1.7	2000	172.2	3.4
1921	17.9	−10.5	1961	29.9	1.0	2001	177.1	2.8
1922	16.8	−6.1	1962	30.2	1.0	2002	179.9	1.6
1923	17.1	1.8	1963	30.6	1.3	2003	184.0	2.3
1924	17.1	0.0	1964	31.0	1.3	2004	188.9	2.7
1925	17.5	2.3	1965	31.5	1.6	2005	195.3	3.4
1926	17.7	1.1	1966	32.4	2.9	2006	201.6	3.2
1927	17.4	−1.7	1967	33.4	3.1	2007	207.3	2.8
1928	17.1	−1.7	1968	34.8	4.2	2008	215.3	3.8

Notes:
1900 CPI 8.1
1950 CPI 24.1 (50-year triple)
2000 CPI 172.2 (50-year up 7 fold) (100-year up 21 fold)

Source: Consumer Price Index, U.S. Bureau of Labor Statistics.

■ BROADBAND SUBSCRIBERS PER 100 INHABITANTS, 2001–2007

Rank	Country	2001	2002	2003	2004	2005	2006	2007	2008	Total Subscribers
1	Denmark	4.4	8.2	13.0	19.0	24.9	31.9	35.1	36.7	1,996,408
2	Netherlands	3.8	7.0	11.8	19.0	25.2	31.8	34.8	35.5	5,806,595
3	Norway	1.9	4.2	8.0	14.8	21.8	27.5	31.2	33.4	1,554,993
4	Switzerland	2.0	5.6	10.1	17.5	24.1	28.5	31.0	32.7	2,471,592
5	Iceland	3.7	8.4	14.3	18.2	26.4	29.7	32.2	32.3	98,361
6	Sweden	5.4	8.1	10.7	14.5	20.2	26.0	30.3	32.3	2,933,014
7	South Korea	17.2	21.8	24.2	24.8	25.2	29.1	30.5	31.2	15,059,029
8	Finland	1.3	5.5	9.5	14.9	22.4	27.2	30.7	30.7	1,616,200
9	Luxembourg	0.3	1.5	3.5	9.8	14.9	20.4	26.7	28.3	133,736
10	Canada	8.9	12.1	15.1	17.6	21.0	23.8	26.6	27.9	9,201,998
11	United Kingdom	0.6	2.3	5.4	10.5	16.4	21.6	25.8	27.6	16,710,169
12	Belgium	4.4	8.7	11.7	15.5	18.2	22.5	25.7	26.4	2,789,579
13	France	1.0	2.8	5.9	10.5	15.1	20.3	24.6	26.4	16,700,000
14	Germany	2.3	4.1	5.6	8.4	13.0	17.1	23.8	26.2	21,618,300
15	United States	4.5	6.9	9.7	12.9	16.3	19.6	23.3	25.0	75,009,521

16	Australia	0.9	1.8	3.5	7.7	13.8	19.2	23.3	23.5	4,981,656
17	Japan	2.2	6.1	10.7	15.0	17.6	20.2	22.1	23.0	29,341,909
18	Austria	3.6	5.6	7.6	10.1	14.3	17.3	19.6	20.6	1,704,769
19	New Zealand	0.7	1.6	2.6	4.7	8.1	14.0	18.3	20.4	853,020
20	Spain	1.2	3.0	5.4	8.1	11.5	15.3	18.0	19.8	8,738,793
21	Ireland	0	0.3	0.8	3.3	6.7	12.5	18.1	19.1	832,590
22	Italy	0.7	1.7	4.1	8.1	11.8	14.8	17.2	18.2	10,727,651
23	Czech Rep.	0.1	0.2	0.5	2.5	6.4	10.6	14.6	15.8	1,626,000
24	Hungary	0.3	0.6	2.0	3.6	6.3	11.9	13.6	15.7	1,583,102
25	Portugal	1.0	2.5	4.8	8.2	11.5	13.8	14.4	14.8	1,568,247
26	Greece	0	0	0.1	0.4	1.4	4.6	9.1	11.2	1,245,974
27	Poland	0.1	0.3	0.8	2.1	2.4	6.9	8.8	9.6	3,650,000
28	Slovak Republic	0	0	0.3	1.0	2.5	5.7	7.6	8.9	480,375
29	Turkey	0	0	0.3	0.7	2.1	3.8	6.0	6.8	5,012,999
30	Mexico	0.1	0.3	0.4	0.9	2.2	3.5	4.3	4.7	4,980,184
OECD Countries		2.9	4.9	7.3	10.2	13.5	16.9	20.0	21.3	251,026,764

■ CASUALTIES IN PRINCIPAL U.S. WARS

WARS	U.S. Pop. (mil.)	Number Serving	Deaths	Wounded	Casualties (% serving)	Deaths** All Sides
Revolutionary* 1775–1783	3.0	250,000	4,435	6,188	4.2%	108,000
War of 1812 1812–1815	8.0	286,730	2,260	4,505	2.4%	20,000
Mexican War 1846–1848	21.5	78,718	13,283	4,152	22.1%	38,283
Civil War 1861–1865	33.0	2,213,363	364,511	281,881	29.2%	618,000
Spanish-American 1898	75.0	306,760	2,446	1,662	1.3%	7,000
World War I 1917–1918	103.4	4,734,991	116,516	204,002	6.8%	20,000,000

World War II 1941–1946	145.0	16,112,566	405,399	670,846	6.7%	72,000,000
Korean War 1950–1953	161.3	5,720,000	36,574	103,284	2.4%	4,000,000
Vietnam 1964–1973	213.3	8,744,000	58,220	303,604	4.1%	5,400,000
Persian Gulf 1990–1991	258.7	2,225,000	382	467	0.04%	200,000
Iraq 2003–2008	305.9	152,350	4,213	30,848	23.0%	1,000,000
		TOTALS	1,008,239	1,611,439	—	103,391,283

Sources: U.S. Dept. of Defense.

* Number serving estimated.
**Estimated military & civilian deaths.

Note that the deaths from all sides in the 20th century equals 102,600,000, making the twentieth century the bloodiest century of all time.

■ COUNTRIES RANKED BY POPULATION, 2008*

Rank	Country	Mils.	Rank	Country	Mils.	Rank	Country	Mils.
1	China	1330.0	39	Uganda	31.4	77	Tunisia	10.4
2	India	1148.0	40	Peru	29.2	78	Czech Republic	10.2
3	United States	304.2	41	Iraq	28.2	79	Rwanda	10.2
4	Indonesia	237.5	42	Nepal	28.2	80	Chad	10.1
5	Brazil	196.3	43	Saudi Arabia	28.1	81	Hungary	9.9
6	Pakistan	172.8	44	Uzbekistan	27.3	82	Guinea	9.8
7	Bangladesh	154.0	45	Venezuela	26.4	83	Belarus	9.7
8	Nigeria	146.3	46	Malaysia	25.3	84	Bolivia	9.6
9	Russia	140.7	47	Ghana	23.4	85	Somalia	9.6
10	Japan	127.3	48	Yemen	23.0	86	Dominican Repub.	9.5
11	Mexico	110.0	49	Taiwan	22.9	87	Sweden	9.0
12	Philippines	96.1	50	Korea, North	22.6	88	Haiti	8.9
13	Vietnam	86.1	51	Romania	22.2	89	Burundi	8.7
14	Ethiopia	82.5	52	Mozambique	21.3	90	Benin	8.5
15	Germany	82.4	53	Sri Lanka	21.1	91	Austria	8.2
16	Egypt	81.7	54	Australia	21.0	92	Azerbaijan	8.2
17	Turkey	75.8	55	Cote d'Ivoire	20.2	93	Honduras	7.6
18	Democratic Republic of the Congo	66.5	56	Madagascar	20.0	94	Switzerland	7.6

19	Iran	65.9	57	Syria	19.7	95	Serbia	7.4
20	Thailand	65.5	58	Cameroon	19.7	96	Bulgaria	7.3
21	France	64.1	59	Netherlands	18.5	97	Tajikistan	7.2
22	United Kingdom	60.9	60	Chile	16.6	98	Israel	7.1
23	Italy	58.1	61	Kazakhstan	16.5	99	El Salvador	7.1
24	South Africa	48.8	62	Burkina Faso	15.3	100	Hong Kong	7.0
25	South Korea	48.4	63	Niger	15.3	101	Paraguay	6.8
26	Burma	47.8	64	Ecuador	14.8	102	Laos	6.7
27	Ukraine	45.5	65	Cambodia	14.2	103	Sierra Leone	6.3
28	Colombia	45.0	66	Malawi	13.9	104	Jordan	6.2
29	Spain	40.5	67	Senegal	13.3	105	Libya	6.2
30	Argentina	40.5	68	Guatemala	13.0	106	Papua New Guinea	5.9
31	Sudan	40.2	69	Angola	12.5	107	Togo	5.9
32	Tanzania	40.2	70	Mali	12.3	108	Nicaragua	5.8
33	Poland	38.5	71	Zambia	11.7	109	Eritrea	5.5
34	Kenya	38.0	72	Cuba	11.4	110	Denmark	5.5
35	Morocco	34.3	73	Zimbabwe	11.4	111	Slovakia	5.5
36	Algeria	33.8	74	Greece	10.7	112	Kyrgyzstan	5.4
37	Canada	33.2	75	Portugal	10.7	113	Finland	5.2
38	Afghanistan	32.7	76	Belgium	10.4	114	Turkmenistan	4.8

(*Continued*)

Rank	Country	Mils.	Rank	Country	Thous.	Rank	Country	Thous.
115	Norway	4.6	153	Mauritius	1,274.1	191	Virgin Island, US.	109.8
116	Georgia	4.6	154	Trinidad/Tobago	1,231.3	192	Micronesia	107.7
117	United Arab Emirates	4.6	155	Swaziland	1,128.8	193	St.Vincent and Grenadines	104.9
118	Singapore	4.6	156	Timor-Leste	1,108.8	194	Aruba	101.5
119	Bosnia/Herzegovina	4.6	157	Fiji	931.7	195	Jersey	91.4
120	Croatia	4.5	158	Qatar	824.8	196	Grenada	90.3
121	Central African Rep.	4.4	159	Cyprus	792.6	197	No. Mariana Islands	86.6
122	Moldova	4.3	160	Guyana	770.8	198	Seychelles	86.6
123	Costa Rica	4.2	161	Comoros	731.8	199	Antigua/Barbuda	84.5
124	New Zealand	4.2	162	Bahrain	718.3	200	Andorra	82.6
125	Ireland	4.2	163	Bhutan	682.3	201	Isle of Man	76.1
126	Lebanon	4.0	164	Montenegro	678.2	202	Dominica	72.5
127	Puerto Rico	4.0	165	Equatorial Guinea	616.5	203	Bermuda	67.4
128	Rep. of the Congo	3.9	166	Solomon Islands	581.3	204	Guernsey	65.7
129	Albania	3.6	167	Macau	545.7	205	American Samoa	64.8
130	Lithuania	3.6	168	Djibouti	506.2	206	Marshall Islands	63.2
131	Uruguay	3.5	169	Luxembourg	486.0	207	Greenland	57.6
132	Liberia	3.3	170	Suriname	476.0	208	Faroe Islands	48.7
133	Oman	3.3	171	Cape Verde	427.0	209	Cayman Islands	47.9

134	Panama	3.3	172	Malta	403.5	210	Saint Kitts and Nevis	39.8
135	Mauritania	3.1	173	Western Sahara	393.8	211	Liechtenstein	34.5
136	Mongolia	3.0	174	Maldives	385.9	212	Monaco	32.8
137	Armenia	3.0	175	Brunei	381.4	213	San Marino	30.0
138	Jamaica	2.8	176	Bahamas	307.5	214	Saint Martin	29.4
139	Kuwait	2.6	177	Iceland	304.4	215	Gibraltar	28.0
140	West Bank	2.4	178	Belize	301.3	216	Virgin Islands, British	24.0
141	Latvia	2.2	179	Barbados	283.5	217	Turks and Caicos Islands	22.4
142	Lesotho	2.1	180	French Polynesia	283.0	218	Palau	20.7
143	Namibia	2.1	181	Neth. Antilles	225.4	219	Wallis and Futuna	15.2
144	Macedonia	2.1	182	New Caledonia	224.8	220	Anguilla	14.1
145	Slovenia	2.0	183	Samoa	217.1	221	Nauru	13.8
146	Botswana	2.0	184	Mayotte	216.3	222	Cook Islands	12.3
147	Kosovo	1.8	185	Vanuatu	215.4	223	Tuvalu	12.2
148	Gambia	1.7	186	São Tomé/Principe	206.2	224	Saint Helena	7.6
149	Guinea-Bissau	1.5	187	Guam	176.0	225	Saint Barthelemy	7.5
150	Gaza Strip	1.5	188	Saint Lucia	159.6	226	St. Pierre and Miquelon	7.0
151	Gabon	1.5	189	Tonga	119.0	227	Montserrat	5.1
152	Estonia	1.3	190	Kiribati	110.4			

*Includes some Territories

Source: U.S. Census Bureau.

FORBES COUNTS 793 BILLIONAIRES IN 2009

Their Entire Net Worth Is $3.0 Trillion

Forbes 2009 Billionaires List contains 793 individuals. The billionaires' combined net worth declined by $1.4 trillion Since 2008. And would you believe of the top 25 that 10 don't have college degrees?

Rank	Name	Citizen of	Age	Worth ($bil)	Coll. Deg.	Wealth Source
1	William Gates III	United States	53	40.0		Microsoft (software)
2	Warren Buffett	United States	78	37	X	Berkshire Hathaway
3	Carlos Slim Helu & family	Mexico	69	35.0	X	Cellphones
4	Lawrence Ellison	United States	64	22.5		Oracle Systems
5	Ingvar Kamrad & family	Sweden	83	22.0		Ikea (Retail)
6	Karl Albrecht	Germany	89	21.5		Aldi Supermarkets
7	Mukesh Ambani	India	51	19.5.	X	Communications
8	Lakshmi Mittal	India	58	19.3	X	Steel
9	Theo Albrecht	Germany	87	18.8.		Aldi Supermarkets
10	Amancio Ortega	Spain	73	18.3		Fashion Stores
11	Jim Walton	United States	61	17.8	X	Wal-Mart

12	Alice Walton	United States	59	17.6		Wal-Mart
13	Christy Walton	United States	54	17.6	X	Wal-Mart
14	S. Robson Walton	United States	65	17.6	X	Wal-Mart
15	Bernard Arnault	France	60	16.5	X	Christian Dior, etc.
16	Li Ka-shing	Hong Kong	80	16.2		Diversified
17	Michael Bloomberg	United States	67	16.0	X	Bloomberg News
18	Stefan Persson	Sweden	61	14.5	X	Fashion Retail
19	Charles Koch	United States	73	14.0	X	Koch Industries
20	David Koch	United States	68	14.0	X	Koch Industries
21	Liliane Bettencourt	France	86	13.4		L'Oreal
22	Prince Alwaleed*	Saudi Arabia	54	13.3	X	Diversified
23	Michael Otto	Germany	65	13.2	X	Shopping Centers
24	David Thomson	Canada	51	13.0	X	Thomson Corp. (Media)
25	Michael Dell	United States	44	12.3		Dell Computers

* Full name Prince Alwaleed Bin Talal Alsaud.

Source: Reprinted by Permission of *Forbes* magazine copyright 2009 Forbes LLC. The entire list is available at http://www.forbes.com/lists/2009/10/billionaires-2009-richest-people_The-Worlds-Billionaires_Rank.html.

FORBES 100 MOST POWERFUL WOMEN, 2009 (TOP 35)

Rank	Name	Occupation	Country
1	Angela Merkel	Chancellor of Germany	Germany
2	Sheila C. Bair	Chairman, Federal Deposit Ins. Corp.	U.S.
3	Indra K. Nooyi	Chairman, CEO, PepsiCo	U.S.
4	Cynthia Carroll	CEO, Anglo American	U.K.
5	Ho Ching	CEO, Temasek Holdings	Singapore
6	Irene B. Rosenfeld	Chairman, CEO, Kraft Foods	U.S.
7	Ellen Kullman	CEO, DuPont	U.S.
8	Angela Bray	CEO, President, WellPoint	Singapore
9	Anne Lauvergeon	CEO, Areva	France
10	Lynn Elsenhans	CEO, Sunoco	U.S.
11	Cristina Fernandez	President	Argentina
12	Carol Bartz	CEO, Yahoo!	U.S.
13	Sonia Gandhi	President, Indian National Congress Party	India
14	Ursula Burns	CEO, Xerox Corp.	U.S.
15	Anne Mulcahy	Chairman, Xerox Corp.	U.S.
16	Safra Catz	President, Oracle	U.S.
17	Christine Lagarde	Minister of Economy, Finance and Employment	France
18	Gail Kelly	CEO, Westpac	U.S.

19	Marjorie Scardino	CEO, Pearson, PLC	U.K.
20	Chanda Kochhar	CEO, Pearson, PLC CEO, ICICI Bank	India
21	Mary Sammons	CEO, Rite Aid Corp,	U.S.
22	Michelle Bachelet	President	Chile
23	Paula Reynolds	Chief Restructuring Officer, AIG	U.S.
24	Carol Meyrowitz	CEO, TJX Companies	U.S.
25	Andrea Jung	CEO, Avon	U.S.
26	Patricia Woertz	CEO, Archer Daniels Midland	U.S.
27	Guler Sabanci	Chairman, Sabanci Holding	Turkey
28	Barbara Desoer	President, Bank of America Home Loans & Insurance	U.S.
29	Brenda Barnes	CEO, Sara Lee Corp.	U.S.
30	Risa Lavizzo-Mourey	CEO, The Robert Wood Johnson Foundation	U.S.
31	Ann Livermore	Executive VP, Hewlett-Packard	U.S.
32	Cathie Lesjak	Executive VP, Hewlett-Packard	U.S.
33	Marina Berlusconi	Chairman, Finivest GroupCo-chairman,	Italy
34	Melinda Gates	Bill & Melinda Gates Foundation	U.S.
35	Nancy Pelosi	Speaker, House of Representatives	U.S.

Source: Reprinted by Permission of *Forbes* Magazine copyright 2009 Forbes LLC. *To see the entire list go to* http://www.forbes.com/lists/2009/11/power-women-09_The-100-Most-Powerful-Women_Rank.html.

■ FREEDOM HOUSE COUNTRY RANKINGS, 2008 (1.0 TO 7.0)

90 FREE

1.0

Andorra
Australia
Austria
Bahamas
Barbados
Belgium
Canada
Cape Verde
Chile
Costa Rica
Cyprus
Czech Republic
Denmark
Dominica
Estonia
Finland
France
Germany
Hungary
Iceland
Ireland
Italy
Kiribati
Latvia
Liechtenstein
Lithuania
Luxembourg
Malta
Marshall Islands
Micronesia
Nauru
Netherlands
New Zealand
Norway
Palau
Poland
Portugal
Saint Kitts/Nevis
Saint Lucia
San Marino
Slovakia
Slovenia
Spain
Sweden
Switzerland
Tuvalu
United Kingdom
United States
Uruguay

1.5

Belize
Bulgaria
Ghana
Greece
Grenada
Israel
Japan
Monaco
Panama
St. Vincent and Grenadines
South Korea
Taiwan

2.0

Antigua/Barbuda
Argentina
Benin
Botswana
Brazil
Croatia
Dominican Rep
Mali
Mauritius
Mongolia
Namibia
Romania
Samoa
Sao Tome/Principe
South Africa
Suriname
Trinidad/Tobago
Vanuatu

2.5

El Salvador
Guyana
India
Indonesia
Jamaica
Lesotho
Mexico
Peru
Senegal
Serbia
Ukraine

60 PARTLY FREE	Niger	Moldova	Sri Lanka	Morocco
3.0	Papua N Guinea	Mozambique	Tonga	Nepal
Albania	Paraguay	Sierra Leone	Venezuela	Singapore
Bolivia	Philippines	Solomon Islands	**4.5**	Uganda
Bosnia-Herzegovina	Seychelles	Tanzania	Armenia	**5.0**
Colombia	Turkey	Zambia	Burundi	Afghanistan
Ecuador	**3.5**	**4.0**	Central Afr. Rep.	Bahrain
Georgia	Comoros	Bangladesh	The Gambia	Djibouti
Honduras	East Timor	Burkina Faso	Haiti	Ethiopia
Kenya	Guatemala	Guinea-Bissau	Jordan	Fiji
Macedonia	Liberia	Kuwait	Kyrgyzstan	Gabon
Montenegro	Madagascar	Malaysia	Lebanon	Yemen
Nicaragua	Malawi	Nigeria	Mauritania	
43 NOT FREE	Egypt	Thailand	Vietnam	Zimbabwe
5.5	Guinea	Togo	**6.5**	**7.0**
Algeria	Kazakhstan	Tunisia	Belarus	Burma
Angola	Maldives	Utd Arab Emirates	China	Cuba
Azerbaijan	Oman	**6.0**	Cote d'Ivoire	Libya
Bhutan	Pakistan	Cameroon	Equatorial Guinea	North Korea
Brunei	Qatar	Chad	Eritrea	Somalia
Cambodia	Russia	Iran	Laos	Sudan
Congo (Brazzaville)	Rwanda	Iraq	Saudi Arabia	Turkmenistan
Congo (Kinshasa)	Tajikistan	Swaziland	Syria	Uzbekistan

Source: Freedom House.

■ FREEDOM HOUSE COUNTRY RANKINGS (SINCE 1973)

Edition	Year/dates Covered*	Total Countries	Free		Part Free		Not Free	
			#	%	#	%	#	%
2008	2007	193	90	47	60	31	43	22
2007	11/05–12/06	193	90	47	58	30	45	23
2006	11/04–11/05	192	89	46	58	30	45	24
2005	11/03–11/04	192	89	46	54	28	49	26
2004	12/03–11/03	192	88	46	55	29	49	25
2003	2002	192	89	46	55	29	48	25
2001–2002	2001	192	85	44	59	31	48	25
2000–2001	2000	192	86	45	58	30	48	25
1999–2000	1999	192	85	44	60	31	47	25
1998–1999	1998	191	88	46	53	28	50	26
1997–1998	1997	191	81	42	57	30	53	28
1996–1997	1996	191	79	41	59	31	53	28
1995–1996	1995	191	76	40	62	32	53	28
1994–1995	1994	191	76	40	61	32	54	28
1993–1994	1993	190	72	38	63	33	55	29
1992–1993	1992	186	75	40	73	39	38	21
1991–1992	1991	183	76	42	65	35	42	23

1990–1991	1990	165	65	40	50	30	50	30
1989–1990	11/88–12/89	167	61	37	44	26	62	37
1988–1989	11/87–11/88	167	60	36	39	23	68	41
1987–1988	11/86–11/87	167	58	35	58	35	51	30
1986–1987	11/85–11/86	167	57	34	57	34	53	32
1985–1986	11/84–11/85	167	56	34	56	34	55	33
1984–1985	11/83–11/84	167	53	32	59	35	55	33
1983–1984	7/82–11/83	166	52	31	56	34	58	35
1982	1/81–7/82	165	54	33	47	28	64	39
1981	1980	162	51	31	51	31	60	37
1980	1979	161	51	32	54	33	56	35
1979	1978	158	47	30	56	35	55	35
1978	1977	155	43	28	48	31	64	41
Jan./Feb. 1977	1976	159	42	26	49	31	68	43
Jan/Feb/1976	1975	158	40	25	53	34	65	41
Jan/Feb/1975	1974	152	41	27	48	32	63	41
Jan/Feb/1974	1973	151	44	29	42	28	65	43

*Unless otherwise noted, year/dates each edition are January 1 through December 31.
Bottom four are from previous publication, *Freedom at Issue*.

Source: Freedom House.

GLOBAL GENDER GAP INDEX, 2008 RANKINGS

This is a tool for benchmarking and tracking global gender-based inequalities in five critical areas: economic participation and opportunity, political empowerment, education, health, and survival.

Rank	Country	Rank	Country	Rank	Country
1	Norway	44	Jamaica	87	Albania
2	Finland	45	Kazakhstan	88	Kenya
3	Sweden	46	Croatia	89	Tajikistan
4	Iceland	47	Honduras	90	Bangladesh
5	New Zealand	48	Peru	91	Maldives
6	Philippines	49	Poland	92	Zimbabwe
7	Denmark	50	Colombia	93	Indonesia
8	Ireland	51	Slovenia	94	Cambodia
9	Netherlands	52	Thailand	95	Mauritius
10	Latvia	53	Macedonia	96	Malaysia
11	Germany	54	Uruguay	97	Mexico
12	Sri Lanka	55	Uzbekistan	98	Japan
13	United Kingdom	56	Israel	99	Brunei
14	Switzerland	57	China	100	Paraguay
15	France	58	El Salvador	101	Kuwait
16	Lesotho	59	Venezuela	102	Nigeria
17	Spain	60	Hungary	103	Tunisia
18	Mozambique	61	Azerbaijan	104	Jordan
19	Trinidad/Tobago	62	Ukraine	105	United Arab Emirates
20	Moldova	63	Botswana	106	Zambia

21	Australia	64	Slovak Republic	107	Syria
22	South Africa	65	Chile	108	Korea, Rep.
23	Lithuania	66	Luxembourg	109	Mali
24	Argentina	67	Italy	110	Mauritania
25	Cuba	68	Vietnam	111	Algeria
26	Barbados	69	Czech Republic	112	Guatemala
27	United States	70	Romania	113	India
28	Belgium	71	Nicaragua	114	Angola
29	Austria	72	Dominican Republic	115	Burkina Faso
30	Namibia	73	Brazil	116	Iran
31	Canada	74	Madagascar	117	Cameroon
32	Costa Rica	75	Greece	118	Oman
33	Belarus	76	Cyprus	119	Qatar
34	Panama	77	Ghana	120	Nepal
35	Ecuador	78	Armenia	121	Bahrain
36	Bulgaria	79	Suriname	122	Ethiopia
37	Estonia	80	Bolivia	123	Turkey
38	Tanzania	81	Malawi	124	Egypt
39	Portugal	82	Georgia	125	Morocco
40	Mongolia	83	Malta	126	Benin
41	Kyrgyz Republic	84	Singapore	127	Pakistan
42	Russian Federation	85	Gambia	128	Saudi Arabia
43	Uganda	86	Belize	129	Chad
				130	Yemen

Source: World Economic Forum as of November 12, 2008, http://www.weforum.org/pdf/gendergap/report2008.pdf.

HOW CAN ANYONE HAVE SO MANY ANCESTORS?

Every child has two parents, four grandparents, eight great-grandparents, and sixteen great-great-grandparents, and so on, and so on. We all lose track of to whom we are related after second and third cousins. Many people marry fourth, fifth, sixth, and seventh cousins without realizing it. Come to think of it, we are all related to each other more or less. With four generations per 100 years, we dare not go beyond 1,000 years and 1 trillion ancestors, as that would add 12 more zeros, which is mathematically difficult to comprehend.

Assuming Four Generations per Century

				Milestones	World Population
1	You	1,048,576			
2	Your parents	2,097,152		1804	1 billion
4	Grandparents	4,194,304		1927	2 billion
8	100 years	8,388,608	600 yrs.	1960	3 billion
16	etc.	16,777,216		1974	4 billion
32	etc.	33,554,432		1987	5 billion
64	etc.	67,108,864		1999	6 billion
128	200 years	134,217,728	700 yrs.	e2011	7 billion
256		268,435,456		e2024	8 billion
512		536,870,912		e2042	9 billion
1,024		1,073,741,824		????	10 billion
2,048	300 years	2,147,483,648	800 yrs.		
4,096		4,294,967,296			
8,192		8,589,934,592			
16,384		17,179,869,184			
32,768	400 years	34,359,738,368	900 yrs.		
65,536		68,719,476,736			
131,072		137,438,953,472			
262,144		274,877,906,944			
524,288	500 years	549,755,813,888	1,000 yrs.		
	Total	1,099,511,627,776	etc.		

> If there are any culprits partly to blame for this humongous population growth, it has to be both capitalism and medical science.

USEFUL WEB SITES

www.snopes.com. Check outrageous email to see if it is true or false—or an urban myth.

www.google.com. Surely the most amazing information source in human history.

www.wikipedia.com. A great site for information hounds, with special emphasis on biographical data.

zipskinny.com. U.S. Census data for your ZIP code, and comparisons with neighboring areas.

www.poodwaddle.com/realage.swf. Determine lifespan based on your lifestyle and genes.

www.census.gov/main/www/popclock.html. Up-to-the-minute population for both the United States and the world.

www.imdb.com. The Internet movie database. Up-to-the-minute movie news, actor, and filmmaker bios.

www.economicindicators.gov. Access to the daily releases of key economic indicators, plus a calendar of dates for future releases.

www.timeanddate.com. Find current local times for any place in the world, plus weather, temperature, and forecasts. This site also features a calendar for any year between 1 and 3999.

www.peterrussell.com/Odds/WorldClock.php. Up-to-the minute deaths from each of 17 diseases, number of injuries from nine different causes (wars are the least), and number of abortions worldwide to date (I estimate 45 million 2009).

■ BILLIONAIRES RANKED BY COUNTRY, 2008

No.	Country	Popul. (mil.)	Per (mil).	No.	Country	Popul. (mil.)	Per (mil.)
469	United States	301.1	1.56	6	United Arab Emirates	4.4	1.36
87	Russia	141.4	0.62	5	Indonesia	234.7	0.02
59	Germany	82.4	0.72	5	Netherlands	16.6	0.30
53	India	1129.9	0.05	5	Singapore	4.6	1.09
42	China	1322.0	0.03	4	Austria	8.2	0.49
35	Turkey	71.2	0.49	4	Chili	16.3	0.25
35	United Kingdom	60.8	0.58	4	Egypt	80.3	0.05
26	Hong Kong	7.0	3.71	4	Greece	10.7	0.37
25	Canada	33.4	0.75	4	Kuwait	2.5	1.60
24	Japan	127.4	0.19	4	New Zealand	4.1	0.98
18	Brazil	190.0	0.09	4	Norway	4.6	0.87
18	Spain	40.4	0.45	4	Portugal	10.6	0.38
14	Australia	20.4	0.69	4	South Africa	44.0	0.09

14	France	63.7	0.22	3	Thailand	65.1	0.05
13	Italy	58.1	0.22	2	Belgium	10.4	0.19
13	Saudi Arabia	27.6	0.47	2	Colombia	44.4	0.05
12	South Korea	49.0	0.24	2	Cyprus	0.8	2.50
11	Switzerland	7.6	1.45	2	Iceland	0.3	6.67
10	Mexico	108.7	0.09	2	Philippines	91.1	0.02
10	Sweden	9.0	1.11	2	Romania	22.3	0.09
9	Israel	6.4	1.41	2	Venezuela	26.0	0.08
8	Malaysia	24.8	0.32	1	Argentina	40.3	0.02
7	Lebanon	3.9	1.79	1	Belize	0.3	3.33
7	Taiwan	22.9	0.31	1	Czech Republic	10.2	0.10
7	Ukraine	46.3	0.15	1	Denmark	5.5	0.18
6	Ireland	4.1	1.46	1	Monaco	⋆	30.61
6	Kazakhstan	15.3	0.39	1	Nigeria	135.0	0.01
6	Poland	38.5	0.16	1	Oman	3.2	0.31

⋆Monaco's population is 32,671.

Source: Reprinted by permission of *Forbes* magazine copyright 2009 Forbes LLC.

MILLIONAIRE HOUSEHOLDS: TOP 15 COUNTRIES, 2008

Rank	Country	Population	Millionaire Households	Per 10,000	$100 Million Households	GDP ($ millions)
1	USA	301,139,947	4,585,000	152	2,300	13,201,819
2	Japan	127,433,494	830,000	65	1,300	4,340,133
3	UK	60,776,238	610,000	100	810	2,345,015
4	Germany	82,400,996	350,000	42	620	2,906,681
5	China	1,321,851,888	310,000	2	180	2,668,071
6	Italy	58,147,733	270,000	46	530	1,844,749
7	France	63,713,926	265,000	42	260	2,230,721
8	Taiwan	22,858,872	220,000	96	140	680,500
9	Switzerland	7,554,861	205,000	271	300	379,758
10	Brazil	190,010,647	190,000	10	210	1,067,962
11	Netherlands	16,570,613	145,000	88	200	657,590
12	Belgium	10,392,226	135,000	130	140	392,001
13	Australia	20,434,176	135,000	66	150	768,178
14	Spain	40,448,191	125,000	31	330	1,223,988
15	Canada	33,390,141	110,000	33	140	1,251,463

Source: The Boston Consulting Group.

■ MILLIONAIRES RANKED BY NUMBER PER 10,000

Rank	Country	Population	Millionaire Households	Per 10,000	$100 Million Households	GDP ($ millions)
1	Switzerland	7,554,861	205,000	271	300	379,758
2	USA	301,139,947	4,585,000	152	2,300	13,201,819
3	Belgium	10,392,226	135,000	130	140	392,001
4	UK	60,776,238	610,000	100	810	2,345,015
5	Taiwan	22,858,872	220,000	96	140	680,500
6	Netherlands	16,570,613	145,000	88	200	657,590
7	Australia	20,434,176	135,000	66	150	768,178
8	Japan	127,433,494	830,000	65	1,300	4,340,133
9	Italy	58,147,733	270,000	46	530	1,844,749
10	Germany	82,400,996	350,000	42	620	2,906,681
11	France	63,713,926	265,000	42	260	2,230,721
12	Canada	33,390,141	110,000	33	140	1,251,463
13	Spain	40,448,191	125,000	31	330	1,223,988
14	Brazil	190,010,647	190,000	10	210	1,067,962
15	China	1,321,851,888	310,000	2	180	2,668,071

Source: The Boston Consulting Group.

■ THE BEAUTY OF MATH!

$1 \times 8 + 1 = 9$
$12 \times 8 + 2 = 98$
$123 \times 8 + 3 = 987$
$1234 \times 8 + 4 = 9876$
$12345 \times 8 + 5 = 98765$
$123456 \times 8 + 6 = 987654$
$1234567 \times 8 + 7 = 9876543$
$12345678 \times 8 + 8 = 98765432$
$123456789 \times 8 + 9 = 987654321$
$1 \times 9 + 2 = 11$
$12 \times 9 + 3 = 111$
$123 \times 9 + 4 = 1111$
$1234 \times 9 + 5 = 11111$
$12345 \times 9 + 6 = 111111$
$123456 \times 9 + 7 = 1111111$
$1234567 \times 9 + 8 = 11111111$
$12345678 \times 9 + 9 = 111111111$
$123456789 \times 9 + 10 = 1111111111$
$9 \times 9 + 7 = 88$
$98 \times 9 + 6 = 888$
$987 \times 9 + 5 = 8888$
$9876 \times 9 + 4 = 88888$
$98765 \times 9 + 3 = 888888$
$987654 \times 9 + 2 = 8888888$
$9876543 \times 9 + 1 = 88888888$
$98765432 \times 9 + 0 = 888888888$
$1 \times 1 = 1$
$11 \times 11 = 121$
$111 \times 111 = 12321$
$1111 \times 1111 = 1234321$
$11111 \times 11111 = 123454321$
$111111 \times 111111 = 12345654321$
$1111111 \times 1111111 = 1234567654321$
$11111111 \times 11111111 = 123456787654321$
$111111111 \times 111111111 = 12345678987654321$

U.S. CENSUS SINCE 1790 BY DECADES

Census Year	Total Population	Increase	Increase (%)	Urban (%)	Rural (%)
1790	3,929,214	—	—	5.1	94.9
1800	5,308,483	1,379,269	35.1	6.1	93.9
1810	7,239,881	1,931,398	36.4	7.3	92.7
1820	9,638,453	2,398,572	33.1	7.2	92.8
1830	12,860,702	3,222,249	33.4	8.8	91.2
1840	17,063,353	4,202,651	32.7	10.8	89.2
1850	23,191,876	6,128,523	35.9	15.4	84.6
1860	31,443,321	8,251,445	35.6	19.8	80.2
1870	38,558,371	7,115,050	22.6	25.7	74.3
1880	50,189,209	11,630,838	30.2	28.2	71.8
1890	62,979,766	12,790,557	25.5	35.1	64.9
1900	76,212,168	13,232,402	21.0	39.6	60.4
1910	92,228,496	16,016,328	21.0	45.6	54.4
1920	106,021,537	13,793,041	15.0	51.2	48.8
1930	123,202,624	17,181,087	16.2	56.1	43.9
1940	142,164,569	18,961,945	15.4	56.5	43.5
1950	161,325,798	19,161,229	14.5	64.0	36.0
1960	189,323,175	27,997,377	18.5	69.9	30.1
1970	213,302,031	23,978,856	13.4	73.6	26.3
1980	236,542,199	23,240,168	11.4	73.7	26.3
1990	258,709,873	22,167,674	9.8	75.2	24.8
2000	291,421,906	32,712,033	13.2	81.0	19.0
2010*	311,000,000	est.			

*2010: 6,850,000,000 world estimate.

Source: U.S. Census Bureau.

■ WONDERS OF THE HUMAN BODY

Nothing matches the miracles that constitute you, a living human being. Research from many sources shows many opportunities to build future careers.

- 50–100 trillion cells in the body, each containing DNA, most pump out and receive radio frequency signals all the time
- 100 billion neurons (nerve cells) in the brain
- 100,000 hairs on average head, each one living 2–4 years
- 5 million or more hair follicles on the body
- 30 feet length of a beard if left to grow indefinitely (males)
- 7 miles of body hair grown every year
- 100,800 heartbeats a day, 2.5 billion in an average lifetime
- 21 square feet of skin, containing 45 miles of nerves, 60,000 miles of blood vessels, 650 sweat glands in each square inch
- 32 million bacteria on every square inch of the body
- 12,000 nerve endings per square inch of skin on back of hand
- 2 million holes in the body skin, 10 billion capillaries
- 300 million cells die in the human body every minute
- 500 million dead skin cells fall off daily
- 640 muscles, 206 bones, 187 separate joints
- 77¼ pints of fluid in the body
- 62,500 miles, the distance of all the nerves if laid end to end.
- 10,000 different odors can be identified by sense of smell
- 5,000 taste buds in the mouth
- 25,000 quarts of saliva produced in a human lifetime, which could fill two swimming pools
- 130 million photoreceptors in the retina of the eye
- 20,000 pints of air inhaled daily delivering oxygen to trillions of cells
- 99% of the body consists of six elements: oxygen 65%, carbon 18%, hydrogen 10%, nitrogen 3%, calcium 1.5%, and phosphorus 1.2%
- 14 minutes of your life lost smoking just one cigarette
- 22 feet is the length of the small intestine
- 50 tons of food and 13,000 gallons of liquid consumed in a lifetime
- 60 mph is the speed of a cough's explosive charge of air

- 100 mph or more can be the speed of a sneeze
- 17 muscles are required to smile, but it takes 43 to frown
- 123,205,750 words are spoken in the average lifetime
- Humans shed and regrow outer skin cells about every 27 days—almost 1,000 new skins in a lifetime
- 700 million breaths in a lifetime, 20 per minute, 10 million a year
- Brain is 85% water and the body 66%
- Brain triples in size during the first few years of childhood
- 25 tons of force produced, if all body muscles pull in one direction
- Span of both arms stretched is usually equal to your height

GROSS DOMESTIC PRODUCT (GDP) BY COUNTRY (RANKED)

Rank	Country	GDP millions of $US	% of World GDP	Cum	Rank	Country	GDP millions of $US	% of World GDP	Cum
1	United States	13,843,825	25.49	25.5	31	Argentina	259,999	0.48	88.7
2	Japan	4,383,762	8.07	33.6	32	Ireland	258,574	0.48	89.2
3	Germany	3,322,147	6.12	39.7	33	Thailand	245,659	0.45	89.6
4	China	3,250,827	5.99	45.7	34	Finland	245,013	0.45	90.1
5	United Kingdom	2,772,570	5.10	50.8	35	Venezuela	236,390	0.44	90.5
6	France	2,560,255	4.71	55.5	36	Portugal	223,303	0.41	90.9
7	Italy	2,104,666	3.88	59.4	37	Hong Kong	206,707	0.38	91.3
8	Spain	1,432,140	2.64	62.0	38	United Arab Emirates	192,603	0.35	91.7
9	Canada	1,438,959	2.65	64.6	39	Malaysia	186,482	0.34	92.0
10	Brazil	1,313,590	2.42	67.1	40	Czech Republic	175,309	0.32	92.3
11	Russia	1,289,582	2.37	69.4	41	Columbia	171,607	0.32	92.6
12	India	1,098,945	2.02	71.5	42	Nigeria	166,778	0.31	93.0

13	South Korea	957,053	1.76	73.2	43	Romania	165,983	0.31	93.3
14	Australia	908,826	1.67	74.9	44	Chile	163,792	0.30	93.6
15	Mexico	893,365	1.64	76.5	45	Israel	161,935	0.30	93.9
16	Netherlands	768,704	1.42	78.0	46	Singapore	161,349	0.30	94.2
17	Turkey	663,419	1.22	79.2	47	Philippines	144,129	0.27	94.4
18	Sweden	455,319	0.84	80.0	48	Pakistan	143,582	0.26	94.7
19	Belgium	453,636	0.84	80.9	49	Ukraine	140,484	0.26	94.9
20	Indonesia	432,944	0.80	81.6	50	Hungary	138,388	0.25	95.2
21	Switzerland	423,938	0.78	82.4	51	Algeria	131,568	0.24	95.4
22	Poland	420,284	0.77	83.2	52	New Zealand	128,141	0.24	95.7
23	Norway	391,498	0.72	83.9	53	Egypt	127,930	0.24	95.9
24	China (Taiwan)	383,307	0.71	84.6	54	Kuwait	111,339	0.21	96.1
25	Saudi Arabia	376,029	0.69	85.3	55	Peru	109,069	0.20	96.3
26	Austria	373,943	0.69	86.0	56	Kazakhstan	103,840	0.19	96.5
27	Greece	314,615	0.58	86.6	57	Slovakia	74,988	0.14	96.6
28	Denmark	311,905	0.57	87.2	58	Morocco	73,429	0.14	96.8
29	Iran	294,089	0.54	87.7	59	Bangladesh	72,424	0.13	96.9
30	South Africa	282,630	0.52	88.2	60	Vietnam	70,022	0.13	97.0

(Continued)

Rank	Country	GDP millions of $US	% of World GDP	Cum	Rank	Country	GDP millions of $US	% of World GDP	Cum
61	Qatar	67,763	0.12	97.2	91	Cameroon	20,646	0.038	99.1
62	Angola	61,356	0.11	97.3	92	El Salvador	20,373	0.038	99.1
63	Libya	57,064	0.11	97.4	93	Iceland	20,003	0.037	99.2
64	Croatia	51,356	0.09	97.5	94	Panama	19,740	0.036	99.2
65	Luxembourg	50,160	0.09	97.6	95	Bahrain	19,660	0.036	99.2
66	Sudan	46,155	0.08	97.7	96	Côte D'Ivoire	19,598	0.036	99.3
67	Slovenia	46,084	0.08	97.7	97	Ethiopia	19,431	0.036	99.3
68	Belarus	44,773	0.08	97.8	98	Tanzania	16,184	0.030	99.3
69	Ecuador	44,184	0.08	97.9	99	Jordan	16,011	0.029	99.4
70	Serbia	41,679	0.08	98.0	100	Ghana	14,863	0.027	99.4
71	Oman	40,059	0.07	98.1	101	Bosnia/Herzegovina	14,780	0.027	99.4
72	Bulgaria	39,609	0.07	98.1	102	Myanmar	13,529	0.025	99.5
73	Lithuania	38,345	0.07	98.2	103	Bolivia	13,192	0.024	99.5
74	Syria	37,760	0.07	98.3	104	Brunei	12,386	0.023	99.5
75	Dominican Republic	36,396	0.07	98.3	105	Botswana	12,313	0.023	99.5

76	Tunisia	35,010	0.06	98.4	106	Honduras	12,279	0.023	99.5
77	Guatemala	33,694	0.06	98.5	107	Gabon	11,301	0.021	99.6
78	Azerbaijan	31,321	0.06	98.5	108	Uganda	11,227	0.021	99.6
79	Sri Lanka	30,012	0.06	98.6	109	Jamaica	11,206	0.021	99.6
80	Kenya	29,299	0.05	98.6	110	Zambia	11,156	0.021	99.6
81	Latvia	27,341	0.05	98.7	111	Senegal	11,123	0.020	99.7
82	Turkmenistan	26,909	0.05	98.7	112	Paraguay	10,870	0.020	99.7
83	Costa Rica	26,238	0.05	98.8	113	Albania	10,619	0.020	99.7
84	Lebanon	24,640	0.05	98.8	114	Georgia	10,293	0.019	99.7
85	Uruguay	22,951	0.04	98.9	115	Democratic Republic of The Congo	10,144	0.019	99.7
86	Uzbekistan	22,307	0.04	98.9	116	Nepal	9,627	0.018	99.7
87	Yemen	21,664	0.04	99.0	117	Afghanistan	8,842	0.016	99.8
88	Cyprus	21,303	0.04	99.0	118	Cambodia	8,604	0.016	99.8
89	Estonia	21,278	0.04	99.0	119	Armenia	7,974	0.015	99.8
90	Trinidad/Tobago	20,700	0.04	99.1	120	Rep. Congo	7,657	0.014	99.8

(*Continued*)

Rank	Country	GDP millions of $US	% of World GDP	Cum	Rank	Country	GDP millions of $US	% of World GDP	Cum
121	Mozambique	7,559	0.014	99.8	151	Sierra Leone	1,664	0.003	100.1
122	Macedonia	7,497	0.014	99.8	152	Lesotho	1,600	0.003	100.1
123	Malta	7,419	0.014	99.9	153	Cape Verde	1,428	0.003	100.1
124	Namibia	7,400	0.014	99.9	154	Eritrea	1,316	0.002	100.1
125	Madagascar	7,322	0.013	99.9	155	Bhutan	1,308	0.002	100.1
126	Chad	7,095	0.013	99.9	156	Belize	1,274	0.002	100.1
127	Burkina Faso	6,977	0.013	99.9	157	Antigua/Barbuda	1,089	0.002	100.1
128	Mauritius	6,959	0.013	99.9	158	Maldives	1,049	0.002	100.1
129	Mali	6,745	0.012	99.9	159	Guyana	1,039	0.002	100.1
130	Bahamas	6,586	0.012	99.9	160	Burundi	1,001	0.002	100.1
131	Papua New Guinea	6,001	0.011	100.0	161	St. Lucia	958	0.002	100.1
132	Nicaragua	5,723	0.011	100.0	162	Djibouti	841	0.002	100.1
133	Haiti	5,435	0.010	100.0	163	Liberia	730	0.001	100.1
134	Benin	5,433	0.010	100.0	164	Seychelles	710	0.001	100.1
135	Guinea	4,714	0.009	100.0	165	Gambia	653	0.001	100.1
136	Moldova	4,227	0.008	100.0	166	Zimbabwe	641	0.001	100.1
137	Niger	4,174	0.008	100.0	167	Grenada	590	0.001	100.1

138	Laos	4,028	0.007	100.0	168	St. Vincent and the Grenadines	559	0.001	100.1
139	Mongolia	3,905	0.007	100.0	169	St. Kitts/Nevis	527	0.001	100.1
140	Kyrgyzstan	3,748	0.007	100.0	170	East Timor	459	0.001	100.1
141	Barbados	3,739	0.007	100.0	171	Vanuatu	455	0.001	100.1
142	Tajikistan	3,712	0.007	100.0	172	Comoros	442	0.001	100.1
143	Malawi	3,538	0.007	100.0	173	Samoa	397	0.001	100.1
144	Fiji	3,409	0.006	100.1	174	Solomon Islands	358	0.001	100.1
145	Rwanda	3,320	0.006	100.1	175	Guinea-Bissau	343	0.001	100.1
146	Swaziland	2,936	0.005	100.1	176	Dominica	311	0.001	100.1
147	Mauritania	2,756	0.005	100.1	177	Tonga	219	0.000	100.1
148	Togo	2,497	0.005	100.1	178	São Tomé/Principe	144	0.000	100.1
149	Suriname	2,404	0.004	100.1	179	Kiribati	67	0.000	100.1
150	Central African Republic	1,714	0.003	100.1					

Gross world product: $54,311,608 million

Note: GDP includes value of goods and services produced by a country in 2007 in U.S. dollars. Some are International Monetary Fund estimates.

Source: International Monetary Fund, World Economic Outlook Database, April 2008.

WORLD POPULATION AND FACT SHEET

Year	Population	Year	Population	Year	Population
1	200 million	1955	2.8 billion	1999	6.0 billion
1000	275 million	1960	3.0 billion	2000	6.1 billion
1500	450 million	1965	3.3 billion	2005	6.5 billion
1650	500 million	1970	3.7 billion	2008	6.7 billion+
1750	700 million	1975	4.0 billion	2010	6.8 billion+
1804	1.0 billion	1980	4.5 billion	2012	7.0 billion
1850	1.2 billion	1985	4.9 billion	2020	7.6 billion
1900	1.6 billion	1987	5.0 billion	2030	8.2 billion
1927	2.0 billion	1990	5.3 billion	2040	9.0 billion
1950	2.6 billion	1995	5.7 billion	2050	9.2 billion

Facts

4,153,922	Billion quarts water consumed yearly
4,997,210	Deaths from water-related diseases
1,465,278,173	People with no access to safe drinking water
890,636,328	Undernourished people in the world
51,472,000	Cars produced this year
283,250,000	Computers sold this years
14,270	People who die of hunger each day
1.200,000	Deaths from auto accidents this year
6,246,757	Deaths caused by cancer this year
999,482	Deaths caused by malaria this year
3,123,385	Deaths caused by smoking this year
10,931,857	Deaths of children under five this year
624,678	Deaths of mothers during birth this year
45,601,541	Abortions this year
128,367,685	Births this year
52,783,673	Deaths this year
75,584,012	Net population gain
207,079	Daily population gain
937,028	Books published this year
274.1	Billion packs of cigarettes produced

Source: WorldOMeters.info and WorldWater.org.

CHAPTER 15

A TREASURY OF MOTIVATIONAL QUOTES

■ LISTEN TO CHURCHILL (Winston Churchill)

The 320 motivational quotes that follow are an important part of this book. Pore over them. You will find their messages useful. They are a font of wisdom and motivate people. They provide ways to get important concepts and points across to colleagues and supervisors in the workplace—and in the family, wives, husbands, children, parents, indeed, anyone you want to reach—including yourself. Quotes are useful in speeches that you might be called upon to make, and in future papers and books you may write. These quotes are a valuable tool to help you succeed far beyond your dreams.

I mentioned the following quote earlier: "Inside each of us are POWERS so strong, TREASURES so rich, and POSSIBILITIES so endless, . . ." May I suggest that you recite it ALOUD with genuine feeling.

Inside each of us are *powers* so strong, *treasures* so rich, and <u>possibilities</u> so endless, if I command them all to action I could MAKE A GIANT DIFFERENCE to millions of people in the world.

To have a great impact on your life and your future, find some quotes that are especially meaningful to you. Then retype each of them on separate pages and blow them up to the largest type size that will fit a single 8½ × 11 in. sheet of paper, and make a poster as I have done at the beginnings of each chapter. You will be amazed at the impact a quote will have on you through the years. Also, you can be a tremendous influence on people in your family or on your friends, by giving or e-mailing them a copy. When you meet interesting people over the years, you can give them a lift by sharing these inspiring quotes.

Another way "you can make a giant difference in the world" is to suggest to friends that you care about that they get a copy of this book. And, if you are an adult, you probably know many young people who could use a little push or "shove." By giving a young person a copy of this book, you will show that you feel very highly about him or her. Each time you do, you will be making that ***GIANT DIFFERENCE*** in someone's life.

Think of all these quotes as your private collection. Whether you read one or two pages every day, week, or month, make sure you mark up those that ring a loud bell in your mind. There is nothing more magical than a big, bold inspirational quotation hitting you in the face when it is hanging on your wall, or someone else's whom you have inspired to aim higher.

Since I began using daily quotations in the diary pages of my annual *Stock Trader's Almanac,* I have acquired about 100 different books of quotations. Practically every single one of them is divided by categories or by author. This, I suppose, is to help readers find specific quotes by subject matter or by the originators of these quotes.

Usually quotation books are reference books. Most of the time people are trying to locate a famous quote by a particular individual or one that pertains to a certain subject matter. I would like people to actually read the quotations without any preconceived notions. That way, they discover more about themselves by finding quotations that reach out to them personally. This is why I have decided to be original and have them appear in a random order.

The first quotation is by Winston Churchill. Look what reading quotations did for him. Just imagine what a few great quotations could do for you.

If you would like to receive three great 8½ × 11 inch inspirational posters, just email me at: yale@thecapitalistspirit.com. Its FREE to all readers of this book. Think of these three free motivational posters as a thank you for making an effort to improve the world! —*Y.H.*

LISTEN TO CHURCHILL!

It is a good thing for any individual to read books of quotations. The quotations when engraved upon the memory give you great thoughts.

—Winston Churchill (1874–1965),
one of the twentieth century's greats

We are responsible for what we are, and whatever we wish ourselves to be, we have the power to make ourselves. If what we are now has been the result of our own past actions, it certainly follows that whatever we wish to be in future can be produced by our present actions; so we have to know how to act.

—Swami Vivekananda (1863–1902), Hindu philosopher

All our dreams can come true, if we have the courage to pursue them.

—Walt Disney (1901–1966), cartoonist, motion picture producer, and founder Disneyland and Disney World

The thoughts we choose to think are the tools we use to paint the canvas of our lives.

—Louise L. Hay (b. 1927), founder of Hay House and author or *The Power Is Within You, You Can Heal Your Life*

You are today where your thoughts have brought you; you will be tomorrow where your thoughts take you.

—James Allen (1864–1912), author of the self-help classic, *As a Man Thinketh*

To continue the journey of life is the journey of self-discovery. It's our personal journey through the unknown possibilities of our existence, the realization of who we are, and our unlimited capabilities.

—Jefferson Mesidor (b. 1977), entrepreneur

Accept responsibility for your life. Know that it is you who will get you where you want to go, no one else.

—Les Brown (b. 1945), motivational speaker

If we listened to our intellect, we'd never have a love affair. We'd never have a friendship. We'd never go into business, because we'd be cynical. Well, that's nonsense. You've got to jump off cliffs all the time and build your wings on the way down.

—Ray Bradbury (b. 1920), science fiction writer

Many believe that self-help and self-improvement is about rags to riches, failure to success, and so forth, when indeed it is the beginning of a journey

into self-discovery. Inside every human being is an eternal truth and a life purpose. Using our mind power is simply starting the engine on that journey of self-discovery and highest self-actualization.

—Eldon Taylor, author of *Choices and Illusions*

When you get into a tight place and everything goes against you, till it seems as though you could not hang on a minute longer, never give up then, for that is just the place and time that the tide will turn.

—Harriet Beecher Stowe (1811–1896),
American writer and abolitionist

Having once decided to achieve a certain task, achieve it at all costs of tedium and distaste. The gain in self-confidence of having accomplished a tiresome labor is immense.

—Arnold Bennett (1867–1931), English novelist and author of *How to Live on 24 Hours a Day*

It is one of the strange ironies of this strange life that those who work the hardest, who subject themselves to the strictest discipline, who give up certain pleasurable things in order to achieve a goal, are the happiest women.

—Brutus Hamilton (1900–1970), U.S. Olympic athlete

Limitations live only in our minds. But if we use our imaginations, our possibilities become limitless.

—Jamie Paolinetti (b. 1964), bicycle racer

If you aren't good at loving yourself, you will have a difficult time loving anyone, since you'll resent the time and energy you give another person that you aren't even giving to yourself.

—Barbara De Angelis (b. 1951), self-help author

I write an email about every week to ten days . . . and within about 24 hours everyone will have read it. The amazing thing is how I can change the direction of the entire company within 24 hours. Ten years ago I couldn't do that.

—Michael Marks (b. 1950), CEO Flextronics

Everyone has inside of him or her a piece of good news. The good news is that you don't know how great you can be! How much you can love! What you can accomplish! And what your potential is!

—Anne Frank (1929–1945), German Jewish girl, diarist, and victim of the Nazis

Success is not measured by money or fame but by how you feel about your own goals and accomplishments and the time and effort you put into them.

—Willie Stargell (1940–2001), professional baseball player

Your mental attitude is something you can control outright and you must use self-discipline until you create a positive mental attitude. Your mental attitude attracts to you everything that makes you what you are.

—Napoleon Hill (1883–1970), legendary motivational speaker, author of *Think and Grow Rich*

Be sure to set your goals so high that you can't possibly achieve them in your lifetime. That way you'll always have something ahead of you.

—Robert Edward Turner II, the father of Ted Turner, to his son

Any young man who wants to make America over, has within himself the energy that will do it. He lives in his country; it is all around him; his energy is acting upon it now. His daily use of his energy is making America.

—Rose Wilder Lane (1886–1968), American writer, founding mother of the Libertarian movement, author of *The Discovery of Freedom*

Our bodies contain approximately 100 million sensory receptors that allow us to see, hear, taste, touch and smell physical reality. But the brain contains 10 thousand billion synapses. This means we're roughly 100,000 times better equipped to experience a world that does not exist, than a world that does.

—William Lederer (b. 1912), author of *The Ugly American* [What enormous possibilities each and every one of us has.—Y.H.]

Inspiration grows into full-scale creation through persistence and imagination.

—Carol Lloyd (b. 1963), *Creating a Life Worth Living*

People begin to become successful the minute they decide to be.

—Harvey Mackay (b. 1932), *Swim with the Sharks without Being Eaten Alive: Outsell, Outmanage, Outmotivate, and Outnegotiate Your Competition*

If only the people who worry about their liabilities would think about the riches they do possess, they would stop worrying. Would you sell both your eyes for a million dollars . . . or your two legs . . . or your hands . . . or your hearing? Add up what you do have, and you'll find that you won't sell them for all the gold in the world. The best things in life are yours, if you can appreciate yourself.

—Dale Carnegie (1888–1955), *How to Win Friends and Influence People*

One of the most essential things you need to do for yourself is to choose a goal that is important to you. Perfection does not exist—you can always do better and you can always grow.

—Les Brown (b. 1945), motivational speaker

The people who keep old rags, old useless objects, who hoard, accumulate: are they also hoarders and keepers of old ideas [and] useless information? I have the opposite obsession . . . I feel one has to learn to discard. If one changes internally, one should not continue to live with the same objects. They reflect one's mind and psyche of yesterday.

—Anaïs Nin (1903–1977)

Compared to what we ought to be, we are only half awake. We are making use of only a small part of our mental and physical resources. The human individual thus lives far within his limits. He possesses power of various sorts, which he habitually fails to use.

—William James (1842–1910), American philosopher, psychologist, and author of *Principles of Psychology* and *The Will to Believe*

Each of us is great insofar as we perceive and act on the infinite possibilities which lie undiscovered and unrecognized within us.

—James Harvey Robinson (1863–1936)

One machine can do the work of fifty ordinary men. No machine can do the work of one extraordinary man.

—Elbert Hubbard (1856–1915), American author, *A Message to Garcia*

Procrastination is opportunity's natural assassin.

—Victor Kiam (1926–1991), *Going for It: How to Succeed as an Entrepreneur*

One can have no smaller or greater mastery than mastery of oneself.

—Leonardo da Vinci (1452–1519), Italian Renaissance polymath

Only those who will risk going too far can possibly find out how far one can go.

—T. S. Eliot (1888–1965), poet, dramatist

Whatever you vividly imagine, ardently desire, sincerely believe, and enthusiastically act upon must inevitably come to pass!

—Paul J. Meyer (b. 1928), founder Success Motivation Institute

Nothing can stop the man with the right mental attitude from achieving his goal; nothing on earth can help the man with the wrong mental attitude.

—Thomas Jefferson (1743–1826), 3rd U.S. President

If you want to make good use of your time, you've got to know what's most important and then give it all you've got.

—Lee Iacocca (b. 1924), American industrialist and former CEO of Chrysler

Within you right now is the power to do things you never dreamed possible. This power becomes available to you just as you can change your beliefs.

—Maxwell Maltz (1899–1975), author, *Psycho-Cybernetics*

There is vitality, a life force, an energy, a quickening, that is translated through you into action, and because there is only one of you in all time, this expression is unique. And if you block it, it will never exist through any other medium and will be lost.

—Martha Graham (1893–1991), American choreographer, dancer, and teacher

Flatter me, and I may not believe you. Criticize me, and I may not like you. Ignore me, and I may not forgive you. Encourage me, and I may not forget you.

—William Arthur Ward (1921–1994), British novelist

So at last I was going to America! Really, really going, at last! The boundaries burst. The arch of heaven soared! A million suns shone out for every star. The winds rushed in from outer space, roaring in my ears, "America! America!"

—Mary Antin (1881–1949), immigrant writer, *The Promised Land*

If you will not settle for anything less than your best, you'll be amazed at what you can accomplish in your life.

—Vince Lombardi (1913–1970), head coach of the Green Bay Packers, 1959–1967

Often the difference between a successful person and a failure is not one has better abilities or ideas, but the courage that one has to bet on one's ideas, to take a calculated risk, and to act.

—Maxwell Maltz (1899–1975), author, *Psycho-Cybernetics*

You can do anything you wish to do, have anything you wish to have, be anything you wish to be.

—Robert Collier (1885–1950), self-help author

Bear in mind, if you are going to amount to anything, that your success does not depend upon the brilliancy and the impetuosity with which you take hold, but upon the everlasting and sanctified bull-doggedness with which you hang on after you have taken hold.

—Rev. Andrew B. Meldrum (1857–1928), Old Stone Church

The average man is always waiting for something to happen to him instead of setting to work to make things happen. For one person who dreams of making 50,000 pounds, a hundred people dream of being left 50,000 pounds.

—A. A. Milne (1882–1956), author of the Winnie-the-Pooh books

Whether or not you reach your goals in life depends entirely on how well you prepare for them and how badly you want them. You're eagles! Stretch your wings and fly to the sky.

—Ronald E. McNair (1950–1986), astronaut, died in the 1986 *Challenger* explosion

If you don't have a vision for the future, then your future is threatened to be a repeat of the past.

—A. R. Bernard (b. 1953),
CEO of the Christian Cultural Center

It's up to you! You can claim your own power now. You can take control of your thoughts, words, and the focus of your attention and consciously create the Life you want to live. The tools are right here. The way before you is wide open. So be bold. Be brave. Take control of your destiny now. Think for yourself and get going. Nobody else can do it for you. Nobody else can take it from you. This is the Road to power.

—Barbara Berger (b. 1945), *The Road to Power*

As human beings, our greatness lies not so much in being able to remake the world, as in being able to remake ourselves.

—Mahatma Gandhi (1869–1948),
spiritual leader of India's independence movement

I never could have done what I have done without the habits of punctuality, order, and diligence, without the determination to concentrate myself on one subject at a time.

—Charles Dickens (1812–1870), the author of
A Christmas Carol, Oliver Twist,
Pickwick Papers, and other classic novels

Winners compare their achievements with their goals, while losers compare their achievements with those of other people.

—Nido R. Qubein (b. 1948),
President of High Point University

In order to succeed, we must first believe that we can.

—Michael Korda (b. 1933), author,
Success! Power! How to Get It, How to Use It

Pretend that every single person you meet has a sign around his or her neck that says, "Make me feel important." Not only will you succeed in sales, you will succeed in life.

—Mary Kay Ash (1918–2001),
founder Mary Kay Cosmetics

Life is to be lived. If you have to support yourself, you had bloody well better find some way that is going to be interesting. And you don't do that by sitting around wondering about yourself.

—Katharine Hepburn (1907–2003), American actress

If you lose hope, somehow you lose the vitality that keeps life moving, you lose that courage to be, that quality that helps you go on in spite of it all. And so today I still have a dream.

—Martin Luther King, Jr. (1929–1968), Civil rights leader, 1964 Nobel Peace Prize

The greatest crime in the world is not developing your potential. When you do what you do best, you are helping not only yourself, but also the world.

—Roger Williams (1603–1683), English theologian

People who have attained things worth having in this world have worked while others have idled, have persevered while others gave up in despair, and have practiced early in life the valuable habits of self-denial, industry, and singleness of purpose. As a result, they enjoy in later life the success often erroneously attributed to good luck.

—Grenville Kleiser (1863–1953), *Fifteen Thousand Useful Phrases*

Every memorable act in the history of the world is a triumph of enthusiasm. Nothing great was ever achieved without it because it gives any challenge or any occupation, no matter how frightening or difficult, a new meaning. Without enthusiasm you are doomed to a life of mediocrity but with it you can accomplish miracles.

—Og Mandino (1923–1996), inspirational author, *The Greatest Salesman in the World*

Let me tell you the secret that has led me to my goal. My strength lies solely in my tenacity.

—Louis Pasteur (1822–1895), French chemist, founder of microbiology

A successful man is one who can lay a firm foundation with the bricks that others throw at him.

—Sidney Greenberg (1918–2003), rabbi and author

If you develop the absolute sense of certainty that powerful beliefs provide, then you can get yourself to accomplish virtually anything, including those things that other people are certain are impossible.

—Anthony Robbins (b. 1960), American motivator

What is it that attracts me to the young? When I am with mature people I feel their rigidities, their tight crystallizations. They have become . . . like the statues of the famous. Achieved. Final.

—Anaïs Nin (1903–1977), author and diarist

Do not tell us before we are born, even, that our province is to cook dinners, darn stockings, and sew on buttons!

—Abolitionist Lucy Stone (1818–1893), at the Woman's Rights convention in Cincinnati, Ohio, 1855

Our business in life is not to get ahead of others, but to get ahead of ourselves—to break our own records, to outstrip our yesterday by our today.

—Stewart B. Johnson, Scottish artist

Whatever the mind of man can conceive and believe, it can achieve.

—Napoleon Hill (1883–1970), Legendary motivational speaker, author, *Think and Grow Rich*

Life is not a journey to the grave with the intention of arriving safely in a pretty and well-preserved body, but rather to skid in broadside, thoroughly used up, totally worn out, and loudly proclaiming—WOW, what a ride!!!

—Anonymous

Confronting and overcoming challenges is an exhilarating experience. It does something to feed the soul and the mind. It makes you more than you were before. It strengthens the mental muscles and enables you to become better prepared for the next challenge.

—Jim Rohn (b. 1930), Business philosopher, motivational speaker, author

One only gets to the top rung on the ladder by steadily climbing up one at a time, and suddenly all sorts of powers, all sorts of abilities, which

you thought never belonged to you, suddenly become within your own possibility.

—Margaret Thatcher (b. 1925),
British Prime Minister 1979–1990

The size of the future you actually experience will largely be determined by one factor: the people you choose to connect with. When you invite people who are truly committed to growth into every aspect of your life, your own potential for growth becomes truly unlimited.

—Dan Sullivan (b. 1944), coach to entrepreneurs

It's impossible to imagine the heights to which, a thousand years from now, man's powers over matter will be carried. We will learn to deprive large masses of matter of their gravitation and to give them an absolute lightness that will make them easier to carry. Agriculture will lower its work and double the production. All our diseases, including old age, will be avoided or cured. Our lives will be lengthened at will, even beyond the time they lasted in the days before the flood. And I hope that moral science will be perfected too, so that we will stop being wolves instead of men and that human beings will finally learn to practice what they now mistakenly call humanity.

—Benjamin Franklin (1706–1790)
U.S. Founding Father, diplomat, inventor, in a letter to Joseph Priestly) [Talk about foresight!—Y.H.]

Success is the ability to go from one failure to another with no loss of enthusiasm.

—Winston Churchill (1874–1965), British Prime Minister

Only one who devotes himself to a cause with his whole strength and soul can be a true master. For this reason mastery demands all of a person.

—Albert Einstein (1879–1955),
German-American physicist and winner of the Nobel Prize in 1921

You are accountable for your actions, your decisions, your life; no one else is, but you.

—Catherine Pulsifer (b. 1957), self-improvement author

If we did all the things we are capable of doing, we would literally astound ourselves.

—Thomas Alva Edison (1847–1931),
American inventor and holder of 1,093 patents

Permanence, perseverance and persistence in spite of all obstacles, discouragements, and impossibilities: It is this, that in all things distinguishes the strong soul from the weak.

—Thomas Carlyle (1795–1881), English essayist, historian,
biographer, and philosopher

I take rejection as someone blowing a bugle in my ear to wake me up and get going, rather than retreat.

—Sylvester Stallone (b. 1946), actor, screenwriter, and director

Nothing splendid has ever been achieved except by those who dared believe that something inside of them was superior to circumstances.

—Bruce Barton (1886–1967), advertising tycoon author

Somehow I can't believe there are many heights that can't be scaled by a man who knows the secret of making dreams come true. This special secret can be summarized in four C's. They are: curiosity, confidence, courage, and constancy, and the greatest of these is confidence.

—Walt Disney (1901–1966), cartoonist, motion picture
producer, and founder Disneyland and Disney World

This is the true joy in life—being used for a purpose recognized by yourself as a mighty one; being thoroughly worn out before you are thrown on the scrap heap; being a force of nature instead of a feverish selfish little clod of ailments and grievances complaining that the world will not devote itself to making you happy.

—George Bernard Shaw (1856–1950), Irish dramatist and the
greatest playwright since Shakespeare

You may be disappointed if you fail, but you are doomed if you don't try.

—Beverly Sills (1929–2007), coloratura soprano

The willingness to accept responsibility for one's own life is the source from which self-respect springs.

—Joan Didion (b. 1934), *The Year of Magical Thinking*

From very early on, I understood that you can touch a piece of paper once . . . if you touch it twice, you're dead. Therefore, paper only touches my hand once. After that, it's either thrown away, acted on or given to somebody else.

—Manuel A. Fernandez (b. 1947), businessman and director of Black & Decker, Cisco, Brunswick Corp., and *Investor's Business Daily*

Learning is the beginning of wealth. Learning is the beginning of health. Learning is the beginning of spirituality. Searching and learning is where the miracle process all begins.

—Jim Rohn (b. 1930), business philosopher, motivational speaker, author

Attitude is an important part of the foundation upon which we build a productive life. A good attitude produces good results, a poor attitude poor results. We each shape our own life, and the shape of it is determined largely by our attitude.

—M. Russell Ballard (b. 1928)

Man alone has the power to transform his thoughts into physical reality; man alone, can dream and make his dreams come true.

—Napoleon Hill (1883–1970), legendary motivational speaker, and author of *Think and Grow Rich*

Whatever you do, do it with all your might. Work at it, early and late, in season and out, not leaving a stone unturned, and never deferring for a single hour that which can be done just as well now.

—P. T. Barnum (1810–1891), founder of Barnum and Bailey Circus

If we do not rise to the challenge of our unique capacity to shape our lives, to seek the kinds of growth that we find individually fulfilling, then we can have no security; we will live in a world of sham in which our selves are determined by the will of others, in which we will be constantly buffeted and increasingly isolated by the changes round us.

—Nena O'Neil (1923–2006), *Open Marriage* (35 million copies sold)

Are you disappointed, discouraged and discontented with your present level of success? Are you secretly dissatisfied with your present status? Do you want to become a better and more beautiful person than you are today? Would you like to be able to really learn how to be proud of yourself and still not lose genuine humility? Then start dreaming! It's possible! You can become the person you have always wanted to be!

—Robert H. Schuller (b. 1926), American minister and author

Every new way of getting wealth more quickly, every machine that lessens work, every means of diminishing the costs of production, every invention that makes pleasures easier or greater, seems the most magnificent accomplishment of the human mind.

—Alexis de Tocqueville (1805–1859), *Democracy in America*

Supposing you have tried and failed again and again. You may have a fresh start any moment you choose, for this thing that we call "failure" is not the falling down, but the staying down.

—Mary Pickford (1892–1979), Canadian actress and cofounder of United Artists

All successful employers are stalking men who will do the unusual, men who think, men who attract attention by performing more than is expected of them.

—Charles M. Schwab (1862–1939), founder of Bethlehem Steel

When school teachers held high expectations of their students, that alone was enough to cause an increase of 25 points in the students' IQ scores.

—Warren Bennis (b. 1925), pioneer leadership studies and author of *The Unconscious Conspiracy: Why Leaders Can't Lead*

You wake up in the morning and lo! Your purse is magically filled with twenty-four hours of the magic tissue of the universe of your life. No one can take it from you. No one receives either more or less than you receive.

—Arnold Bennett (1867–1931), English novelist, *How to Live on 24 Hours a Day*

One quality all successful people have is persistence.

—Dr. Joyce Brothers (b. 1928), psychologist and columnist

I do not think there is any other quality so essential to success of any kind as the quality of perseverance. It overcomes almost everything, even nature.

—John D. Rockefeller (1839–1937), American industrialist

Some people dream of great accomplishments, while other stay awake and do them.

—Anonymous

You gain strength, courage and confidence by every experience in which you really stop to look fear in the face. You must do the thing, which you think you cannot do.

—Eleanor Roosevelt (1884–1962), humanitarian, columnist, wife of FDR, and "First lady of the world" according to Harry Truman

The world is full of abundance and opportunity, but far too many people come to the fountain of life with a sieve instead of a tank car . . . a teaspoon instead of a steam shovel. They expect little and as a result they get little.

—Ben Sweetland (b. 1976), *Grow Rich While You Sleep*

When you're one step ahead of the crowd you're a genius. When you're two steps ahead, you're a crackpot.

—Rabbi Shlomo Riskin (b. 1940)

Dreams are renewable. No matter what our age or condition, there are still untapped possibilities within us and new beauty waiting to be born.

—Dale E. Turner (1917–2006), author

All successful men and women are big dreamers. They imagine what their future could be, ideal in every respect, and then they work every day toward their distant vision, that goal or purpose.

—Brian Tracy (b. 1944), motivational speaker, self-help author, *The 21 Success Secrets of Self-Made Millionaires*

One of the few things in life over which we have total control is our own attitude . . . our attitude determines whether we love or hate, tell the truth

or lie, act or procrastinate, advance or recede, and by our own attitude we, and we alone, actually decide whether we succeed or fail.

—Jim Rohn (b. 1930), motivational speaker, author

The act of taking the first step is what separates the winners from the losers.

—Brian Tracy (b. 1944), motivational speaker, self-help author, *21 Success Secrets of Self-Made Millionaires*

Success is being praised by others, and that's nice, too, but not as important or satisfying. Always aim for achievement and forget about success.

—Helen Hayes (1900–1993), American actress

Don't ask what the world needs. Ask what makes you come alive and go out and do it. Because what the world needs is people who have come alive.

—Howard Thurman (1899–1981)

You don't learn to hold your own in the world by standing on guard, but by attacking and getting well hammered yourself.

—George Bernard Shaw (1856–1950), Irish dramatist and the greatest playwright since Shakespeare

Some men give up their designs when they have almost reached the goal, while others, on the contrary, obtain a victory by exerting, at the last moment, more vigorous efforts than ever before.

—Herodotus (490 BCE–431 BCE), Greek historian

It's a very funny thing about life; if you refuse to accept anything but the best, you very often get it.

—W. Somerset Maugham (1874–1965), British writer, author of *The Moon and Sixpence* and *Of Human Bondage*

No horse gets anywhere until he is harnessed. No stream or gas drives anything until it is confined. No Niagara is ever turned into light and power until it is tunneled. No life ever grows great until it is focused, dedicated, disciplined.

—Harry Emerson Fosdick (1878–1969), American clergyman

Success is not measured by what you accomplish, but by the opposition you have encountered, and the courage with which you have maintained the struggle against overwhelming odds.

—Orison Swett Marden (1850–1924), motivational writer and founder of *Success* magazine

Success is waking up in the morning, whoever you are, wherever you are, however old or young, and bounding out of bed because there's something out there you love to do, that you believe in, that you're good at—something that's bigger than you are, and you can hardly wait to get at it again today.

—Whit Hobbs, author, *I Love Advertising, Harvard, 1941*

Without a strong sense of passion, purpose and direction, you have no true AMBITION.

—Eric R. Haas (b. 1945), CEO of ThinkTQ.com

Consult not your fears but your hopes and your dreams. Think not about your frustrations, but about your unfulfilled potential. Concern yourself not with what you tried and failed in, but with what it is still possible for you to do.

—Pope John XXIII (1881–1963)

Man is so made that when anything fires his soul, impossibilities vanish.

—Jean de la Fontaine (1621–1695), French poet

The critical ingredient is getting off your butt and doing something. It's as simple as that. A lot of people have ideas, but there are few who decide to do something about them now. Not tomorrow. Not next week. But today. The true entrepreneur is a doer, not a dreamer.

—Nolan Bushnell (b. 1943), founder Atari and Chuck E. Cheese's

Whatever you can do, or dream you can do, begin it; boldness has genius, power and magic in it.

—Johann Wolfgang von Goethe (1749–1832), German poet and polymath

We have an approximate structure of five stages in the creative process: 1) First Insight, 2) Saturation, 3) Incubation, 4) Illumination, 5) Verification. These stages progress over time from one stage to the next. Each stage may occupy varying lengths of time.

—Betty Edwards (b. 1926), *Drawing on the Artist Within*

Learn from yesterday, live for today, hope for tomorrow. The important thing is to not stop questioning.

—Albert Einstein (1879–1955), German-American physicist and winner of the Nobel Prize in 1921

The more you seek security, the less of it you have. But the more you seek opportunity, the more likely it is that you will achieve the security that you desire.

—Brian Tracy (b. 1944), motivational speaker, self-help author, *The 21 Success Secrets of Self-Made Millionaires*

Only the person who risks is truly free. A man's conquest of himself dwarfs the conquest of Mt. Everest.

—Norman Vincent Peale (1898–1993), preacher and author, *The Power of Positive Thinking*

People, who have kept on trying, when there seemed to be no hope at all, have accomplished most of the important things in the world.

—Dale Carnegie (1888–1955), *How to Win Friends and Influence People*

I was fourteen years old the night my daddy died. He had holes in his shoes and a vision that he was able to convey to me, even lying in an ambulance, dying, that I as a black girl could do and be anything, that race and gender are shadows, and that character, determination, attitude are the substances of life.

—Marian Wright Edelman (b. 1939), founder of the Children's Defense Fund

Every truth passes through three stages before it is recognized. In the first it is ridiculed; in the second it is opposed; in the third it is recognized as self-evident.

—Arthur Schopenhauer (1788–1860), German philosopher

I know of no more encouraging fact than the unquestionable ability of a man to elevate his life by a conscious endeavor.

—Henry David Thoreau (1817–1862), American writer, naturalist, and philosopher

All of the great achievers of the past have been visionary figures; they were men and women who projected into the future. They thought of what could be, rather than what already was, and then they moved themselves into action to bring these things into fruition.

—Bob Proctor (b. 1934), motivational speaker and author of *You Were Born Rich*

TWO GREAT INSIGHTS: Innovation is the driving force not only of capitalism but also of economic progress in general; and entrepreneurs are the agents of innovation.

—Joseph A. Schumpeter (1883–1950), Austrian-American economist, *Theory of Economic Development*

People of mediocre ability sometimes achieve outstanding success because they don't know when to quit. Most men succeed because they are determined to.

—George E. Allen (1896–1973), speechwriter for President Truman

The common idea that success spoils people by making them vain, egotistic and self-complacent is erroneous; on the contrary it makes them, for the most part, humble, tolerant and kind.

—W. Somerset Maugham (1874–1965), British writer, author of *The Moon and Sixpence* and *Of Human Bondage*

It is not because things are difficult that we do not dare; it is because we do not dare that they are difficult.

—Seneca (4 BCE–64 CE), Roman philosopher

Time is the coin of your life. It is the only coin you have, and only you can determine how it will be spent. Be careful lest you let other people spend it for you.

—Carl Sandburg (1878–1967), American writer and editor

There are no secrets to success. Don't waste your time looking for them. Success is the result of perfection, hard work, learning from failure, loyalty to those for whom you work, and persistence.

—General Colin Powell (b. 1937), Chairman of the Joint Chiefs 1989–1993 and Secretary of State 2001–2005

Without goals, and plans to reach them, you are like a ship that has set sail with no destination.

—Fitzhugh Dodson (1924–1993), clinical psychologist

The will to win, the desire to succeed, the urge to reach your full potential . . . these are the keys that will unlock the door to personal excellence.

—Eddie Robinson (1919–2007), football coach

We grow great by dreams. All big men are dreamers. They see things in the soft haze of a spring day or in the red fire of a long winter's evening. Some of us let these great dreams die, but others nourish and protect them, nurse them through bad days till they bring them to the sunshine and light, which come always to those who sincerely hope that their dreams will come true.

—Woodrow Wilson (1856–1924), 28th U.S. President

It's not the strongest of the species that survive, nor the most intelligent, but the one most responsive to change.

—Charles Darwin (1809–1882), *The Origin of Species*

There is no failure except in no longer trying. There is no defeat except from within, no really insurmountable barrier save our own inherent weakness of purpose.

—Frank McKinney "Kin" Hubbard (1868–1930), Humorist and cartoonist

You've got to say, "I think that if I keep working at this and want it badly enough I can have it." It's called perseverance.

—Lee Iacocca (b. 1924), American industrialist and former CEO of Chrysler

The men who have done big things are those who were not afraid to attempt big things, who were not afraid to risk failure in order to gain success.

—B.C. Forbes (1880–1954), founder of *Forbes* magazine

I learned about the strength you can get from a close family life. I learned to keep going, even in bad times. I learned not to despair, even when my world was falling apart. I learned that there are no free lunches. And I learned the value of hard work.

—Lee Iacocca (b. 1924), American industrialist and former CEO of Chrysler

Your ideas are like diamonds without the refining process, they are just a dirty rock, but by cutting away the impurities, they become priceless.

—Paul Kearley (b. 1959), American motivator

It's the same every time with progress. First they ignore you, then they say you're mad, then dangerous, then there's a pause, and then you can't find anyone who disagrees with you.

—Tony Benn (b. 1925), British Labor Party

We should be taught not to wait for inspiration to start a thing. Action always generates inspiration. Inspiration seldom generates action.

—Frank Tibolt (1897–1989), *A Touch of Greatness*

We ask ourselves, "Who am I to be brilliant, gorgeous, talented, fabulous?" Actually, who are you not to be?

—Marianne Williamson (b. 1952), author

It is no sin to attempt and fail. The only sin is to fail to make the attempt.

—SuEllen Fried (b. 1932), bullying prevention expert, *Bullies and Victims*

Desire is the key to motivation, but it's determination and commitment to an unrelenting pursuit of your goal—a commitment to excellence—that will enable you to attain the success you seek.

—Mario Andretti (b. 1940), Italian-American car racing legend

Most people have no idea of the giant capacity we can immediately command when we focus all of our resources on mastering a single area of our lives.

—Anthony Robbins (b. 1960), American motivator

There is one quality one must possess to win, and that is definiteness of purpose, the knowledge of what one wants, and a burning desire to possess it.

—Napoleon Hill (1883–1970), Legendary motivational speaker and author, *Think and Grow Rich*

The pessimist complains about the wind; the optimist expects it to change and the realist adjusts the sails.

—William Arthur Ward (1921–1994), British novelist

Excellence is not a destination; it is a continuous journey that never ends.

—Brian Tracy (b. 1944), motivational speaker and self-help author, *21 Success Secrets of Self-Made Millionaires*

A pessimist sees the difficulty in every opportunity; an optimist sees the opportunity in every difficulty.

—Winston Churchill (1874–1965), British Prime Minister

Think of yourself as on the threshold of unparalleled success. A whole, clear glorious life lies before you. Achieve! Achieve!

—Andrew Carnegie 1835–1919), Scottish-born U.S. industrialist and philanthropist, *The Gospel of Wealth*

I believe life is constantly testing us for our level of commitment, and life's greatest rewards are reserved for those who demonstrate a never-ending commitment to act until they achieve. This level of resolve can move mountains, but it must be constant and consistent. As simplistic as this may sound, it is still the common denominator separating those who live their dreams from those who live in regret.

—Anthony Robbins (b. 1960), American motivator

Schools everywhere are organized on the assumption that there is only one right way to learn and that it is the same way for everybody. But to be forced to learn the way a school teaches is sheer hell for students who learn differently.

—Peter Drucker (1909–2005),
Austria-born management guru

Cherish your vision! Cherish your ideals! Cherish the music that stirs in your heart, the beauty that forms in your mind, the loveliness that drapes your purest thoughts. If you remain true to them, your world will at last be built.

—James Allen (1864–1912), author of the self-help classic,
As a Man Thinketh

Knowing others is intelligence; knowing yourself is true wisdom. Mastering others is strength; mastering yourself is true power.

—Lao-Tzu (about 6th century BCE), monk, philosopher, and
founder of Taoism, *Translates to Old Master*

When you see a thing clearly in your mind, your creative "success mechanism" within you takes over and does the job much better than you could do it by conscious effort or "willpower."

—Maxwell Maltz (1899–1975), author, *Psycho-Cybernetics*

Entrepreneurs work hard, driven by an intense commitment and determined perseverance. They burn with the competitive desire to excel and win. They use failure as tool for learning, and would rather be effective than perfect. They respond to setbacks and defeats as if they were temporary interruptions, and rely on resiliency and resourcefulness to rebound and succeed. They have enough confidence in themselves to believe they can personally make a decisive difference in the final outcome of their ventures, and in their lives.

—Jeffry A. Timmons (1942–2008),
The Entrepreneurial Mind

Far better it is to dare mighty things, to win glorious triumphs, even though checkered by failure, than to rank with those poor spirits who neither enjoy much nor suffer much because they live in that gray twilight that knows neither victory nor defeat.

—Theodore Roosevelt (1858–1919), 26th U.S. President

Some men see things as they are and say "why?" I dream things that never were and say "why not?"

—George Bernard Shaw (1856–1950), Irish dramatist and greatest playwright since Shakespeare

Disciplining yourself to do what you know is right and important, although difficult, is the high road to pride, self-esteem and personal satisfaction.

—Brian Tracy (b. 1944), motivational speaker and self-help author, *The 21 Success Secrets of Self-Made Millionaires*

The first requisite for success is the ability to apply your physical and mental energies to one problem incessantly without growing weary.

—Thomas Alva Edison (1847–1931), American inventor and holder of 1,093 patents

Nothing in this world can take the place of persistence. Talent will not; nothing is more common than unsuccessful men with talent. Genius will not; unrewarded genius is almost a proverb. Education alone will not; the world is full of educated derelicts. Persistence and determination alone are omnipotent. The slogan "press on" has solved and always will solve the problems of the human race.

—Calvin Coolidge (1872–1933), 30th U.S. President

The people who try to do something and fail are infinitely better than those who try to do nothing and succeed.

—Lloyd Jones (b. 1955), New Zealand author

To laugh often and much; to win the respect of intelligent people and the affection of children; to earn the appreciation of honest critics and endure the betrayal of false friends; to appreciate beauty, to find the best in others; to leave the world a little better; whether by a healthy child, a garden patch or a redeemed social condition; to know even one life has breathed easier because you have lived. This is the meaning of success.

—Ralph Waldo Emerson (1803–1882), American author, poet, and philosopher, *Self-Reliance*

The strongest single factor in prosperity consciousness is self-esteem: believing you can do it, believing you deserve it, believing you will get it.

—Jerry Gillies (b. 1940), *Money Love*

Genius is 1% inspiration and 99% perspiration.

—Thomas Alva Edison (1847–1931), American inventor and holder of 1,093 patents

The best years of your life are the ones in which you decide your problems are your own. You do not blame them on your mother, the ecology, or the president. You realize that you control your own destiny.

—Albert Ellis(1913–2007), American psychologist

True motivation comes from within—from the willingness to see a dream fulfilled—from the desire to leave the world better than you found it.

—Steve Brunkhorst (b. 1962), success coach and motivational author

The greatest good you can do for another is not just to share your riches, but to reveal to him his own.

—Benjamin Disraeli (1804–1881), British Prime Minister

The discipline of writing something down is the first step toward making it happen.

—Lee Iacocca (b. 1924), American industrialist and former CEO of Chrysler

If one advances confidently in the direction of his dreams, and endeavors to live the life he has imagined, he will meet with a success unexpected in common hours.

—Henry David Thoreau (1817–1862), American writer, naturalist, and philosopher

A person should set his goals as early as he can and devote all his energy and talent to getting there. With enough effort, he may achieve it. Or he may find something that is even more rewarding. But in the end, no matter what the outcome, he will know he has been alive.

—Walt Disney (1901–1966), cartoonist, motion picture producer, and founder Disneyland and Disney World

What a curious phenomenon it is that you can get men to die for the liberty of the world who will not make the little sacrifice that is needed to free themselves from their own individual bondage.

—Bruce Barton (1886–1967), advertising tycoon author

We are what we think. We become what we believe. Our life is what we visualize. Our life is what we say it is. We can change our lives by changing our thoughts.

—Barbara Berger (b. 1945), *The Road to Power*

Twenty years from now you will be more disappointed by the things that you didn't do than by the ones you did do. So throw off the bowlines. Sail away from the safe harbor. Catch the trade winds in your sails. Explore. Dream. Discover.

—Mark Twain (1835–1910), American novelist and satirist, pen name of Samuel Langhorne Clemens

These are the times in which a genius would wish to live. It is not in the still calm of life that great characters are formed. The habits of a vigorous mind are formed in contending with difficulties. Great necessities call out great virtues.

—Abigail Adams (1774–1818) to her son John Quincy Adams, future U.S. president

The boss drives people; the leader coaches them. The boss depends on authority; the leader on good will. The boss inspires fear; the leader inspires enthusiasm. The boss says "I," the leader says "WE." The boss fixes the blame for the breakdown; the leader fixes the breakdown. The boss says, "GO," the leader says "LET'S GO!"

—H. Gordon Selfridge (1858–1947), retail magnate

Sit down and put down everything that comes into your head and then you're a writer. But an author is one who can judge his own stuff's worth, without pity, and destroy most of it.

—Colette (1873–1954), French novelist

Destiny is not a matter of chance; but a matter of choice. It is not a thing to be waited for; it is a thing to be achieved.

—William Jennings Bryan (1860–1925), three-time presidential candidate

Never give in, never give in, never, never, never, never, in nothing, great or small, large or petty, never give in except to convictions of honor and good sense.

—Winston Churchill (1874–1965), British Prime Minister

Life without risks is not worth living.

—Charles A. Lindbergh (1902–1974), achieved instant fame by flying solo from New York to Paris in 1927

You see things that are and say "Why?" But I dream things that never were and say "Why not?"

—George Bernard Shaw (1856–1950), Irish dramatist and greatest playwright since Shakespeare

A person's greatest virtue is his ability to correct his mistakes and continually make a new person of himself.

—Yang-Ming Wang (1472–1529), Chinese philosopher

Our destiny is shaped by our thoughts and our actions. We cannot direct the wind but we can adjust the sails.

—Anonymous

It had long since come to my attention that people of accomplishment rarely sat back and let things happen to them. They went out and happened to things.

—Elinor Smith (b. 1911), youngest woman to fly solo at 15

Success begins in the morning. We either "seize the day" or we don't. We seize the initiative, or we don't. We work from a plan, or we don't. If we fail to take charge of our mornings, we allow fate and circumstances, other people and luck to play a huge role, and that's usually a mistake. "If we fail to plan, we are planning to fail."

—Philip E. Humbert, Ph.D. (b. 1950), personal success coach and founder of Resources for Success

Parents can only give good advice or put them on the right paths, but the final forming of a person's character lies in his or her own hands.

—Anne Frank (1929–1945), German Jewish girl, diarist, and victim of the Nazis

No matter what age you are, or what your circumstances might be, you are special, and you still have something unique to offer. Your life, because of who you are, has meaning.

—Barbara De Angelis (b. 1951), self-help author

Give me a stock clerk with a goal and I'll give you a man who will make history. Give me a man with no goals and I'll give you a stock clerk.

—James Cash Penney (1875–1971), founder of J. C. Penney

The natural effort of every individual to better his own condition is so powerful that it is alone, and without any assistance, not only capable of carrying on the society to wealth and prosperity, but of surmounting a hundred impertinent obstructions with which the folly of human laws too often encumbers its operations.

—Adam Smith (1723–1790), *The Wealth of Nations*

You've got to get up every morning with determination, if you're going to go to bed with satisfaction.

—George Lorimer (1869–1937), editor of the *Saturday Evening Post, 1899–1936*

I am convinced that life is 10% what happens to me and 90% of how I react to it. And so it is with you . . . we are in charge of our Attitudes.

—Charles Swindoll (b. 1934), preacher and author of 70 books

Men give me credit for some genius. All the genius I have lies in this: When I have a subject in hand, I study it profoundly. Day and night it is before me. I explore it in all its bearings. My mind becomes pervaded with it. Then the effort, which I have made, is what people are pleased to call the fruit of genius. It is the fruit of labor and thought.

—Alexander Hamilton (1755–1804), U.S. Treasury Secretary 1789–1795, founder of the New York Post, and slain by Aaron Burr in a duel

If you believe you can, you probably can. If you believe you won't, you most assuredly won't. Belief is the ignition switch that gets you off the launching pad.

—Denis Waitley (b. 1933), American motivational author and speaker

Man is made or unmade by himself. In the armory of thought he forges the weapons by which he destroys himself. He also fashions the tools with which he builds for himself heavenly mansions of joy and strength and peace.

—James Allen (1864–1912), author of the self-help classic, *As A Man Thinketh*

Always listen to experts. They'll tell you what can't be done and why. Then do it.

—Robert Heinlein (1907–1988), science fiction writer

In reading the lives of great men, I found that the first victory they won was over themselves . . . self-discipline with all of them came first.

—Harry S. Truman (1884–1972), 33rd U.S. President

Obstacles don't have to stop you. If you run into a wall, don't turn around and give up. Figure out how to climb it, go through it, or work around it.

—Michael Jordan (b. 1963), American professional basketball star

Those who are fired with an enthusiastic idea and who allow it to take hold and dominate their thoughts find that new worlds open for them. As long as enthusiasm holds out, so will new opportunities.

—Norman Vincent Peale (1898–1993), preacher and author, *The Power of Positive Thinking*

One worthwhile task carried to a successful conclusion is worth half-a-hundred half-finished tasks.

—Malcolm S. Forbes (1917–1990), publisher *Forbes* magazine

People become really quite remarkable when they start thinking they can do things. When they believe in themselves they have the first secret of success.

—Norman Vincent Peale (1898–1993), preacher and author, *The Power of Positive Thinking*

Quiet times, reflective times, peaceful times, when your mind is relaxed and somewhat idle, are the times when inner power is best able to gain your attention and release true genius through you. People who constantly

rush about and who never have quiet, peaceful periods of reflection often have to work very hard. If they listened more to their inner promptings, they would receive rich ideas, fresh ideas, intelligent ideas that would make their lives easier and richer.

—Catherine Ponder (b. 1927), *Dynamic Laws of Prosperity*

Any human anywhere will blossom in a hundred unexpected talents and capacities simply by being given the opportunity to do so.

—Doris Lessing (b. 1919), novelist
and winner of the Nobel Prize

People with a sense of fulfillment think the world is good, while the frustrated blame the world for their failure.

—Eric Hoffer (1902–1983), *The True Believer*

Continuous effort—not strength or intelligence—is the key to unlocking our potential.

—Winston Churchill (1874–1965), British Prime Minister

I learned that courage was not the absence of fear, but the triumph over it. The brave man is not he who does not feel afraid, but he who conquers that fear.

—Nelson Mandela (b. 1918), President of South Africa
1994–1999 and winner of the 1993 Nobel Peace Prize

Those who try to do something and fail are infinitely better than those who try to do nothing and succeed.

—Lloyd Jones (b. 1955), New Zealand author

The greater danger for most of us is not that our aim is too high . . . and we miss it. But that it is too low and we reach it.

—Michelangelo (1475–1564), Italian Renaissance painter

Patience and perseverance have a magical effect before which difficulties disappear and obstacles vanish.

—John Quincy Adams (1767–1848), 6th U.S. President

Love yourself first and everything else falls into line. You really have to love yourself to get anything done in this world.

—Lucille Ball (1911–1989), comedienne and actress

Every individual is enthusiastic at times. One has enthusiasm for thirty minutes, another for thirty days, but it is the one who has it for thirty years who makes a success of his or her life.

—Edward B. Butler (1853–1928),
department store founder

The greatest glory in living lies not in never falling, but in rising every time we fall.

—Nelson Mandela (b. 1918),
President of South Africa 1994–1999 and
winner of the 1993 Nobel Peace Prize

With confidence, you can reach truly amazing heights; without confidence, even the simplest accomplishments are beyond your grasp.

—Jim Loehr (b. 1943),
cofounder of the Human Performance Institute

When a woman falls in love with the magnificent possibilities within herself, the forces that would limit those possibilities hold less and less sway over her.

—Marianne Williamson (b. 1952), author

What lies behind us and what lies before us are tiny matters, compared to what lies within us.

—Ralph Waldo Emerson (1803–1882),
American author, poet, and philosopher, *Self-Reliance*

The reasonable man adapts himself to the world; the unreasonable one persists in trying to adapt the world to himself. Therefore, all progress depends on the unreasonable man.

—George Bernard Shaw (1856–1950),
Irish dramatist and greatest playwright since Shakespeare

Realize that true happiness lies within you. Waste no time and effort searching for peace and contentment and joy in the world outside. Remember that there is no happiness in having or in getting, but only in giving. Reach out. Share. Smile. Hug. Happiness is a perfume you cannot pour on others without getting a few drops on yourself.

—Og Mandino (1923–1996),
inspirational author, *The Greatest Salesman in the World*

No one is more interesting to anybody than is that mysterious character we all call me, which is why self-liberation, self-actualization, self-transcendence, etc., are the most exciting games in town.

—Robert Wilson (b. 1941), theater director and playwright

If we hire people bigger than ourselves, we will become a company of giants-smaller than ourselves, a company of midgets.

—David Oglivy (1911–1999), cofounder of the advertising agency Oglivy and Mather

Keep your dreams alive. Understand to achieve anything requires faith and belief in yourself, vision, hard work, determination, and dedication. Remember all things are possible for those who believe.

—Gail Devers (b. 1966), "World's fastest woman," Olympic gold medal winner in 1992 and 1996

Don't worry about people stealing your ideas. If your ideas are any good, you'll have to ram them down people's throats.

—Howard Aiken (1900–1973), computer pioneer

I remember the moment I finally said, "I've had it! I know I'm much more than I'm demonstrating mentally, emotionally, and physically in my life." I made a decision in that moment which was to alter my life forever. I decided to change virtually every aspect of my life. I decided I would never again settle for less than I can be.

—Anthony Robbins (b. 1960), American motivator

There is a kind of greatness that does not depend upon fortune: it is a certain manner that distinguishes us, and which seems to destine us for great things; it is the value we insensibly set upon ourselves; it is by this quality that we gain the esteem of other men, and it is this which commonly raises us more above them, than birth, rank, or even virtue itself.

—François de la Rochefoucauld (1613–1680), French author

Persistence is a big differentiator between someone who succeeds and someone who doesn't.

—Dov Moran (b. 1956), Israeli technologist

I had an unshakable faith. I had it in my head that if I had to, I'd crawl over broken glass. I'd live in a tent, . . . it was gonna happen. And I think when you have that kind of steely determination, people get out of the way.

—Richard S. Newcombe (b. 1950), founder of Creators Syndicate

Resentment is like taking poison and waiting for the other person to die.

—Malachy McCourt (b. 1931), Irish-American actor, writer, and politician, *A Monk Swimming: A Memoir*

What lies behind us and what lies before us are tiny matters, compared to what lies within us.

—Ralph Waldo Emerson (1803–1882), American author, poet, and philosopher, *Self-Reliance*

This became a credo of mine . . . attempt the impossible in order to improve your work.

—Bette Davis (1908–1989), actress

Success: To laugh often and much, to win the respect of intelligent people and the affection of children, to earn the appreciation of honest critics and endure the betrayal of false friends, to appreciate beauty, to find the best in others, to leave the world a bit better, whether by a healthy child, a garden patch, or a redeemed social condition; to know even one life has breathed easier because you have lived. This is to have succeeded!

—Ralph Waldo Emerson (1803–1882), American author, poet, and philosopher, *Self-Reliance*

While one person hesitates because he feels inferior, the other is busy making mistakes and becoming superior.

—Henry C. Link (1889–1952), American psychologist and director of Psychological Corporation

Keep away from people who try to belittle your ambitions. Small people always do that, but the really great make you feel that you, too, can become great.

—Mark Twain (1835–1910), American novelist and satirist, pen name of Samuel Langhorne Clemens

America is the civilization of people engaged in transforming themselves. In the past, the stars of the performance were the pioneer and the immigrant. Today, it is youth and the Black.

—Harold Rosenberg (1906–1978), art critic

What is opportunity, and when does it knock? It never knocks. You can wait a whole lifetime, listening, hoping, and you will hear no knocking. None at all. You are opportunity, and you must knock on the door leading to your destiny. You prepare yourself to recognize opportunity, to pursue and seize opportunity as you develop the strength of your personality, and build a self-image with which you are able to live—with your self-respect alive and growing.

—Maxwell Maltz (1899–1975), author, *Psycho-Cybernetics*

Self-observation brings man to the realization of the necessity of self-change. And in observing himself a man notices that self-observation itself brings about certain changes in his inner processes. He begins to understand that self-observation is an instrument of self-change, a means of awakening.

—George Gurdjieff (1877–1949), mystic and spiritual teacher

Positive thinking won't let you do anything, but it will let you do everything better than negative thinking will.

—Zig Ziglar (b. 1926), American motivational speaker

People often say that this or that person has not yet found himself. But the self is not something one finds, it is something one creates.

—Thomas Szasz (b. 1920), psychiatrist

The greatest discovery of my generation is that human beings can alter their lives by altering their attitudes of mind.

—William James (1842–1910), American philosopher, psychologist, and author of *Principles of Psychology* and *The Will to Believe*

No one is in control of your happiness but you; therefore, you have the power to change anything about yourself or your life that you want to change.

—Barbara De Angelis (b. 1951), Self-help author

I am a great believer in luck, and I find the harder I work, the more I have of it.

—Stephen Leacock (1869–1944),
Canadian economist and humorist

I've continued to recognize the power individuals have to change virtually anything and everything in their lives in an instant. I've learned that the resources we need to turn our dreams into reality are within us, merely waiting for the day when we decide to wake up and claim our birthright.

—Anthony Robbins (b. 1960), American motivator

You have powers you never dreamed of. You can do things you never thought you could. There are no limitations in what you can do except the limitations of your own mind.

—Darwin P. Kingsley (1857–1932), President of New York Life

Ordinary people believe only in the possible. Extraordinary people visualize not what is possible or probable, but rather what is impossible. And by visualizing the impossible, they begin to see it as possible.

—Cherie Carter-Scott, *If Life is a Game, These Are the Rules*

The potential of the average person is like a huge ocean unsailed, a new continent unexplored, a world of possibilities waiting to be released and channeled toward some great good.

—Brian Tracy (b. 1944), Motivational speaker and self-help author, *The 21 Success Secrets of Self-Made Millionaires*

It is common sense to take a method and try it. If it fails, admit it frankly and try another. But above all, try something.

—Franklin D. Roosevelt (1882–1945), 32nd U.S. President

I have a love affair with America, because there are no built-in barriers to anyone in America. I come from a country where there were barriers upon barriers.

—Michael Caine (b. 1933), English actor

I've never been poor, only broke. Being poor is a frame of mind. Being broke is only a temporary situation.

—Mike Todd (1909–1958), American film producer

It's your aptitude, not just your attitude that determines your ultimate altitude.

—Zig Ziglar (b. 1926), American motivational speaker

Einstein's three rules of work: 1. Out of clutter find simplicity, 2. From discord find harmony, 3. In the middle of difficulty lies opportunity.

—Albert Einstein (1879–1955), German-American physicist, and winner of the Nobel Prize in 1971

In the realm of ideas everything depends on enthusiasm; in the real world all rests on perseverance.

—Johann Wolfgang von Goethe, German poet and polymath (1749–1832)

He who knows much about others may be learned, but he who understands himself is more intelligent. He who controls others may be powerful, but he who has mastered himself is mightier still.

—Lao-Tzu, (about 6th century BCE), monk, philosopher, and founder of Taoism, *Translates to Old Master*

The golden opportunity you are seeking is in yourself. It is not in your environment; it is not in luck or chance, or the help of others; it is in yourself alone.

—Orison Swett Marden (1850–1924), motivational writer and founder of *Success* magazine

There isn't a ruler, a yardstick or a measuring tape in the entire world long enough to compute the strength and capabilities inside you.

—Paul J. Meyer (b. 1928), founder of Success Motivation Institute

The mediocre teacher tells. The good teacher explains. The superior teacher demonstrates. The great teacher inspires.

—William Arthur Ward (1921–1994), British novelist

Know the true value of time; snatch, seize, and enjoy every moment of it. No idleness, no laziness, no procrastination: never put off till tomorrow what you can do today.

—Lord Chesterfield (1694–1773), British statesman

You have a right to succeed, and your chances of succeeding are probably just as good as anyone else's, and most certainly better than you think they are.

—Michael Korda (b. 1933), author, *Success!, Power! How to Get It, How to Use It*

The roots of true achievement lie in the will to become the best that you can become.

—Harold Taylor (1914–1993), progressive educator

A man can succeed at almost anything for which he has unlimited enthusiasm.

—Charles M. Schwab (1862–1939), founder of Bethlehem Steel

Deep within man dwell those slumbering powers; powers that would astonish him, that he never dreamed of possessing; forces that would revolutionize his life if aroused and put into action.

—Orison Swett Marden (1850–1924), Motivational writer and founder of *Success* magazine

I'm a great believer in luck, and I find the harder I work the more I have of it.

—Thomas Jefferson (1743–1826), 3rd U.S. President

He who cherishes a beautiful vision, a lofty ideal in his heart, will one day realize it. Dream lofty dreams and as you dream so shall you become.

—James Allen (1864–1912), author of the self-help classic *As a Man Thinketh*

To conquer fear is the beginning of wisdom.

—Bertrand Russell (1872–1970), British mathematician and one of the greatest philosophers of the twentieth century

Every morning you are handed 24 golden hours. They are one of the few things in this world that you get free of charge. If you had all the money in the world, you couldn't buy an extra hour. What will you do with this priceless treasure?

—Anonymous

Women are expected to do twice as much as men in half the time and for no credit. Fortunately, this isn't difficult.

—Charlotte Whitton (1896–1975), Canadian feminist and former Mayor of Ottawa

Attitude is more important than the past, than education, than money, than circumstances, than what people do or say. It is more important than appearance, giftedness, or skill.

—W. C. Fields (1880–1946), actor and comedian

IGNORANCE is not knowing something; STUPIDITY is not admitting your ignorance.

—Daniel Turov (b. 1947), money manager, *Turov on Timing*

To those of you who received honors, awards and distinctions, I say well done. And to the C students, I say you too may one day be president of the United States.

—George W. Bush (b. 1946), 43rd U.S. President

If you employed study, thinking, and planning time daily, you could develop and use the power that can change the course of your destiny.

—W. Clement Stone (1902–2002), cofounder with Napoleon Hill of *Success Unlimited* magazine

To me, success is the peace of mind that comes from knowing that you have achieved your very best under challenging circumstances. To grow as a person, you must continuously raise your expectations. To achieve success you must seize the moment and execute beyond expectation.

—Eric R. Haas (b. 1945), CEO of *ThinkTQ.com*

If you don't like who you are and where you are, don't worry about it because you're not stuck either with who you are or where you are. You can grow. You can change. You can be more than you are.

—Zig Ziglar (b. 1926), American motivational speaker

The future belongs to those who believe in the beauty of their dreams.

—Eleanor Roosevelt (1884–1962),
Humanitarian, columnist, wife of FDR, and
"First lady of the world" according to Harry Truman

Do not go where the path may lead, go instead where there is no path and leave a trail.

—Ralph Waldo Emerson (1803–1882),
American author, poet, and philosopher, *Self-Reliance*

Excellence can be attained if you—care more than others think is wise—risk more than others think is safe—dream more than others think is practical—and expect more than others think is possible.

—Anonymous

Words can never adequately convey the incredible impact of our attitudes toward life. The longer I live the more convinced I become that life is 10 percent what happens to us and 90 percent how we respond to it.

—Charles Swindoll (b. 1934), preacher and author of 70 books

Success isn't measured by the position you reach in life; it's measured by the obstacles you overcome.

—Booker T. Washington (1856–1915), Founder of
Tuskegee Institute

No one can make you feel inferior without your consent.

—Eleanor Roosevelt (1884–1962),
Humanitarian, columnist, wife of FDR, and
"First lady of the world" according to Harry Truman

Make no little plans, they have no magic to stir men's blood and will not be realized. Make big plans; aim high in hope and work, remembering that a noble and logical plan never dies, but long after we are gone will be a living thing.

—Juliet Lita Bane (1887–1957), Dean of Home Economics,
University of Illinois, 1941

Thomas Alva Edison once said, "Genius is 1% inspiration and 99% perspiration!" Unfortunately, many startup "genius" entrepreneurs

mistakenly switch the two percentages around, and then wonder why they can't get their projects off the ground.

—Yale Hirsch

I never take straight-A students. Real scientists tend to be critical, and somewhere along the line, they had to rebel against their teachers.

—Lynn Margolis (b. 1938), science professor, University of Massachusetts

To dream anything that you want to dream, that is the beauty of the human mind. To do anything that you want to do, that is the strength of the human will. To trust yourself, to test your limits, that is the courage to succeed.

—Bernard B. Edmonds (1910–2003), British reverend and organist

The way to get started is to quit talking and begin doing. We keep moving forward, opening new doors, and doing new things, because we're curious and curiosity keeps leading us down new paths.

—Walt Disney (1901–1966), cartoonist, motion picture producer, and founder Disneyland and Disney World

Many people dream of success. To me, success can only be achieved through repeated failure and introspection.

—Soichiro Honda (1906–1991), founder of Honda Motors

Look ahead; envision the beautiful blessings waiting on your distant shores. If you follow your personal stepping-stones with joy, love, faith and gratitude, the swiftest currents will not impede your journey.

—Steve Brunkhorst (b. 1962), success coach and motivational author

What the superior man seeks, is in himself. What the inferior man seeks, is in others.

—Confucius (551–478BC), Chinese philosopher

By virtue of being born to humanity, every human being has a right to the development and fulfillment of his potentialities as a human being.

—Ashley Montagu (1905–1999), anthropologist and humanist

It takes no more effort to expect the best than to fear the worst. It's healthier, more productive, and a lot more fun!

—Philip E. Humbert, Ph.D. (b. 1950), personal success coach and founder of Resources for Success

The real difference between men is energy. A strong will, a settled purpose, an invincible determination, can accomplish almost anything; and in this lies the distinction between great men and little men.

—Buckminster Fuller (1895–1983), American architect and author

It must be borne in mind that the tragedy of life doesn't lie in not reaching your goal. The tragedy lies in having no goal to reach. It isn't a calamity to die with dreams unfulfilled, but it is a calamity not to dream. It is not a disaster to be unable to capture your ideal, but it is a disaster to have no ideal to capture. It is not a disgrace not to reach the stars, but it is a disgrace to have no stars to reach for. Not failure, but low aim is a sin.

—Benjamin E. Mays (1894–1984), president of Morehouse College and civil rights leader

For a man to achieve all that is demanded of him he must regard himself as greater than he is.

—Johann Wolfgang von Goethe (1749–1832), German poet and polymath

The quality of a person's life is in direct proportion to their commitment to excellence, regardless of their chosen field of endeavor.

—Vince Lombardi (1913–1970), head coach of the Green Bay Packers, 1959–1967

No pessimist ever discovered the secrets of the stars, or sailed to an uncharted land, or opened a new heaven to the human spirit.

—Helen Keller (1880–1968), American writer and first deaf and blind college graduate

My father had an extremely difficult life, but he showed me how you can change yourself and your life just by making the choice to do that.

—Ben Affleck (b. 1972), American actor

The thing always happens that you really believe in; and the belief in a thing makes it happen.

—Frank Lloyd Wright (1869–1959), American architect

You may have a fresh start any moment you choose, for this thing we call failure is not the falling down, but the staying down.

—Mary Pickford (1892–1979),
Canadian actress and cofounder of United Artists

Set your sights high, the higher the better. Expect the most wonderful things to happen, not in the future but right now. Realize that nothing is too good. Allow absolutely nothing to hamper you or hold you up in any way.

—Eileen Caddy (1917–2006), spiritual teacher

The man who has no imagination has no wings.

—Muhammad Ali (b. 1942),
world heavyweight boxing champion

Don't be afraid of the space between your dreams and reality. If you can dream it, you can make it so.

—Belva Davis (b. 1932), broadcast journalist

If we make up our mind what we are going to make of our lives, then work hard toward that goal, we NEVER lose.

—Ronald Reagan (1911–2004), 40th U.S. President

If the winds of fortune are temporarily blowing against you, remember that you can harness them and make them carry you toward your definite purpose, through the use of your imagination.

—Napoleon Hill (1883–1970),
legendary motivational speaker and author,
Think and Grow Rich

Only those who dare to fail greatly can ever achieve greatly.

—Robert F. Kennedy (1925–1968),
U.S. Attorney General 1961–1964 and U.S. Senator 1965–1968

A dream is just a dream, but a goal is a dream with a plan and a deadline.
—Harvey Mackay (b. 1932), author of *Swim with the Sharks without Being Eaten Alive: Outsell, Outmanage, Outmotivate, and Outnegotiate Your Competition*

What pays under capitalism is satisfying the common man, the customer. The more people you satisfy, the better for you.
—Ludwig von Mises (1881–1973), Austrian economist

Shoot for the moon. Even if you miss, you'll land among the stars.
—Les Brown (b. 1945), motivational speaker

When a goal matters enough to a person, that person will find a way to accomplish what at first seemed impossible.
—Nido R. Qubein (b. 1948), president of High Point University

Life isn't about finding yourself. Life is about creating yourself.
—George Bernard Shaw (1856–1950), Irish dramatist and greatest playwright since Shakespeare

My life has been filled with terrible misfortune; most of which never happened.
—Michel de Montaigne (1533–1592), French philosopher and essayist

I don't know the key to success, but the key to failure is trying to please everybody.
—Bill Cosby (b. 1937), American comedian

There's only one corner of the universe you can be certain of improving, and that's your own self. Every man who knows how to read has it in his power to magnify himself, to multiply the ways in which he exists, to make his life full, significant and interesting.
—Aldous Huxley (1894–1963), English author, *Brave New World*

Man often becomes what he believes himself to be. If I keep on saying to myself that I cannot do a certain thing, it is possible that I may end by really becoming incapable of doing it. On the contrary, if I have the belief that I can do it, I shall surely acquire the capacity to do it even if I may not have it at the beginning.

—Mahatma Gandhi (1869–1948), spiritual leader of India's independence movement

Low self-esteem is like driving through life with your hand-break on.

—Maxwell Maltz (1899–1975), author, *Psycho-Cybernetics*

To me, the definition of focus is knowing exactly where you want to be today, next week, next month, next year, then never deviating from your plan. Once you can see, touch and feel your objective, all you have to do is pull back and put all your strength behind it, and you'll hit your target every time.

—Bruce Jenner (b. 1949), decathlon winner, 1976 Olympics

The most important key to achieving great success is to decide upon your goal and launch, get started, take action, and move.

—Brian Tracy (b. 1944), motivational speaker, self-help author, *The 21 Success Secrets of Self-Made Millionaires*

Don't wait. Where do you expect to get by waiting? Doing is what teaches you. Doing is what leads to inspiration. Doing is what generates ideas. Nothing else and nothing less!

—Daniel Quinn (b. 1935), *Ishmael*

The real contest is always between what you've done and what you're capable of doing. You measure yourself against yourself and nobody else.

—Geoffrey Gaberino (b. 1962), 1984 Olympic swimming gold medal winner

Take a chance! All life is a chance. The man who goes farthest is generally the one who is willing to do and dare.

—Dale Carnegie (1888–1955), *How to Win Friends and Influence People*

The truth of the matter is that there's nothing you can't accomplish if: (1) You clearly decide what it is that you're absolutely committed to achieving,

(2) You're willing to take massive action, (3) You notice what's working or not, and (4) You continue to change your approach until you achieve what you want, using whatever life gives you along the way.

—Anthony Robbins (b. 1960), American motivator

The way a young man spends his evenings is a part of that thin area between success and failure.

—Robert R. Young (1897–1958),
American financier and railroad tycoon

We all have possibilities we don't know about. We can do things we don't even dream we can do.

—Dale Carnegie (1888–1955), *How to Win Friends and Influence People*

If you wish in the world to advance, your merits you're bound to enhance, you must stir it and stump it, and blow your own trumpet or trust me you haven't a chance!

—W. S. Gilbert (1836–1911), dramatist and librettist for the team of Gilbert & Sullivan, composers of operettas

You can do anything if you have enthusiasm. Enthusiasm is the yeast that makes your hopes rise to the stars. With it, there is accomplishment. Without it there are only alibis.

—Henry Ford (1863–1947), founder of Ford Motors and father of the assembly line

Men often become what they believe themselves to be. If I believe I cannot do something, it makes me incapable of doing it. But when I believe I can, then I acquire the ability to do it even if I didn't have it in the beginning.

—Mahatma Gandhi (1869–1948),
spiritual leader of India's independence movement

Each of us was born with wings and has the ability to go farther than we ever thought possible, to do things beyond our wildest imaginings.

—Barbara Stanny, author of *Secrets of Six-Figure Women: Surprising Strategies to Up Your Earnings and Change Your Life*

If you want to take your mission in life to the next level, if you're stuck and you don't know how to rise, don't look outside yourself. Look inside. Don't let your fears keep you mired in the crowd. Abolish your fears and raise your commitment level to the point of no return, and I guarantee you that the Champion Within will burst forth to propel you toward victory.

—Bruce Jenner (b. 1949), Decathlon winner, 1976 Olympics

If there is someone in your life you wish to motivate every day, just send me their e-mail address with "quote of the day" in the subject box. You may include yourself, if you wish. My e-mail address is yale@thecapitalistspirit.com.